BION IN BRAZIL

BION IN BRAZIL

Supervisions and Commentaries

Edited by

José Américo Junqueira de Mattos,
Gisele de Mattos Brito, and
Howard B. Levine

Routledge
Taylor & Francis Group
LONDON AND NEW YORK

First published 2017 by
Karnac Books Ltd.

Published 2018 by Routledge
2 Park Square, Milton Park, Abingdon, Oxon OX14 4RN
711 Third Avenue, New York, NY 10017, USA

Routledge is an imprint of the Taylor & Francis Group, an informa business

British Library Cataloguing in Publication Data

A C.I.P. for this book is available from the British Library

ISBN-13: 9781782203209 (pbk)

Typeset by V Publishing Solutions Pvt Ltd., Chennai, India

CONTENTS

ACKNOWLEDGMENTS AND DEDICATION

The editors would like to thank the late Francesca Bion and the Bion literary estate for permission to publish these supervisions. It is to the memory of Francesca Bion, whose love and companionship proved so vital in helping Bion recover from the trauma of his war experiences and who helped him to publish and thereby disseminate and preserve his ideas, that we dedicate this book.

ABOUT THE EDITORS AND CONTRIBUTORS

Maria Bernadete Amêndola Contart de Assis is a full member and teaching analyst of the Brazilian Society of Psychoanalysis of Ribeirão Preto and associate member of the Brazilian Psychoanalytic Society of São Paulo (SBPSP).

João Carlos Braga M.D., PhD is a full member, training, and supervising analyst at the Brazilian Psychoanalytic Society of São Paulo and Psychoanalytic Group of Curitiba, Brazil.

Gisèle de Mattos Brito is a full member of the Brazilian Psychoanalytic Society of São Paulo (SBPSP) and the Brazilian Psychoanalytic Society of Minas Gerais (Provisional) (SBPMG). She is training analyst and Teacher of the Training Institute of SBPMG where she leads study groups on the work of W. R. Bion. Since 2009 she coordinates a seminar on Bion's Supervisions at SBPSP. She has published several papers published in Brazil and abroad.

Arnaldo Chuster is a member of the Brazilian Psychiatric Association, training, and teaching analyst at Rio de Janeiro Psychoanalytic Society

(FIPA), full professor at the W. Bion Institute in Porto Alegre. Member of Newport Beach Institute, Irvine, California and has authored eight books published in Portuguese about Bion's work and written chapters in eight further books in Spanish, Italian, and English.

Antônio Carlos Eva, is a physician and psychiatrist trained at the Faculty of Medicine of the University of São Paulo (FMUSP) where his dissertation was on "Aspects of the Establishment of a Therapeutic Community." He is a Full Member and Training Analyst of the Brazilian Psychoanalytic Society of São Paulo (SBPSP) and has studied and taught the work of W. R. Bion for the last twenty five years. Since 2005, he is director of the "Conversas Psicanalíticas" (Psychoanalytical Conversations) seminar at S.B.P.S.P.

Julio Frochtengarten graduated as medical doctor from the University of São Paulo's School of Medicine in 1973. Senior member and training analyst of the Brazilian Psychoanalytic Society of São Paulo since 1994. Instructor at the Psychoanalytic Institute since 1990, coordinating ongoing clinical and theoretical seminars, particularly on the work of Freud and Bion. Member of the Institute's educational committee from 1993 to 2000 and its board of directors. Held positions in numerous scientific and editorial boards. Has published books and articles in Brazilian journals.

Maria Cecilia Andreucci Pereira Gomes is a full member of International Psychoanalytic Association (IPA) and FEPAL and a full member and training analyst of the SBPSP.

José Américo Junqueira de Mattos graduated from the Institute of Psychoanalysis of the SBPSP. He was one of the five founding members of the psychoanalysis group that later became the Brazilian Society of Psychoanalysis of Ribeirão Preto and has been a training analyst in both societies. He has published several papers published both in Brazil and abroad. Since the beginning of his career he has been interested in the ideas of Bion, who was his analyst.

Howard B. Levine, is on the faculty at the Psychoanalytic Institute of New England East (PINE), on the editorial Board of the IJP and

Psychoanalytic Inquiry and in private practice in Brookline, MA. He is a member of the Contemporary Freudian Society, the Newport Psychoanalytic Institute, and a founding member of the Group for the Study of Psychoanalytic Process (GSPP) and The Boston Group for Psychoanalytic Studies, Inc. (BGPS). He is the editor of *Adult Analysis and Childhood Sexual Abuse* (Analytic Press 1990), co-editor (with Lawrence Brown) of *Growth and Turbulence in the Container/Contained* (Routledge, 2013), (with Gail Reed and Dominique Scarfone) of *Unrepresented States and the Construction of Meaning* (Karnac 2013,) (with Gail Reed) *Responses to Freud's Screen Memories Paper* (Karnac 2014), (with Giuseppe Civitarese) *The Wilfred Bion Tradition* (Karnac 2015) and (with David Power) *Engaging Primitive Anxieties Of The Emerging Self. The Legacy Of Frances Tustin* (Karnac 2017).

Ney Marinho is a psychiatrist, training analyst and PhD in philosophy. His doctoral thesis is on *The Case of Schreber* (Freud), revisited from philosophical (Marcia Cavell's and Wittgenstein's) and psychoanalytical (Bion's) contributions. He gives courses on Bion's work in his Institute and has been researching the concept of "madness" in the Portuguese Speaking Country Community (CPLP) since 2009.

Dr. Carmen C. Mion M.D. Full member, supervisor, and training analyst at the Brazilian Psychoanalytic Society of São Paulo. Full member of FEPAL and the International Psychoanalytic Association (IPA). Since 2011 she is a member of IPA education and oversight committee. She is in private practice in São Paulo, and has published articles in Brazilian and international journals.

Leopold Nosek is a training analyst and past president of the Brazilian Psychoanalytic Society of São Paulo (SBPSP), past president of FEPAL and the Federation of Brazilian Psychoanalytic Societies and Institutes (FEBRAPSI), past editor of the Brazilian journal of psychoanalysis, the Latin American journal of psychoanalysis, and the IDE journal of the SBPSP. In 2014, he received the Sigourney Award.

Paulo Cesar Sandler is a training analyst, Sociedade Brasileira de Psicanalise de Sao Paulo; psychiatrist at Institute of Medical

Rehabilitation, Hospital das Clinicas, Faculdade de Medicina da Universidade de Sao Paulo; author of many books and papers, including *The Language of Bion, A Dictionary of Concepts; A Clinical Application of Bion's Concepts*, in three volumes; *An Introduction to A Memoir of the Future by W. R. Bion*, in two volumes—all published by Karnac; *A Apreensao da Realidade Psiquica*, in seven volumes, by Imago ed.

Antônio Sapienza is a full member of International Psychoanalytic Association (IPA) and FEPAL and a full member and training analyst of SBPSP.

Renato Trachtenberg (Brazil) is a psychiatrist, full member, training, and supervising analyst for the Brazilian Psychoanalytical Society of Porto Alegre (IPA). He is full member of the Buenos Aires Psychoanalytical Association (IPA) and full member of the Psychoanalytical Studies Center of Porto Alegre. He is co-author of the books: *The Seven Capital Envies* with Arnaldo Chuster (Artmed, Porto Alegre, 2009 and Lumen, Buenos Aires, 2010) and *W. R. Bion: The Complex Work* with Arnaldo Chuster and Gustavo Soares (2014).

Luiz Carlos Uchôa Junqueira Filho, M.D. (Faculty of Medicine, University of São Paulo) is a former psychiatrist member of the Brazilian Psychiatric Society, a Training Analyst, past President, and chair of the Biennial Meeting of the Brazilian Psychoanalytic Society of São Paulo (SBPSP) and Editor of the corresponding books. He is also the author of: *Sismos e Acomodações: A Clínica Psicanalítica como Usina de Idéias* (Ed. Rosari, 2003), and *Dante e Virgílio: o resgate na selva escura* (Ed. Blucher, 2017).

Ana Maria Stucchi Vannucchi was born in São Paulo, Brazil. She graduated in psychology at the University of São Paulo where she also got her Master`s degree in psychology. Ana went through her psychoanalytical training at the Brazilian Psychoanalytic Society of São Paulo (SBPSP). Presently she is a training analyst and a member elected at the teaching committee at the Institute for Psychoanalysis at the Brazilian Society of Psychoanalysis of São Paulo (SBPSP).

FOREWORD

João Carlos Braga

We have *information* about Wilfred Bion, as much about the man as about the thinker. We also have several sources that allow us to have *knowledge* of his psychoanalytic contributions. However, this collection of supervisions conducted by him during his four visits to Brazil (1973, 1974, 1975, and 1978) belongs to another order, to that of *experiences*. These supervisions allow us close contact with Bion's unique way of approaching mental life from the clinical material. They introduce us to the analyst in action, through careful transcription of what was spoken in English during each supervision, showing what Bion himself heard and spoke. With the careful preservation and transcription of the audio records, this edition allows us to richly recreate what occurred then, both factually and emotionally. For those who listen to them, it is almost a face-to-face experience; for the reader, they offer plenty of fodder for emotional experiences and personal achievements.

In addition to the experiences that these supervisions offer, we find so many conceptual points of interest that it is practically impossible to list them. We can, however, highlight some of them: the perception of the amplitude of Bion's thinking, of his opening beyond the dimensions of knowing/not knowing, for what is not yet born to the mind and for the experiences of enchantment that the direct contact with reality makes possible to experience. It also gives us an opportunity to identify his view of the mind, to follow him drifting in different dimensions while approaching his model of the mind, without losing sight of the immediate moment experienced by the analytic couple. Even more, it allows us to follow how the theories (his and those of other analysts, mainly Freud's and M. Klein's) can be integrated into an analyst's mental resources without disturbing his or her clinical observation. In addition, it allows us to follow the developments of his thoughts, for example, the emergence (after 1976) of his conjectures about the existence of primordial mental states, always present, but subjected to the "impressive caesura of the act of birth" (Bion, 1977, p. 59, in reference to S. Freud, 1926).

Another significant aspect that these supervisions offer us is the opportunity to follow in detail Bion's psychoanalytic thinking in the heat of the clinical moment, and with that, to form an idea about how he conducted himself in practice at that time. It shows us an analyst who is extremely creative, patient, and generous, with impressive clarity of thought, surprising with lively comments and with a privileged emotional contact with the participants. An original thinker, with sharp focus on what is happening at the moment, always formulating his impressions in a colloquial way, rather than using conceptual language. We often witness him saying, as an exercise, what he himself would communicate to the analysand, had he been the analyst in that situation. And, on the other hand, how he weighed whether or not he would say what he thought, carefully evaluating if the analysand could follow his thought.

In addition, these supervisions provide us with elements to evaluate the speculation that Bion conducted himself in his clinical practice as "an orthodox Kleinian" (Vermote, 2011, p. 1115), an idea which suggests that there was a distance between the formulations in his books and seminars and his performance as an analyst. This perspective, obtained from statements from ex-analysands in London (before 1968) and Los Angeles (right after 1968), raises a curious issue, if compared with the view presented by José Américo Junqueira de Mattos (1980a; 1980b), Bion's analysand during his last two years of life (1977–1979). From Junqueira's descriptions, Bion was an unorthodox and understanding analyst, but who made no concessions; he was sensitive to the emotional climate of the session, but true to the traditional psychoanalytic perspective of elaborating the experience lived at the moment by the couple. An illustration (Junqueira de Mattos, 1980a) shows the climate of freedom in which Bion transited within the psychoanalytic parameters: After listening to a French poem recited by Junqueira (*Le Corbeau et le Renard*), Bion said that the theme of seduction had been treated before La Fontaine by Virgil in Aeneid's Book five and begins to recite, in English, the verses that deal with the temptation of the god of sleep to Palinurus. Facing the emotional turmoil experienced by the analysand (described by himself as "ecstasy followed by extreme distress"), Bion says:

> Yes, you became anxious because you realize that if you come here and recite poetry to me and I in the same way recite for you; you fear not supporting and entering into a state of ecstasy, seduced by the beauty of the moment and there is no more analysis ... Our work ceases ... Hence all the anxiety that invades you now. (Junqueira de Mattos, 1980b, p. 18)

A curious possibility that emerges from this controversy is that Bion himself took time to integrate into his practice what he had achieved with the development of his intuition. The analyst in London was no longer the same analyst as the one ten years later, in the early years in Los Angeles (where he was invited as a member of the Kleinian group). That change is not surprising to any experienced analyst, but is certainly an encouragement for all of us who laboriously try to include in our work the technical indications developed by Bion after 1965.

The publication of these supervisions raises yet another area of psychoanalytic interest. For various reasons, of which the language barrier is the most obvious, psychoanalysis as conceived and practiced in Brazil has been little exposed to the analytical world. We can speculate that we have developed among us a few special characteristics, which have a great deal to do with Bion's thinking and latest technical recommendations ("the late Bion"). For example, if we look at the world scene, we can follow in many analysts a form of expression in which the contributions of Bion appear as additions to the Freudian/Kleinian thinking. In contrast, among Brazilian analysts who accept the contributions from Bion, it is common to observe that their formulations bear the hallmarks of a "Bionization" of the thoughts of Freud and M. Klein. The difference is that, in the first case Bion is "thought" through the lens of Freud and M. Klein; in the second, the thoughts of Freud and

Klein are assimilated into Bion's thoughts. This may be observed in the comments that follow each of the supervisions presented in this book, all written by Brazilian analysts who are influenced by Bion's ideas and integrate them into their practice, making them their own.

This brings up yet another subject. Historically, the relationship between Bion and Brazilian analysts was both precocious and long lasting. His ideas began to circulate among Brazilian analysts at an early stage in the development of Brazilian psychoanalysis. The first translations to a foreign language of *Learning from Experience* and *Elements of Psychoanalysis* were in Portuguese, long before Bion's first trip to Brazil (1973). Also the volumes I and II of his controversial trilogy *A Memoir of the Future* (1975–1977) and *Two Papers: The Grid and Caesura* were first edited and published in English in Brazil.

The fact that Bion came to Brazil for four long periods to develop an intense work within his last six years of life does not seem arbitrary. It is possible that something vital was experienced by both sides. So, what could Bion have perceived in Brazilian analysts? Perhaps his personal correspondence or statements from his wife can bring perspective to this question. And what did Brazilian analysts see in Bion's thinking which made his influence so significant? It is certainly not the understanding of the theoretical system that emerged after Bion, something that even today we are still trying hard to reach. Possibly, what happened was an identification. The opinion of D. Meltzer (at his seminar on 8 October 1998 at the Brazilian Psychoanalytical Society of Sao Paulo) that Brazilian analysts idealize Bion's contributions seems relatively superficial, a partial interpretation of a complex set of factors. First of all, Bion always displayed great care to try not to be seen as an object of idealization, despite being very charismatic. The easily recognizable feelings in Brazilian analysts are those of admiration and gratitude for the mind-opening movement that came with Bion's helpful, personal, technical, and theoretical contributions. What could have possibly been more important was the exposure of a significant group of influential analysts to an author presenting a new vision of psychoanalysis waiting for development and pointing to the future. The impact of the acceptance of the later contributions from Bion generated a change-seeking movement that still exists today.

Another potential contribution is the particular blend of thinking and feeling (with emphasis on feeling) that characterizes the way we live our experiences. The ease with which emotions offer themselves during thought and infiltrate the verbal language, causing the unspoken to stand almost at the surface may favour our interest in *being*, since we realize the limitation of *knowing*. To live with doubts and uncertainties, as well as to value intuition, and to be less adherent to logic and intellectualization—these are other general characteristics of our mental functioning. Not by chance, these are characteristics that converge with Bion's proposals of an analytic attitude without memory, without desire and without understanding.

Today, forty years after these supervisions occurred, they may be more accessible than in previous decades, because our ability to keep up with Bion's thinking is improving. Bion spoke of the present to tomorrow's analysts, those who would emerge from the analysts who listened to him, either by psychological changes within themselves or by developments that would gain form only in subsequent generations, which we could see when he quoted Max Planck: "... a new scientific truth does not triumph by convincing its opponents and making them see the light, but rather because its opponents eventually die and a new generation grows up that is familiar to it" (Bion, 1975, p. 135). Even today, to accept Bion's contributions is to accept a challenging exposure to the new, to borders of the mind that are still waiting for analysts to explore them. In these supervisions we find psychoanalysis as we know it today and perhaps how future generations of psychoanalysts will know it as well: Such is the range of thought formulated there. What we find in it has the characteristic of timelessness, the seal of the presence of reality.

I think I have delineated enough reasons to present these more than one hundred and thirty supervisions (thirteen, in this volume) as precious insights into how Bion thought and practiced psychoanalysis in his final years. Along with the seminars conducted in Los Angeles (1976), New York (1977), Rome (1977), and São Paulo (1978), as well as the articles published in these years, they present a set whose sum enhances the richness of each part.

There is still something to be said. How can we express our appreciation, admiration, and gratitude to José Américo Junqueira de Mattos, who dearly collected, preserved, transcribed and edited these supervisions, and to his daughter, Gisèle de Mattos Brito, who is continuing this task? For this publication is not an unearthed lost treasure: what is now available to all of us is the result of patient, dedicated, and meticulous work, an endeavor of more than thirty years, thousands of hours of effort, of thorough attention to detail, substantial financial expense, personal work with the assistance of both information technologists and English teachers. In search of how to express my experience and feelings, Junqueira's (1980a) farewell to Bion at the end of their last session came to my mind. Upon Junqueira's thanking him, Bion replied that there was nothing to thank him for: "There is an English saying: Virtue is its own reward." And then Bion added: "All the reward in you being an analyst is that you are an analyst. With this I feel totally rewarded." Knowing Junqueira, I can recognize that this is also his frame of mind. So, I imagine him telling us: "I did my part and I feel already rewarded. Now it is in your hands to do what is possible for each one of you." To which I would answer: "Right, but whether you want it or not, I recognize the inestimable value of your contribution and I have a strong feeling of gratitude. I cannot find a more direct way to say this to you other than to simply say, 'Thank you very much, Junqueira.'"

References

Bion, W. R. (1975). Brasilia, a new experience. In: *Clinical Seminars and Other Works* (pp. 121–129). London: Karnac, 1994.

Bion, W. R. (1975–1977). *A Memoir of the Future, volume I and II*. Rio de Janeiro: Imago.

Bion, W. R. (1977). *Two Papers: The Grid and Caesura*, Imago: Rio de Janeiro: Imago.

Freud, S. (1926). Inhibitions, symptoms and anxiety. In: *Sigmund Freud The Complete Psychological Works* Vol. XX (pp. 75–175). London: Hogarth.

Junqueira de Mattos, J. A. (1980a). *Impressões de minha análise com Dr. Bion.* 1^{0} Colóquio Científico: W. R. Bion. SBPSP, 1980. [*Impressions of my analysis with Dr. Bion.* 1^{0} Scientific Meeting: W. R. Bion]: Brazilian Psychoanalytic Society of São Paulo.

Junqueira de Mattos, J. A. (1980b) —*Impressões de minha análise com Dr. Bion: Comentários do autor*. 1^{0} Colóquio Científico: W. R. Bion. SBPSP, 1980. [*Impressions of my analysis with Dr. Bion—Commentaries of the author*. 1^{0} Scientific Meeting: W. R. Bion]: Brazilian Psychoanalytic Society of São Paulo.

Vermote, R. (2011). Rudi Vermote's response to David Taylor. *International Journal of Psychoanalysis*, *92*: 1113–1116.

INTRODUCTION

Gisèle de Mattos Brito

That's how it all began …

It was back in 1973, and the Sao Paulo Society had newly emerged and was in the process of consolidating its own unique psychoanalytic identity. Dr. Frank Julian Philips took the initiative. Trained in London, analyzed by both Melanie Klein and Bion, he was at that time analyzing many others who would become the pioneering analysts in São Paulo and help spread analysis and Bion's ideas throughout Brazil. Together with Professor Virgínia Leone Bicudo, director of the Sao Paulo Institute, Phillips organized the first of Bion's four visits to Brazil in 1973 (the other three were in 1974, 1975, and 1978). The impact of those visits was to prove enormously influential, both in Sao Paulo and in many other Brazilian psychoanalytic Societies that the Sao Paulo group went on to help develop.

On his first visit Bion stayed at Phillips's house, and Phillips served as translator and interpreter of Bion's conferences at the Society. Dr. Philips was held in high esteem in psychoanalytic circles and his influence with the São Paulo Society helped in the introduction and acceptance of Bion's ideas. At the time, we had 122 members in the society, sixteen of whom were full members—half analyzed by Phillips, thirty-six were associates and seventy were candidates. Some had already studied Bion and were familiar with his ideas, while others were encountering his thinking for the first time. But the series of conferences not only represented contact with ideas and psychoanalytic concepts to be learned. Something much more important happened. It was to be a vital and generative *experience.*

Many of the analysts who attended these conferences and clinical seminars were deeply affected, not only by their contact with the ideas and theories that Bion laid out, but with their experience of the man. Some have reported feeling astonished, even dumbfounded. One senior analyst recalled that his experience at hearing Bion speak over the weekend, was so powerful that he cancelled all of his sessions the following Monday! He spent the day trying to digest what he had experienced and heard, rethinking what he was trying to do in analysis, and wondering how to continue to work in his practice!

Bion's initial supervisions and lectures produced a considerable hubbub in the society and many members from Sao Paulo and elsewhere, even Buenos Aires, eventually came to the later sessions. But what was it that specifically created that state of animation? Just what impact was everyone talking about that so strongly influenced theoretical and clinical positions in the São Paulo Society and throughout Brazil and Latin America? The feeling was that we were having a unique *experience,* seeing and listening to a very special person: Bion, the Man and the Thinker.

The man

As a man Bion was tall, serious, and circumspect, always available to listen. He was interested, curious, and possessed a wry sense of humor. He preferred asking questions rather than bringing answers and was careful to remind his audience that only those who participated in an experience could really know what that experience felt like. Motivated by his curiosity, he questioned, and with his reflections, he broadened our field of discussion. He constantly brought in new aspects, new points of view, One colleague, a candidate at the time, told me about the impact she felt when she realized that Dr. Bion was able to recognize and understand the feeling that had brought her to the supervision session. Essentially she did not know what was going on with a certain patient. Yes, Bion was able to say he didn't know either, and then helped us talk about our own ignorance without criticizing or attacking us, without putting himself in the role of someone who was bringing the truth, or offering a palliative or a prescription as to how psychoanalysis should be practiced.

We can see in the supervision sessions transcribed here the deep respect with which he treated both patients and colleagues. He was a wise and generous individual and used his culture and knowledge to expand the capacity of his listeners to recognize the complexity of each human being. In this way, he broadened and integrated the knowledge that emerged. This aspect of Dr. Bion's personality can be seen when reading many of his comments.

Something that caught the attention of a number of colleagues was that Bion seemed to be in the same state of mind from the moment he got up in the morning to the moment he finally went to bed at night. Junqueira Uchôa described an unusual incident that took place after one of Bion's conferences in 1973.

> [The conference] had taken up the greater part of a very long day of work and I asked him if he would like to retire for the night. Without batting an eye he answered: "But at night our mind is always working actively!" (Junqueira Uchôa, 2012, p. 77)

He also commented that, "Years later I realized that what I had seen was the 24-hour functioning of the process he described as 'dreamwork alpha'" (Junqueira Uchôa, 2012, p. 78).

The thinker

In an article published in the *Jornal do Brasil* newspaper Bojunga noted that Dr. Bion's gaze and voice were firm. He opened one conference by saying: "What can I offer you? What can I say this evening? In what area shall I display my ignorance?" (Bojunga, 1978, p. 3).

During one conference Dr. Bion told about the time when two thieves raided a sacred tomb in the cemetery at Ur. Then he asked the audience: "Was the thieves' act courageous? Could it be considered a model for science? Might those thieves serve as patrons for the scientific method?" He then wondered out loud and asked:

> What did the thieves feel? They must have been courageous to dare to dig up treasures in a place guarded by evil spirits. To summarize, each one of you who sees a patient tomorrow should feel fearful

> of the experience. And, in fact, in each psychoanalytic office there should be two frightened people: the psychoanalyst and the patient. If they are not anxious it is because they are limiting themselves to talk about what everybody already knows anyway. The familiar is a temptation, a temptation that is greater for the analyst than for the patient. And this is because psychoanalysis is one of the few frightening occupations that don't require us to leave home to carry it out. (Bojunga, 1978, p. 3)

That is beautiful! He uses the model of an attack on a tomb in the cemetery at Ur to describe the scene he imagined was present in an analyst's office, namely, tension, fear, and the courage to move ahead.

At another point Junqueira Uchôa wrote that:

> Bion's lively presence stirred up respectful expectations in his listeners. Taken up by the magnetism of his solidly structured body and circumspect facial expression, people seemed to be holding their breath in his presence, waiting for the paused distillation of the ideas that flowed from his mind like volcanic lava. The atmosphere around him was dreamlike, as if he were continually weaving a network to catch psychic objects and guide them to the best possible destination. (Junqueira Uchôa, 2012, p. 77)

True to his formulation of the importance of trying to use multiple vertices to discern new relationships between familiar elements, Bion would play freely with ideas and invert points of view. We might say he used *bi-ocular vision*[1] or that he had a modernistic gestalt, like Samuel Beckett or Ludwig Wittgenstein. In other words, he would often switch viewpoints, take ideas to their final consequences or go beyond what was already thought to be known. He possessed the ability to lead us along paths that have never been taken before. I associate this capacity to the famous poem by the Brazilian poet Carlos Drummond de Andrade, transcribed below:

José

What now, José?
The party's over,
the lights are off,
the crowd's moved on,

the night's grown cold,
what now, José?
what now, you?
you who are nameless,
who make fun of others,
you who write verses,
who love, protest,
what now, José?

Got no woman,
got no speech,
got no love,
can't drink,
can't smoke,
can't even spit,
the night's grown cold,
the day didn't come,
the tram didn't come,
laughter didn't come
utopia didn't come
and everything ended
and everything fled
and everything rotted
what now, José?

What now, José?
Your sweet words,
your moment of fever,
your feasting and fasting,
your library,
your gold mine,
your suit of glass,
your incoherence,
your hatred—what now?

Key in hand
you want to open the door,
but no door exists;
you want to die in the sea,

but the sea has dried;
you want to go to Minas,
Minas no longer exists;
José, what now?

If you could scream,
if you could groan,
if you could play
a Viennese waltz,
if you could sleep,
if you could tire,
if you could die …
But you don't die,
you are stubborn, José!

Alone in the dark
like a beast of the wild,
without any theogony,
without even a naked wall
to lean against,
without a black horse
to gallop away,
You march, José!
José, where to?

You march, José!
José, where to?[2]

—Carlos Drummond de Andrade

My impression when reading these supervision sessions is that Bion, like Drummond de Andrade, makes us wonder about the meaning of our own existence and the existence of the world. He challenges us to try to be in contact with the unknown, the unknowable and, at the same time, calls us, as responsible analysts, to work on this enormous—often terrifying and confusing—undertaking of being a psychoanalyst.

Was it coincidental that this poem was written during World War II, at which time Brazil lived under the repression of the Vargas dictatorship? Like José, Bion lived in times of the agony of war. Two wars. And yet he managed to make a good deal from it. He had the strength to move ahead even without knowing where he might be headed, deep in doubt and insecurity, alone in the dark, but with faith and the conviction that we must move ahead.

Traveling along strange and original paths, Bion talked to us about ourselves, and even today he continues to have an impact on us, as he unmasks and illuminates our complicated existence with deep and revealing comments. Through these supervision sessions, he helped us, then, and still helps us today, to make contact with our own unique and individual experiences.

We move ahead, open, expectant, frightened, hopeful, vulnerable … with Bion as our companion …[3]

Notes

1. "Bi-ocular" rather than "binocular" in that he preserved the distinction between different points of view as his attention oscillated back and forth between them, rather than resolving them into a distinct and flawless image the way an optical instrument would.
2. English translation: Tsotha (http://forum.literotica.com/showthread.php?t=1035734&page=2) last accessed 14 October 2016.
3. I would like to extend my special thanks to our colleagues José Américo Junqueira de Mattos, Luiz Carlos Uchôa Junqueira Filho, Mayer Snitcovsky, and Antonio Luiz Serpa Pessanha, for their information and impressions which helped greatly in drawing up this introduction.

References

Andrade, C. D. (2012). José. In: *Antologia poética* (pp. 28–29). First edition. São Paulo: Companhia das Letras.

Bojunga, C. (1978). One of the best psychoanalyst in the world is in São Paulo. Does anyone know? *Jornal do Brasil*, 3.

Junqueira Uchoa, L. C. (2012). Dimensions, Psychoanalyze, Brazil. São Paulo: Brazilian Society of São Paulo, p. 77.

CHAPTER ONE

Supervision A1

In the text that follows, T stands for translator; P1 and P2 stand for participants in the audience of the supervision.

T: This patient came to analysis concerned about all the lies he had told to the people with whom he lived in order, to appear as a "normal" person. One of the lies was that he met a girlfriend when he went away on vacation. When he returned from one of these trips, he was with his school friends and they were mostly girls. On the way up in the lift, they asked how things were going with his girlfriend and he became very disturbed. So, he didn't go up the lift, he went up the escalator. Then, when he found the girls waiting for him, he realized that he had made up the story and felt ill with anguish and then he didn't know who he really was, where he came from, or if he was meeting the same people again that he had met down below. This, the patient told to the analyst, in his first interview, while sitting on a chair, and moving about, posing as if he were a clown.

Bion: Can we just pause there? Supposing all of us saw this patient for the first time, does anybody have any idea what your impression would be about it? Take a guess. I'd like to suggest … Have you all got paper? Because, I think it might be quite interesting for you, if you'll write here, how, in any order, the first impression that you get about this patient. Now, when you've done that … turn it over and hide it from yourself—like that! Just hide it from yourself. Just fold it over, so you don't see it, turn it back, whichever you like! Shall we go on?

T: In his experience with this client, A came to know a fact that was very important. The story the patient told was that he had observed his father constantly worrying about economic security and how much money he had in the bank. The patient had similar worries and when he realized this he also realized that he wished that his father—whom he didn't like, who was a very unlikable person, would die so that he could inherit his father's wealth. Six months, later, when he was conscious of this death wish, in relation to his father, his father died unexpectedly of a very sudden illness.

Bion: Did he call it a death wish?

T: He called it a death wish and felt as if he had done something that, in fact, had killed his father.

Bion: … Anything about this case? Any impression that you get?

T: [At this point, the translator informs the group in Portuguese that she has an opinion] It's not so much about the case, but (A) had said that he had the impression that the patient was a young man, but he actually was not a young man. What I noticed is that A is still speaking about him, as if he were a very young man.

P2: Like prince Hamlet! Denmark.

T: Now he is twenty-six years old.

Bion: I don't know if you'd like to write again, once more, your diagnosis and fold it over again. Write it and hide it from yourself. We started by making our first correction of the impression, from the very first, the first goal and then hiding that. This is the second time we're giving our impression. I'll give you my impressions if you like. I don't know whether you'd like me to give you my impressions now, because I've also changed in the same way!

P1: Give your impressions!

T: Yes!

Bion: I don't want to make any pronouncements about the patient, but I would like to give you an idea of the way that I think about this patient. Now, one point is: why does he look young? Is it his skin? Is it his small muscles of the face? Is it his posture? Because none of that has to do with what he said—but it is what his body says. It's what we can see, with our eyes, without touching him. There are one or two other things, which I would expect to notice. For example: was there an odor, a smell? Language corporal and psychic body language? Similarly, if I were a musician, how would I record the sounds that he makes? However, the first point is: how does the patient make you think what his age is? And how does he contradict that? If you feel that the patient is younger than he looks like.

P2: Is it a question that you are asking?

Bion: Well, I'm asking you to think of this; this is what I would be doing. Now, suppose the patient hasn't said that he is twenty-six? Is there any way in which his body has said, that he is older than twenty-six? What part of his body has said, that he is younger than twenty-six? Now, if that is the case, does the body conflict with the body? Or are conflicts only up here? [Bion indicates his head].

We talked about conflicts and we usually mean mental conflicts. What I'm suggesting is that we forget all that and remember this idea of conflict. For example: the patient might disagree with me—in which case, he would certainly be disagreeing with himself *and* with me. I don't want to bother about that. What I'm bothering about is that he looks younger than he is. What part of his body tells me he is older than he looks? What part of his body tells me that he looks younger than another part of his body tells me he is?

T: What was the second option … could you …?

Bion: Simply: the two sides of it! What says that he is old? What says that he is young? For example, if his voice and manner were that of the young man, but shall we say, that his hair was gray, would his hair be disagreeing with his muscles? That's just to give an idea of why I would want to know how his body is contradicting his body. Now, the other point that strikes me is that he talks as if he had learnt how to imitate everybody, in relation with being aware of difference, imitates everybody else. But as if he were aware that he is not like everybody else. He's learnt to look like everybody else, but he is not like everybody else—he is not in fact. Now, I don't think I would want to say anything to him, but there is a difficulty, because if I were there, if I didn't say anything, the patient might become too anxious. Therefore, I would want to watch in silence, but if the analyst's silence is making the patient feel anxious, then he might leave the room and not come back again. So, this becomes a matter of difficulty for the analyst, because the analyst needs also to help the patient stay in the room. It might be a good thing to consider whether you would say anything or not, so far.

T: A would like to add something now.

Bion: Yes.

T: A is very grateful, in a way, because of the way we are talking about speaking and not speaking, in the session, because this arises, even today in his relation with the patient: speak and not speak. The patient, when he is silent, gets so anxious that he has the impression …

Bion: When who is silent?

T: When the analyst, is silent, the patient gets so anxious that he himself starts speaking, saying things like, for example: the interpretation he imagines he would hear if the analyst should speak to him. He says to the analyst: "Speak, tell me anything, make even a noise, because I can't stand the silence."

Bion: Now, here again, musicians have certain advantages, because they can make notes on paper, which represent notes of music. Musical sounds that patients make. But amongst these marks they make, they also have what they call: rests, breath stops, and so on … I don't know if anybody is a musician, so, it would be quite a good thing to notice that the patient can't stand the *silence.* Why some patients cannot tolerate silence ... Now that is a very common thing. If you are dealing with a child patient, the parents find it very difficult to tolerate the analyst's silence, having known you only through their child. So, very often, it is useful if the analyst can say to the parents: "Don't talk to me, talk to Dr. X he'll help you." With a grown man, with the adult, it's more difficult because he is the parent. But the statement the patient has made is, in fact, putting pressure on the analyst to make him talk—because if the analyst doesn't talk, the patient might go away and never come back again. On the other hand, if the analyst does talk, he may be compelled to talk prematurely before he wants to. Now, why can't this patient stand a silence?

T: P2 asked if he can speak to you?

Bion: Oh, yes!

T: P2 thinks that the patient, in this moment, is reviving some experience with his primary love object; in this case, his mother, and therefore he couldn't know what was happening to him. He didn't have a symbol to signify in the beginning what he wanted to say and he was demanding that the mother should ... communicate with him. He asks Dr. X if the client expressed anything through his actions. It seems that the client doesn't speak or doesn't have much symbolic capacity.

Bion: Now, to get on to this second point, which I'm working on all the time, namely: the practice of analysis! Suppose we all agree, that we would think that, about the patient what would we do? What would you say to the patient? Would you say anything or not?

T: A would like to say, what he has been doing and P2 suggests he should say this at the end.

Bion: Well, again, I'd like to suggest that you write down, on a bit of paper, whether you'd say anything or not and if you would say something, what would that be—and again, turn it over! To fold a piece of paper is rather similar to forgetting. Notes, taking notes, memory, and desire. What I said before in terms of not keeping to memory or desire.

Memory: the past; desire: anticipation. So, by hiding what you've written, is like forgetting it. Memory and desire in relation to taking notes. Now, here again, I'd like to tell you how I think about it. I would consider that the patient is having a very unpleasant experience. The unpleasant experience is being dependent and being all-alone. Being dependent and all-alone. They're indistinguishable. The patient is all-alone with the analyst. He is both dependent on the analyst being there—which is a nasty feeling—and he is all-alone, which is also a nasty experience. If I thought the patient might walk out and leave the room, I think, although I mightn't want to say anything, I would say what I've just said. I would say: "You are finding this very frightening to be all-alone in this room with me. Perhaps we shall find out, perhaps we shall understand this more later." I would prefer, if I could, not to say anymore—but I would prefer, if I could, not to increase the patient's anxiety, either by remaining silent, or by saying too much. But I would like to make it clear that, while I would like to be able to do that, I would hate to give the impression that I knew *how* to do it. Here, in this group, it's much easier to talk about this. It's much easier for me than for me with the patient. It's different from being the analyst. I don't think that I would be, at all, surprised if such a patient didn't come back again—whichever I did.

T: P2 is asking if it wouldn't be very bad for the patient, if this situation were repeated, from his childhood, in which he didn't receive words or something from his primary love object and now the situation happens again. If it doesn't repeat the situation of the frustrating object in the present situation?

Bion: There's always that risk. That is why it is so much easier to talk about this, when the patient isn't here. Psychoanalysis is extremely difficult. The theory is quite easy; it's easy to theorize about this. That is why I don't want to give the impression that I think that the practice of analysis is easy. So often and unfortunately, it is encouraged by institutions of psychoanalysis, that it's considered to be a bad thing to lose a patient. Practice of analysis is much more difficult than the theory. Theory of psychoanalysis is much easier than practice. It may be a bad thing: but practicing analysts lose patients. There is no such thing, as a practicing analyst, who isn't always losing patients. Losing patients … is it a bad thing losing a patient? When one is young and inexperienced, then one thinks it's terrible to lose a patient! When you are my age you've gotten used to it. For the patient, it is also a terrible experience to get lost. He isn't used to getting lost; feelings of getting lost. Frustrations that the patient experiences. Now, I think that this particular patient also, may not be at all familiar with frustrations, because I suspect, very strongly, that he has learnt to behave like everybody else, in the way that a good mimic can. The sort of mimic, who can professionally take up an acting profession. He isn't good enough to be able to do that. So he's not a professional actor/actress. But he isn't good enough to be real either. So, this matter is difficult, because part of the analytic situation is, for the patient to get used to frustration and it helps him to feel that the analyst, likewise, is frustrated, but is not so frightened of it.

Now, I'm afraid it's time, isn't it? Hum ... if you've got a moment, can you now write down what, in any order, any thoughts you have about this patient and then, if you'll compare, what you've written on your first bit, with the second and also, if you'll compare the order; if you take whatever the impressions were, the first two, or three impressions that we've formed, what order did you put them down on the paper in the first time and what order have you put them in this time.

Well, there we'll have to stop, I'm afraid!

Supervision A1 commentary

Julio Frochtengarten

The observations that follow are made with the deepest affection, respect, and appreciation for Bion's valuable contributions to psychoanalysts.

The first question I asked myself concerns which aspects of this supervision I ought to emphasize and comment on in order to give life to a written document. It is certainly not a matter of supervising Bion, or adding comments to the supervision of the analyst. I think the material that we now have allows us to become reasonably acquainted with Bion's psychoanalytic way of thinking. A reader familiar with his ideas will recognize that *hallucinosis* is a paramount issue in this supervision, although many other interesting aspects—for example, the termination of analysis—also came up at the time. I have organized these comments around three main lines of ideas that came to me while reading the transcript of Bion's meeting with Brazilian psychoanalysts.

First line of approach

In his first intervention, Bion suggests that group members write down their "impression" of the patient. During the meeting, he repeats this suggestion three other times, with only minor variations: they should put their "diagnoses" in writing; record "what they would say to the patient"; and, finally, jot down "any thoughts" they might have on the patient. I see this proposal as a psychoanalytic game, an approximation of what takes place in the mind of the analyst when she attains the state of free-floating attention. Experience shows us that, because of the stimuli that arise during the course of a session—internal and external stimuli from within and from outside—new thoughts emerge or are added, successively modifying how one sees what occurs in the consulting room.

At the end of the transcript, as part of the proposed psychoanalytic game, Bion suggests that participants compare the various notes they took in sequence. This process, by which our view of a situation changes, occurs regardless of contradictions, logic or consequences. I think Bion is encouraging the analyst to welcome the emotional experience that takes place over the course of a session between herself and the patient. The proposal he made to the participants is now reproduced in the experience of reading the transcript.

I see here one of the main features of Bion's contributions: descriptively, to give heed to the emotional experience and learn from it; or, conceptually, to use the α function. This is the analyst's tool in a session. I think this is the process he refers to in a footnote in *Learning from Experience*: "The process that the analyst is activating is, in the cases in which he is investigating disorders of thought, designed to investigate the same process in the patient" (Bion, 1962, p. 103).

As the analyst presents the clinical report, he establishes a relation between three elements: the savings of the patient's father; the patient's desire that his father die so he can appropriate them; and the father's sudden death due to an illness. The analyst assigns a causal character to this relation, originating from the patient's system of lies (hallucinosis). Bion does not share this viewpoint and, as I see it, it is clear that learning from the emotional experience precludes a causal relationship of this kind. I believe the psychoanalytic game mentioned above had already made it clear that learning from emotional experience does not involve logic, consistency or consequences.

I believe that all the thoughts (in the broadest sense) of the participants, as proposed in the psychoanalytic game, are their *transformations*. As such, they can then be classified, *a priori*, anywhere in the grid—including column 2[1] that includes the β[2] elements, which the analyst uses in her work. These thoughts gradually create a receptive environment for the emergence of the *selected fact*. "By selected fact I mean that by which coherence and meaning is given to facts already known but whose relatedeness has not hitherto been seen" (Bion, 1963, p. 19).

> The selected fact is the name of an emotional experience, the emotional experience of a sense of discovery of coherence; its significance is therefore epistemological and the relationship of selected facts must not be assumed to be logical. (Bion, 1963, p. 73)[3]

It seems to me we arrive here at a new conjunction, one that will continue to be developed until the end of Supervision A1, namely, the emotion that accompanies the analyst when he has two dissonant, contradictory, and simultaneous impressions about the patient—he seems young and he seems not to be young. Bion insists that both impressions be kept in mind, that neither be discarded. To examine these impressions, he both resorts to sensory elements and approaches the patient's mental elements—the contact with the individual as a whole, mental, and physical. His thoughts are inquiring and he "wanders" through the hair, the body, the resemblance to an ordinary person, the youngish posture, the clownish poses in the first interview—the similarity to a mimic. Progressively, this mental movement maintains the contradictory impressions side by side, without emphasizing one or the other, leading Bion to the idea of *imitation*—"being like everyone else"—and to the patient's perception of it ("as if aware that he is not like everyone else").

In this first line approach, I have tried to describe how I saw Bion, the analyst, working, approaching something that I have come to equate with the concept of *hallucinosis*, a singular "vision" of the emotional experience.

Second line of approach

In a second stance, I highlight what Bion referred to as "the practice of analysis." He examines the question of the analyst feeling compelled to speak before desiring to do so, and how this pressure interferes with analytical observation. He states he would rather not *have to* (italics mine) say anything, or not say much, but is sensitive to the fact that this would make the patient unsustainably anxious: "the analyst must also help the patient remain in his office."

I understand the expression "not have to say anything" as "true north" for the analyst, not as a practical suggestion. The same reference to the freedom of the analyst can be found in many other passages of Bion's writings. I quote, as an example, the following excerpt from Bion:

> The analyst, to observe correctly, must be sensitive to as many of the phenomena that are included in these headings as possible. The more nearly he is able to approximate to this ideal, the nearer he is to the first essential in psychoanalysis—or, for that matter, any other science—namely, correct observation. The complement of the first essential is the last essential—correct interpretation. By "first" essential I mean not only priority in time but priority in importance, because if an analyst can observe correctly there is always hope; it is of course a big "if". Without the last essential he is not an analyst, but if he has the first essential he may become one in time; without it he can never become one, and no amount of theoretical knowledge will save him. (Bion, 1997, p. 14)

Third line of approach

As my final approach to Bion's supervision, I begin with a question put forth by one of the members of the group, who asked whether the patient's *expression* occurred through *actions* or through *symbols*. This participant said, "[The patient] is *demanding* that his mother should communicate with him" (italics mine). If, this is correct and the patient expresses himself through actions, not through symbolic language, what should the analyst do?

Bion suggested, for the last time on that occasion, that each participant write down whether he would say something and what it would be. I imagine that I would like to intervene in the session in order to "create" an interlocutor and, thus, contribute to get the analysis underway. To this end, there would have to be a division in the patient that enabled him to see what was going on. What I am suggesting is that if the analyst finds something to say, he has at his disposal an alternative to silence which could lead to an interruption of the analysis—although this possibility should always be taken into account.

Finally, we should remember Bion's intervention almost at the end of the meeting: "You are finding this very frightening, being all alone in the office with me. We may discover, we may understand this better later on." It is a short, simple remark, seemingly unpretentious, in which he talks *to* the patient and, in doing so, indicates the possible existence of a certain feeling. His intervention does not assume the patient already has symbolic abilities—as would the intervention, "the patient is reliving some experience with his primary love object, his mother, who must not know what's going on with him"—but, by "making" the interlocutor, the analyst leads, in the direction I have proposed above, to the commencement of analysis.

Notes

1. "... the theory used as a barrier against the unknown will remain the armoury of analyst." Bion, 1963, p. 18.
2. "I reserve the term, 'Knowledge', for the sum total of α and β- elementes. It is a term that therefore covers everything the individual knows and does not know." Bion, 1992, p. 182.
3. See in *Bion*, 1992, p. 275*: The cause and the selected fact.*

References

Bion, W. R. (1962). Learning from experience. In: *Seven Servants* (pp. 1–105). New York, NY: Jason Aronson.

Bion, W. R. (1963). Elements of psycho-analysis. In: *Seven Servants* (pp. 1–104). New York, NY: Jason Aronson.

Bion, W. R. (1992). *Cogitations.* London: Karnac.

Bion, W. R. (1997). *Taming Wild Thoughts.* London: Karnac.

CHAPTER TWO

Supervision S12

In the text that follows, T stands for translator; A stands for analyst; P1, P2, P3, P4, and P5 stand for participants in the audience of the supervision.

A: The patient is a female approximately forty years old, who dresses too young for her age. As she is a foreigner, she speaks Portuguese with a strong accent. She's been consulting me for more than one year, but only two months ago we have been able to start analysis at four times a week.

Bion: When you say: "her dress is not in conformity with her age," is that her opinion, or is that the impression you get?

A: It is mine.

Bion: I see. So she thinks it's all right?

A: Yes. Before we began treatment, she phoned me twice. She was very interested and wanted to begin the treatment. When she first came to my office to arrange the treatment, she was very excited and happy because I had an hour to spare. Just before beginning the treatment, she was in Europe on holiday. In a big city shopping street, amongst all the crowds, she suddenly felt ill and frightened of being alone and of something happening to her, with no one to turn to.

Bion: May I interrupt a moment? I think that this is quite fundamental! It seems to me that even a baby—although it can't verbalize it, of course—can feel dependant and all-alone. They go together, they're both unpleasant feelings and in fact, the feeling that is unpleasant is: being dependant and being all-alone you have both at once. So, one could say: you can be all-alone with yourself, all-alone with your analyst, all-alone with a crowd of people in a shopping street. It's a curious combination of being all-alone and dependant on people and things that are not you. We seem to be the kind of animal that has to have a society, that has to have brothers and sisters, fathers and mothers, or the whole apparatus of society. We depend on that and we're all-alone at the same time. So, I think that this point is right up-to-date, it's at the age of forty, it's also at the age of four and the age of nought. So, I think this is straight away a fundamental point!

A: So, you want to say that it always remains in us?

Bion: I think so. But, I think it is something to which the analyst tries to introduce the patient, because, the patient has either: forgotten it or has never been conscious of it. It's like having the experience, but never being aware of the experience. The advantage of the analytic discussion is: the patient gets a chance of being aware of a feeling that they have never really been consciously aware of.

A: Well, she informed me that she travelled alone. Her father died four years ago and her mother last year. The patient lived with them for some years. Here, we need more information on that. Before this, she lived for a long time on her own. She had an independent life, a long way from her parents. She was an only child. In the session before that one, from which we extracted the text given below, she explained that she had kept her parent's bedroom intact, ever since her mother's death. She never moved anything, not even the clothes, the furniture, the ornaments or the photographs.

P1: Now, I'm thinking about the furniture, the ornaments ... it's the presence of the parents, it's necessary, the presence of the parents in the house.

A: They're in the photograph.

P1: No change, because she needed the parents.

Bion: The advantage of the facts is that, it's easier to say: "It's me" and "It's this photograph" or whatever it is. It's easier to talk about the furniture of the room, than to talk about the furniture of her mind or character; but, it's a step in that direction. It's a sort of way of getting to know, in which, the patient can get to know who he or she herself is. It's a sort of transient relationship. It's a sort of transference. When there is an actual analyst, then it can be, it can become again transient, he can know who the analyst is and so on ... Or who may be the father, the mother, the brother, the sister, everybody ...—a crowd of people; but, it's on the way to something else ...

P2: Would it mean that the objects mobilize less emotion than people?

Bion: No, I think it's a matter of feeling that it would be more bearable if, what we would say, to know yourself and to be ignorant of yourself. Even the inscriptions at Delphi says: "Know thyself."**[1] So, it's a very old story, which would somehow be useful to know yourself. But, on the way to knowing yourself, it's easier to know the furniture of your house. You might get to know the furniture of your mind in time ... but, it's a step on the way. Similarly, it's a step on the way if the analyst can say: "You feel that I am like your father or mother" or whatever it is. We don't mean that *that* is what you think and that is what you'll think forever, but it's on the way, it's one of the stepping stones on the way to knowing yourself. But, like the Ancient Greeks we still think that it is helpful for patients and ourselves to *know ourselves.* Only the analytic procedure is carrying that ambition, or that aspiration, a step, we hope, further. We hope that by these analytic conversations we shall get a bit closer to knowing who we are. Mind you, I'm doubtful whether any of us will ever live long enough to know ourselves, but, on the way ... We're one little bit of the story we started with Delphi and far earlier than that.

A: So, we would be substituting an ancient religious institution, through which people try to know themselves, the Delphic Oracle?

Bion: No, the Delphic religion, the worship of Apollo, would be a step on the way, to what we know now. Mind you, I don't say that we are better than the ancient Hebrews, or Greeks or Chinese and so on ... That is a matter of opinion. We can, really, ask ourselves where the human race is improving or deteriorating. That's a matter of opinion. If we knew a bit more about ourselves and a bit more about the ancient human beings, like the Egyptians or the Greeks, or the Chinese and so on ... then, we could get some idea as to which way we are going.

P1: So, the photos and other things, related ornaments, they are a step, an intermediate object between parents and the childhood and the analyst?

Bion: And between the parents and between the patient and the patient. Between the unmarried patient and the patient who is a father and mother. This patient hasn't yet got a husband or a wife. The patient hasn't yet got sons and daughters, but this may be on the way to having one, or becoming one.

A: By the way, the patient, on another occasion, informed me that she was married at seventeen, for one year. She had a child. She said that she couldn't stand that life: tied to a child and home. She wanted to travel and enjoy life. She separated herself from her husband and her husband's family kept the child. They are people of means and of education, greater than her own family. She went to another country, where she lived for some years alone. She has never seen her child since, nor is she interested in doing so.

Bion: I think that she is afraid that if she goes on with these conversations with the analyst, she will get to know herself as a child and then, she may think that the clothes that she is wearing aren't really appropriate to whom she is. That is easier for you to see, than for her.

P1: To show the filicide to her?

A: I have my doubts if she had this son, mentally.

Bion: Yes. Quite. Yes.

A: Although, I don't think it's a filicide, because I don't think she had a son.

P1: That it wasn't a son is not important; it's a filicide …

Bion: Because the feeling that a mother might have about a son or a daughter could be very powerful. So, what's happened to them? In the meantime, she is hoping to escape from them by coming to Brazil, or wherever it is. You can move about the surface of the earth, but, whether you can really escape is different. There might be some reason why she comes to see an analyst. I don't suppose she knows …

A: Really, the impression I have of this patient is that she's passing her life escaping.

Bion: Yes. She's probably more expert at that than anything else …

A: More expert at escaping?

Bion: Yes.

A: Escaping from herself.

May I go on? Well, we have a small part of a session from Monday. She came in looking very miserable and said: "When will I get better? I don't think that anything is pleasurable. I feel so alone. It was just a weekend like all the others … I'm worried about the future. I feel as if I am becoming more and more alone, all the time. Yesterday my friends picked me up at home and we went to city X [X is a small city near ours], but I got no pleasure from it at all. They were all very kind, but what help was it?" And she cries a little.

Bion: I think that this is, again, part of this *fundamental* story, that she can't tolerate a situation in which she is all-alone with herself, even when she is with other people. In other words, this self won't leave her alone. That self goes with her, but we don't yet know what this *self* is. It certainly isn't a self that she wants to be alone with, so, she is always reaching out for somebody else. If she couldn't come to you, she would certainly go to somebody else. If she couldn't find anybody else, then, she'd find a crowd of people like on the shopping street. Anywhere, where there are masses of people, so as to avoid being aware that she is with herself, whether she likes it or not.

A: I have an idea about this. I heard her saying that all those people in city X were very kind, very nice, but, they are all the same, like the furniture that are always the same in the room of her parents. The people are felt by her as furniture. They are dead objects; she can't distinguish them. Very kind, beautiful and nice; but there isn't life. It's always the same, like that. Objects just don't change. Like in R the shopping street, there is a crowd, they are just furniture, not persons, just objects. Like inanimate objects, ornaments and she is alone, between them, in the middle of a dead life. She has no relation to life. The child is an object for her. For this, she may leave the child alone, her own child. It's just the same that she is not in contact with itself. With the life, or people around her position. She's alone. "Perhaps with you too, in your session, in your Monday, just the same, always the same. You're sitting there, you're a furniture for me too." Something like this.

Bion: I would like to suggest that, to me, it appears that this self—that she is so anxious to escape from is a very difficult thing, even for me, to describe. I feel pretty sure that I know what it is that she's talking about, but, I find it difficult to describe. The best way that I can describe it is: it's a sort of *urge to exist*. Now, the *urge to exist* of which I'm talking about seems to me to be completely indifferent to mere human beings. The urge to exist does not care whether we die, or die in childbirth or in any other way. Her parents similarly: the urge to exist forces them to give birth to a child, whether they want one or not. So, she herself is a product of that same urge to exist. So, she herself is at the mercy of that same urge to exist. So, she herself is frightened of being all-alone with that urge to exist—which doesn't mind what happens to her. It's completely ruthless. That's the sort of impression that I get. So, I think that she is terrified of something to which her parents were enslaved and to which she is afraid of being enslaved herself. She is a slave to the urge, to the impulse. She, herself, is just an object on the way. Of course, it's all very theoretical, it's very problematic!! Impulses may seem completely indifferent to the human being. If they're wiped out, then, another kind of thing will exist, instead.

T: A is asking if it is the client's conjecture. We have the impression it's your words. Are you saying it's the client's?

Bion: I'm saying it's mine, but I suspect this is something of which we are all victims. The patient notices it, or the patient hates it. Hates just being a slave to this impulse. It doesn't matter whether she dies in childbirth or not, or whether she's seventeen or seventy. At seventeen she gets a baby, even if she can't look after it. Even at seventeen she has to have a sexual mate, whether she wants him or not, or whether the sexual mate wants her or not. But, I think she's got reasons to be afraid of that urge, which will make use of her to produce another life. I think it is really felt to be a very frightening force. A very frightening sort of dominant master of—not only the human being—but all forms of life, whether the forms of life are algae or germs or cocci. If the human race was wiped out, these impulses would still find something or another to exist by.

A: Something, like an incarnation theory?

Bion: Yes, quite. But, if it's not incarnation, then, it's *implantation*. Plants will do just as well. It's not only bacilli it's also the coccus. It's not only animal life, but, also, botanical life. Recently, it's been suggested that there's a form of animate object, which is neither animal nor vegetable.

A: There would be two kinds of self or ego. The one that pre-exists; the other that uses this urge to life, herself or the patient oneself too and that comes into and uses this other life …

Bion: I think that the Id or the Ego has a kind of resemblance to it, but this is, I suspect, relatively superficial. I think that this is something, which is more than the human being and we are all, after all, only investigating human beings. That's all we can do, we can just, psychoanalytically, investigate a particular human being.

T: Why? Would you put what Freud sometimes worked at as the instinct of self-preservation? Because, I have the impression we're talking about the impulse in the general sense of species …

Bion: I think one could place that in the human being, but, it's because the human being wants to go on existing. But, this impulse to which I'm going to draw attention and which, I think she is frightened of, doesn't mind what happens to her. That's why you get, these states of affairs, in which you get: maternal mortality, infant mortality. It doesn't matter what happens to the mother or child, provided life goes on … The mere fact that the mother or child dies, it doesn't matter, just find another mother and child and so on … through the list. If you run out of human beings, you fall back on plants.

P3: Would it be the *negative capability* that you once mentioned, responsible for us being able to think about it?

Bion: No. I think it is the peculiarity of the human animal that has got into the way of thinking and it caused an awful lot of trouble! I think that we *hate* being the sort of animal that thinks. We don't know what to do with it.

P3: With thinking?

Bion: It's a sort of *curse* that we live under … We think! "Cogito ergo sum, sum ergo cogito."[2]

You can look at it any way you like. But, we're just part and parcel of this story. When this business started, or how it came about, I don't know … But we are involved in a decision, which has been taken … Heaven knows when!!! So, we are under the obligation to go on thinking … And now, we have this difficulty: that we want to be able to think properly. We have this apparatus of thought, but we also want to know how to think … or how to think clearly!!

P4: Please, I want to ask a question about that. This is a very serious problem, how to think. But the human being forgets that it's better for him to think …

Bion: I don't think he knows it.

P4: Well, that's only an opinion …

Bion: I think it's a very small number of people who, like us, think that we ought to think. I think the vast majority of people would like it if you could put yourself in the position of Freud's paper on "Two principles of mental functioning" (1915), to go straight from the impulse to action, without thinking.

P4: But, the question is: is this a moral statement? This one that I made, that it's better for the human beings to think …?

Bion: It's hard to know, because there seems to be a kind of *inborn moral statement*. In the way for example, I think that the Roman Catholic Church talks about the *original sin*. I think that that's what they mean. We are born with a feeling of guilt, we are born with that, which some day turns into a kind of *conscience*. But the *primordial original sin* isn't really a conscience exactly; it becomes one, or seems to do. So, I think it's another of these basic fundamental things like this point that I mentioned before. It seems to me that the feeling of *dependence and being all-alone*, is also fundamental. So is *guilt*.

A: Did you say that we are born, we're been born with this feeling of guilt?

Bion: It seems to be. Of course, later it becomes concerned with matters like: discriminating between *Good* and *Evil*.

P1: Sounds like the story of the original sin, *Expulsion of Paradise*, would be rather a good version of the origin of this dynamic …

Bion: Well, I think that there is a wish to believe that there is or will be, a kind of *Paradise*. Or that there was a time when we were in Heaven … there will be a time when we will be in Heaven! The awkward thing is about *now* … and *now* we are not in Heaven … we are not in Paradise …

A: You said that you feel like that, you feel that you have been cursed. We hate our situation of being able to think.

Bion: Hmm, Hmm … (During this comment, the analyst is speaking very rapidly. From the rhythm of this speech we grasp that he is tense, emotional to a point that Dr. Bion tried to intervene. We hear Dr. Bion uttering some characteristic sounds, but A keeps on talking).

A: We hate this urge to live, in a way, in this way I thought that we feel guilty, a kind of primary guilt; born feeling guilty. As if we would have been cursed, *expelled* from another state, that would be just like being guilty.

Bion: I think, it's not so much our urge to live, as being the *slaves* to the urge to live. We have to feed ourselves, clothe ourselves, cure ourselves.

P5: What would your opinion be about the observation that so few people apparently think?

Bion: It's largely to do with what your standard of comparison is. The idea is based on a standard: that of thinking properly. So, you might feel that many people could think, but, they don't think properly, or they don't think clearly. But, the fact is that: the human being is a very imperfect animal. I mean, this point is clear with an infant: an infant has to have a mother or father, but there's no mother or father to the grown man or woman. There's nobody to look after them, except themselves … The result is that they have to provide themselves with clothes, food, work … and even have to keep their bodies and their minds in working order—whether we like it or not. But, we don't all go at the same speed.

The same thing seems to apply to ourselves; for example: our genital apparatus may not travel at the same speed as our ability to see. Our ability to hear, may not travel at the same speed as the apparatus of the adrenal bodies. In the embryo, as you know, one can get some kind of idea about the development of the adrenal bodies, the development of the gonads. Then, after that, after we are born, then again, our alimentary canal takes over. The importance is: whether our alimentary system is feeling hungry, feeling it wants something in it. Then, it is complicated by the fact that we become aware of thinking. Then, we get into trouble because we do become aware of the fact that we need to think clearly and then, you get people that have what we, nowadays, call a "scientific view." That only means an aspiration towards knowing what the Truth is.

It doesn't matter whether we are religious, or artistic or musical. All of us find a pressure of this need to do it properly. The imitation music, imitation painting, imitation sculpture, isn't good enough, nor is imitation analysis. Lots of people learn how to use words like: Oedipus complex, inferiority … We don't know what those words mean … That's the whole point about the analytic training is that we try to know what these words mean … Not just have words, which are noises which sound as if we could think, but being able to think, as well as sounding as if we could think. It's summed up by the rather sarcastic statement of: "people who mistake deep noises from the chest for profound thoughts from the mind."

P5: Could I ask a question since the time is almost over? I tried to work out, if guilty feelings, as you said, are something … are a peculiar human inheritance, like thinking is also peculiarly human, in the sense you're meaning. I was wondering if original sin or this guilt feeling, could be related to the fact that we can't think clearly, that if this basic guilt feeling we are born with doesn't come, because we feel that we can't think perfectly, ever?

Bion: No. I don't think so. I think that the difficulty is how to harmonize or how to marry our ability to think with our ability to feel. Now, it's no good becoming so intellectual that we don't have any human feeling at all. On the other hand, there's the problem that if we allow ourselves to be feeling people, then how is it possible to avoid a situation in which our capacity to feel overwhelms our capacity to think? So, I think that there is always this sort of *storm* going on inside us. Sometimes the waves of thought rise so high that our capacity to feel is submerged. Sometimes our capacity to feel rises so high that our capacity to think is submerged!

This is the sort of thing that happens to me, or any of us, when we lose our abilities to think, because of the experience of panic, fear … or lose our capacity to fear, so that we do extremely dangerous things, like waging war—in which after all chances are that we can get ourselves killed. So, from that point of view, you can't very well decide to be a completely unfeeling person. Because, if one could do that, then, one would end up by being a sort of psychiatric case, one that could be, I suppose, indistinguishable from a state of panic. On the other hand, if you *do allow* yourself to have feelings, then, you can get also somewhere near to being manic depressive; going from: the height of mania to the depths of depression from the depths of depression, to the height of mania and so on … "Fluctuat nec mergitur" as Freud said when he was impressed by the motto of Paris,**[3] "Storm tossed, but not submerged." So far, we managed to keep afloat; so far … But, we can be submerged by becoming too intellectual—like this patient who is afraid of becoming addicted to psychoanalysis—meaning by that: the person that only thinks and never feels, or a person that only feels and never thinks. Those are the extremes. But, from the moment, to moment it's always a problem of how to decide that. Now ... Now, what it is to decide ... I don't know. I don't know if any of you have formed any ideas about this. Superficially, it sounds as if ... I think it is what the Jesuits called *arbitrium* ... What decides? When we decide not to be dominated by a feeling, like fear, or greed, or sex ... What decides that? If it is something to do with our brain ... What brain? The nose brain? The rhinencephalon, diencephalon, cerebellum? The lymphatic system? The spleen? Or this stuff up here.

[A gesture should have been with the hand in direction of the head].

Or is this only a kind of gigantic neural exchange? Like a telephone exchange, where all the wires come together and the exchanges are up in the top end of the body. I don't know whether our analytic investigations may throw some light on this, because, I don't think that the neurosurgeons, or the neurologists can do that. I think the approach has to be through what we can "see" of the mind. So, there is always the problem about the individual patient: the particular patient but, also, the general problem about not that particular patient but all of us; not just all of us, but also that particular one.

Notes

1. Plato (Phaedrus, 230).
2. EDITORS NOTE: "I think therefore I am" is Descartes' famous quote, but here Bion also calls attention to the potential automatic defensive quality of thinking and "story telling" saying it is also true that we think to deal with the potential traumatic nature of existential experience. Therefore, thought cannot be automatically trusted to be truthful or to be a form of avoidance of disturbance and distress.
3. Freud, S.E. XIV, p. 7.

Reference

Freud, S. (1911b). Formulations on the two principles of mental functioning. In: *Sigmund Freud The Complete Psychological Works Vol. XII* (pp. 213–226). London: Hogarth.

Supervision 12[1] commentary

João Carlos Braga

Conquering a facet of the formless infinite: the primordial states of the mind

Some of the highlights of this supervision are the observations about a dimension in the human mind in which records of fetal life experiences remain active. Bion bases this assumption on his clinical experience and suggests the incorporation of a new domain of psychoanalytic investigation, highlighting a face of the self *won from the void and formless infinite* (Bion, 1965, p. 151).

This supervision, conducted one and a half years before Bion's death, shows that he had achieved a vision of the mind beyond the innovative proposals that he had presented in *Transformations* and *Attention and Interpretation*. From 1976 onwards, his articles[2] and seminars[3] included references to manifestations of inborn primordial states of mind, a physical part of the personality separated from the symbolic mind by the caesura of birth—a "fundamental" and "basic"[4] condition of human development, always present in mental life as vestiges of archaic states of mind. They are impenetrable in the sense of movements from the symbolized to the undifferentiated (->), but not the other way around.

To present his ideas, Bion used the model of the physical presence of embryonic remains as in the vestigial tail and branchial cleft tumors.

In this supervision, Bion addresses three types of manifestations of this primordial psychic layer: states of mind of "being all-alone and dependent", the impulse of "urge to exist" and the existence of a primitive conscience. This is possibly the only time in all his work in which these three conditions emerge together, making this supervision particularly meaningful.

Bion qualified these ideas as imaginative conjectures (Bion & Bion, 1981, p. 21), a qualification that continues to be appropriate. They are still ideas awaiting greater critical mass to favor our capacity to think about them. Bion himself left these hypotheses without a major epistemological development, maintaining them at a descriptive-analog level, although he approached them in many moments during his last three years of life.

A personal reading of this supervision

Bion asks questions to the group and the presenter at the beginning of the supervision, as he often used to do. He was probably tuning their minds to seek what they didn't know, like the first violinist who leads the orchestra in tuning their instruments; in this case, to look at the unknown for evidence attempting to emerge. This defines his attitude throughout the supervision: of being oriented, as in a tropism, for something awaiting evolution. He remains loyal to this proposal even when he reveals his thoughts, which he always does in a way to open new issues to allow the emergence of new questions. This attitude of seeking the uncertain demands patience towards inevitable flickering questions and tolerance towards a lack of definitive answers. It contrasts sharply with the position of a supervisor who appeals to known theories to explain what is being identified.

After a short description by the presenter, Bion intervenes with a proposal. He had already identified something meaningful in the description of the analysand's mental movement: "I think that this is quite fundamental!" He then introduces the intuitive psychoanalytic theory of a person facing a primordial manifestation of the mind. I think he is exercising what in another supervision he clarified as his method:

> QUESTION—May I ask a question? I am considering your consideration as very interesting, but I just can't see, I'm not having the

> intuition ... where did you get those contributions in the material you got? (...) (...)
>
> BION: It's partly due to the experience which I've had, which leads me to feel that I'm familiar with people who behave in this kind of way. So, it depends on two things: partly on what I know about myself and what I'm capable of standing, tolerating, putting up with; the other thing, what I think I know about the human race, as it were, human beings." (Bion, 1975b, Supervision S6 (Brasília), from the archives of Dr. José Américo Junqueira de Mattos.)[5]

Returning to Supervision 12, it is worth noting that Bion is once again defining the way he would like the group to follow. Instead of focusing on the analysand's psychopathology—the traditional psychoanalytic approach (panic attack, filicide, emotional immaturity, denial of loss, non-elaborated mourning)—Bion prefers to address what appears to his intuition as the analysand's uncontained emotional experience: the manifestation of two unpleasant feelings combined, "being dependent and being all-alone." He presents them as feelings persistently present in human beings since "the age of nought." These feelings create a need in us to live with an unpleasant self. In the case of the analysand, she tries to avoid and evade this unpleasant self. Bion proposes that these states of the mind are "a step towards knowing ourselves," and "something to which the analyst tries to introduce the patient."

The freedom of the thoughts emerging from Bion's observations is striking, and so is the expanding amplitude of this theme. From a short clinical description to the intuition of a fundamental difficulty in the analysand, which also constitutes a fundamental difficulty of every human being. We are "very imperfect animals" awaiting development, disturbed by the consciousness of our ability to think and by the premonition that we can think clearly. He qualifies this as "a sort of curse that we live under" and offers glimpses of further expansions under this impulse to know: "(...) a step on the way (...) useful to know yourself (...) that only means an aspiration towards knowing what the Truth is." And he points out that the difficulty of *knowing* has to do with something even more basic, that is, our ability to feel: "I think that the difficulty is how to harmonize or how to marry our ability to think with our ability to feel." Therefore, in addition to emphasizing the irreplaceable value of knowing, he also points to its limitation—the distortions in the thinking processes that create a hallucinatory domain.

In the dimension of knowledge, the task is to promote thoughts to gain clarity as a step to approach reality (Truth). In this sense, Bion offers a new vision of transference, "it's a sort of way of getting to know, in which the patient can get to know who he or she herself is. It's a sort of transient relationship. It's a sort of transference." He goes on, elaborating colloquially these ideas, pointing out differences to identify them in manifestations of thoughts, as a kind of a thinking progression scale which inevitably reminds us of the grid: (1) registrations without condition of being thought; (2) impulses that pass directly into action, (3) unclear thoughts, distorted by feelings (hallucinosis), (4) clear thoughts, products of elaboration of emotional experiences and, finally, (5) scientific thinking.

As if driven by a powerful call, Bion once again points to the presence of manifestations of the primordial mind. In addition to deepening his observations about the feelings of "being all-alone and dependent," he emphasizes the presence of states of terror as a basic condition of the mind, and then addresses two other conjectures. First, about the fear of fundamental forces that "urge to exist" and are imposed on us, whether we want it or not, causing fear that they may enslave us. Second, the existence of an "inborn moral statement": "We are born with a feeling of guilt, we are born with that, which someday turns into a kind of conscience." These are conjectures that offer a glimpse of his thoughts about our genetic programming as humans and about the existence of an inborn mind.

In considering the hypothesis that we carry a phylogenetic heritage that programs the fundamental forces that guide life and its tendency to complexity and to end itself, we have been in a well-known terrain since Freud. Bion doesn't add anything to this hypothesis; his attention is focused as always on what is within direct reach of the analytical pair. But regarding these primordial states of mind, the ideas that emerge in this supervision are extremely original and catalytic. Out of all of Bion's recorded manifestations, this may be one of the moments in which these ideas emerge most broadly, clearly and explicitly. Due to the importance of these ideas, I will expand them below.

A few notes on Bion's conjectures about the primordial states of mind

In this supervision, the references to the three manifestations (being all-alone and dependent, urge to exist, and primitive conscience) allow identification of epistemological complexities when we rely on terms and models used by Bion. "Urge to exist" is qualified as "impulse," which suggests a force akin to instincts. "All-alone and dependent" as well as guilt, greed, and sex arise as "feelings" and states of mind, "fundamental" elements present even at "the age of nought." Even without explicitness, he suggests that these are manifestations of early records, pre-mental and proto-experiences of the interaction between somatic sensations and the ordering from the genetic programming.

These different states that Bion describes (states of mind, impulses, feelings) not only show the complexities of identifying experiences at this level, but are similar to his warning in *Transformations*: "*I do not distinguish these terms because no distinction is precise enough,* referring to impulses, emotions and instincts" (Bion, 1965, p. 67, italics added for emphasis). This complexity doesn't happen only in the conceptual dimension. There is also "not enough precise distinction" when the analyst captures these experiences of the primordial level. States of terror and the experience of *something* that urges to exist are always present. Therefore, isolation of these different conditions would be somewhat artificial. The impression is that despite being confident in his observations, Bion felt without words or other means to offer more organized thought about them: "I feel pretty sure that I know what it is that she is talking about, but I find it difficult to describe."

Over the forty years that followed these formulations, there has been much information about prenatal life, both in embryology and in psychoanalysis. However, there is still limited penetration of this knowledge among analysts. Since this is not the proper place to examine the current condition of these ideas, I will limit myself to a summarized examination of how Bion formulated them.

All-alone and dependent—Although appearing in other supervisions (e.g., A7), Bion expounds this idea more explicitly in the current supervision and in the entry "Dependent" in *A Key to "A Memoir of the Future"* (Bion & Bion, 1981, p. 25). His statement here sounds emphatic: "It seems to me that even a baby—although it can't verbalize it, of course—feels dependent and feels all-alone." These experiences are presented as "unpleasant feelings" with which we always live, in which the unpleasantness is in being incomplete, being "dependent on people and things", and at the same time, being all-alone.

"Urge to exist"—This is an idea also expounded in other supervisions conducted in Brazil (e.g., A35, 1978a) as well as in *A Memoir of the Future* (W. R. Bion, 1977b, p. 36). In the current supervision, Bion describes it

as an "impulse" and identifies it with the "self" ("... this self that she is too anxious to escape from ..."). In *A Key to "A Memoir of the Future"* under the entry "Exist", he offers a synthetic and almost conceptual description: *"The impulse to exist is postulated even as an urge to which the individual is 'slave'. It provokes rebellion against its dominance. Such a rebellion finds extreme expression in self-murder"* (Bion & Bion, 1981, p. 31, italics added for emphasis). We observe here the same reference that we find in the manifestation of a primitive conscience: the dramatic way in which this impulse would find self-murdering as an outlet. It is another indication of how these movements of the primordial mind are apprehended with little discrimination.

It is impossible not to correlate this concept of "urge to exist" with the idea of instincts as biological roots of the mind. The difference between the approaches of Freud and Bion, however, is that with Freud, the concept arises in an explanatory perspective of causality and as part of a structure (the id). With Bion, the concept is at an epistemological level and the experience is apprehended by the person in a descriptive perspective. It is noteworthy that both authors seem to be dealing with a somatic part of the personality.

Primitive conscience—Of all these manifestations of the primordial mind, the idea of a "feeling of guilt (...) which someday turns into a kind of conscience" is possibly the one that Bion developed most.[6] Its basic characteristic is being always ready to say what we should not do or think, but never what we should. We find Bion trying to give to this "inborn moral statement" a form in different ways, at different moments, with different names: "sub-thalamic fear" and "thalamic fear," before naming it "primitive conscience." It should be noted that the earliest attempts emphasized the most evident of the manifestations he described, the state of terror while in his later writings, the terror emerges associated with a primordial feeling of guilt.

In this supervision, he brings primitive conscience closer to the idea of the original sin of the Roman Catholic Church: "We are born with a feeling of guilt."

In all manifestations of the primordial mind, we find states of terror requiring additional exploration. There are suggestions in Bion's work (e.g., Bion & Bion, 1981, p. 83: "Terror"; Bion & Bion, 1981, p. 83: "Thalamus") of states of terror both as isolate manifestations and as integral parts of the manifestations of the primordial states of the mind. In the manifestations of "urge to exist," the terror is associated with the capture of the individual by this "impulse"; in the other two ("being dependent and all-alone, and primitive conscience"), it seems to be treated as an integral part of the manifestation.

Some important issues for clinical work

In clinical practice, the contact with primordial states of mind leaves a strong impression that the emotional experiences lived in the session can be symbolically elaborated and represented, but not its primordial content. As fetal remains, they lack the symbolic or proto-symbolic condition to be integrated to the conscious/unconscious systems of the mind. They are manifested as somatizations, acting-outs and hallucinations and do not achieve symbolization. The hypothesis is that they continue to be part of our somatic personality, with no discrimination between body and mind. In practice, we observe that they are conditions unresponsive to our analytical tools.

In several supervisions in 1978, Bion made observations about how he dealt with the emergence of manifestations that he identified as primordial states of mind. From a technical point of view, it is as though Bion had knowledge of the amplitude of the mind and its different domains and was able to follow his experiences, like a musician who knows the importance of the clef to identify the pitch of a musical note. If the demonstrations are on the primordial mind clef, they need to be recognized and treated differently than if they were in the symbolic mind, hallucinatory, or being or becoming reality clef. Therefore, "the problem of the analyst is to intuit the date of the quality he is observing" (Bion & Bion, 1981, p. 25).

In a clinical situation, the identification of these primordial states of the mind paves the way to bringing them closer to the symbolic mind. As Bion states in this Supervision S12: "The advantage of the analytic discussion is: the patient gets a chance of being aware of a feeling that they have never really been consciously aware of." However, in practice, Bion's understandings made him cautious and led him to evaluate the condition of the analysands carefully to establish contact with them. At different moments, he made considerations about the sensitivity of this situation, as in the following passage:

> QUESTION—(...) how would you put this into words? What language would you talk and how would you do it?
>
> BION: That is the practical problem, for practicing psychoanalysts! I think that we ought all to consider what we would say to the patient, if we were treating that patient, if we wanted to tell the patient what we thought was happening and if we want the patient to understand what we said. It's no good saying something, which the patient couldn't hear and couldn't understand. It's no good making that kind of noise. What should we do with our vocal cords, apparatus of phonation for the patient to be able to understand what we have seen, from what she has said. Now, that is an ongoing situation; it's not a closed problem. It depends on us, whether we find a language or means of communication which would be suitable for helping the patient to understand what it is that we have seen, or what we have observed. (Bion, 1975c, Supervision A7)

It seems that our limitation today with primordial states of mind continues to be the same that Bion had pointed out by the awareness of a part of our personality with which we have to live, but can't really change. The most we can achieve is to *know* about primordial states of mind. We are far from able to *become* them.

Notes

1. Given in São Paulo on April 1978.
2. "Caesura" (1977[1975a]), "Emotional turbulence" (1976a), "On a quotation from Freud" (1976b), "Evidence" (1976c), "Making the best of a bad job" (1979), and *A Memoir of the Future* (1975–1979).
3. The first three seminars in Los Angeles (1976), the fourth and the fifth seminars in New York (1977), and from the fifth to the seventh seminars in Sao Paulo (1978), in "Four discussions with W. R. Bion" (1978). Also from the fourth to the eighth seminars in Rome (1977a), in "Italian Seminars."
4. I will use quotes when I cite words or sentences from the present supervision, and italics in other citations by Bion.
5. Kindly offered by Gisèle Mattos Brito.
6. For more data, refer to "Evidence" (1976) and seminars in New York (1977) and Sao Paulo (1978b) in "*Bion in New York and São Paulo*".

For a deeper approach, see Junqueira de Mattos, J. A., & Braga, J. C. (2013). Primitive conscience: a glimpse of the primordial mind. In: H. B. Levine & L. J. Brown (Eds.), *Growth and Turbulence in the Container/ Contained—Bion's Continuing Legacy* (pp. 179–200). New York, NY: Routledge.

References

Bion, W. R. (1965). *Transformations.* London: Maresfield, 1991.
Bion, W. R. (1970). *Attention and Interpretation.* London: Karnac, 1993.
Bion, W. R. (1975a). Caesura. In: *Two Papers: The Grid and Caesura* (pp. 43–59). Rio de Janeiro: Imago, 1977.
Bion, W. R. (1975b). Supervision S6, given in Brasilia. Archives of Dr. José Américo Junqueira de Mattos.
Bion, W. R. (1975c). Supervision A7, given in Brasilia. Archives of Dr. José Américo Junqueira de Mattos.
Bion, W. R. (1976a). Emotional turbulence. In: *Bion, W. R. Clinical Seminars and Other Works* (pp. 295–305). London: Karnac, 1987.
Bion, W. R. (1976b). On a quotation from Freud. In: *Bion, W. R. Clinical Seminars and Other Works* (pp. 306–311). London: Karnac, 1987.
Bion, W. R. (1976c). Evidence. In: *Bion, W. R. Clinical Seminars and Other Works* (pp. 312–320). London: Karnac, 1987.
Bion, W. R. (1977a). *Seminari italiani.* Roma: Borla, 1985.
Bion, W. R. (1977b). *A Memoir of the Future. Book II. The Past Presented.* Rio de Janeiro: Imago Ed.
Bion, W. R. (1978a). Supervision A35, given in Sao Paulo. Archives of Dr. José Américo Junqueira de Mattos.
Bion, W. R. (1978b). *Bion in New York and São Paulo.* Perthshire: Clunie Press.
Bion, W. R. (1979). Making the best of a bad job. In: *Bion, W. R. Clinical Seminars and Other Works* (pp. 321–332). London: Karnac, 1987.
Bion, W. R. (1990). *A Memoir of the Future.* London: Karnac.
Bion, W. R. & Bion, F. (1981). *A Key to "A Memoir of the Future".* Perthshire: Clunie Press.

CHAPTER THREE

Supervision A25

In the text that follows, T stands for Translator; A stands for Analyst.

T: Don't you feel, Dr. Bion that perhaps, with everyone here understanding only a little different bit of the English, from different kinds of "sauces" there can emerge the understanding of something new, although perhaps not exactly what you were saying?

Bion: Maybe, maybe. But, the language that is *spontaneous* it's a sort of language which the French call: "Les grands mots"—the indecent words. If you are taken by surprise, if you are suddenly frightened, the language that comes naturally to you is not polite language. [lots of laughter]

That language is universal, whether you are French, or English, or Portuguese, or German, or Chinese, or whatever. I think you can *immediately* understand that language. Even words like: "God" can be used with a different intonation. If you are swearing, if you are praying, or if you are taking part in a religious service. So, perhaps, the day will dawn where an international psychoanalytic congress conducted in entirely indecent words. [Bion declares this in a laughing tone of voice]

Wouldn't Freud be surprised if he could come back and hear that? After all, these international congresses are nearly always bad tempered.

Well, is there some material that anybody wants to discuss in particular?

T: Yes, It's a patient that's recently begun analysis fifteen days ago and feels very destructive towards the people around her and her environment.

Bion: Did she say that or ...?

T: Yes. She also says that she has had various experiences with other psychotherapies—other methods—and she has always been very destructive, so that the situation had to be broken up. But, nevertheless, she felt very positive towards her new relation with her psychoanalyst—that she's beginning to establish now—because she has a friend that's in analysis with him and has spoken very well about him to her. She complains that she has difficulty in her relationship with her husband and her mother and she complains very much about people sucking away her life from her. A has the feeling that she has a great difficulty in tolerating life together with people that are, in a way that she considers frustrating or disappointing and this will probably be so, even in her relation with the analyst. Although he is already idealized as a "good person" by her—she apparently has a good relationship with him—she has difficulty accepting the fact that he can stop the session and is afraid that he will end the treatment if he does not find her to be a "satisfying" patient. The session that A brings to illustrate these points was their fourth session and took place at the end of the week, at the beginning of a series of holidays, because of Holy Week.

Bion: It is well to be aware that for our purposes it's necessary to conform, more or less, to the ordinary standards of politeness and civil behavior. Otherwise, it becomes impossible to do analysis. At the same time, the kind of talk that takes place between ourselves and the analysand is very provocative. It's very evocative. It's liable to be an emotionally stirring experience. So, the analytic work produces a strain. It's liable to be a situation in which the patient feels angry, hostile, in love and so forth ... The same thing applies to the analyst: an analytic session can be extremely annoying. It can also be extremely attractive. You can like the man or woman who comes to you, so much that, it becomes a kind of provocation—which might be a sort of love affair. But you aren't supposed to have a sexual relationship; you aren't supposed to hit your analyst; or your analysand is not supposed to hit you and so on ... So, in so far as both people, the analyst and the analysand, try to cooperate and try to do this work, it's a trying relationship—for both people. If analysts realize that more often, they wouldn't be surprised to find that they are tired at the end of the day. You often find analysts who think that they can do a day's work, go to supervisions, go to their own analysis, perhaps, go to international congresses and still feel alright! Then, they surprisingly find they're tired. Now, an actor or a singer would understand that what they're acting or singing has to be heard right up there in the gallery—at the end of the theatre; not only at the beginning of the play, or the concert, but also at the end of it. That is true of us. So, if you take this case, it is necessary to be able to say—whatever you have to say—at the beginning of the session and even at the end of the session; at the end of the analysis, just as much as at the beginning of the analysis. That's why it's important to be able to realize that one is spending one's energies. There are limits to the amount of work that you can do, if you propose to go on doing the same kind of work for the rest of your life.

Well, I've spent rather a long time about that, so now shall we get on with this actual case?

T: When she went to the session, she told her analyst that she'd met a friend and they were talking and she was telling her friend that, in the beginning, she thought that four sessions a day would be too much for her.

A: Four sessions a week!

T: [bursts out laughing when she realizes her mistake] That four sessions a week would be too much. But after discussing this with her friend, she realized that four sessions were a correct number—quite alright. Her friend—she was talking about the friend—was telling her that she not only went for four sessions a week, but she also spent most of her time thinking about her analysis. The patient added that she considered that this situation could be similar to hers—although she was not very sure. She thought it could be like a Buddhist practice, or meditation, thinking about it the whole day. Then she told A that this actually happened with her. When she got home and was surrounded by all her children and family, she didn't want to be with them. She wanted to be thinking about her analysis. So, the analyst said to her that although she was apparently enjoying very much her sessions with him, she still was unhappy, because they had to stop. A long weekend was coming and she would like to remain with him the whole time. She didn't want the sessions to end. The client says then that …

Bion: Could we just stop a moment? What's your impression about this, now? Would you like to have this patient or not? Does this patient want to have the analyst or not? Do you think the patient would want to come to you? What's your impression about that?

T: P4 describes the patient as giving him the impression of being a very passionate person. She throws herself entirely inside a situation. She lives this situation so intensely, that by the end, it cannot be enough for her. It cannot give her everything she wants, or give her back everything she puts into it. That's perhaps why she has the impression of being so destructive in her relationships.

Bion: Yes. She starts with this idea that she wouldn't be able to stand having more than two sessions a week, but before long, she's afraid that she likes it too much; she likes her analyst too much. If she wants to have four sessions a week, then perhaps, the analyst doesn't want to—or if the analyst saw her four times a week, the analyst mightn't want to have anything to do with a patient like that. He mightn't like her. That's the trouble of having two people in the same room at the same time, who can have quite strong feelings. In more extreme terms, if she loves the analyst, the analyst may not love her. On the other hand, if the analyst hated her, she mightn't be able to come for analysis. In short, you can think for yourself about the various combinations of feelings, which these two people can have. So, neither, or both of them, may not be able to stand the analytic conversation. As far as the patient is concerned, the patient doesn't know. So, the patient doesn't know if the analyst could stand it, if he got to know her better. But the whole point about the analytic relationship is that it is hoped that the patient would get to know more about who they are, who they themselves are. But it's impossible for her to know more about herself without the analyst also knowing more about her. So, it's quite a problem whether these two people could go on working together, or for that matter, whether they could part. In that way, the analytic situation is itself a frightening situation. It may also be dealing with emotional situations, which have a long history, both in the analysand and in the analyst. So, potentially, it's quite a frightening situation for both people, presumably. But as far as she's concerned she knows something about her difficulties, but she doesn't know how the analyst would take these problems.

T: So, she continued saying that when she got home, she had so many things to think about. Then the analyst made an intervention and he said: "But you know it's not the same thing when you think about the session and when you are in the session with me." So, she went on to describe a situation in which her children would be away from home, for a period of time for the holidays. But she would be staying with her husband. She complained because she thinks that it's a very uncomfortable situation.

Bion: Yes. In a way it's worse than analysis, because it's the *real thing*. It's worse than playing fathers and mothers. It's worse even than playing the psychoanalytic game, because if you play that game, then you can go and have children. So, it's not just like playing sexual games with your brother or sister, because it doesn't just end with a sexual relationship. It doesn't end with a nice sexual experience. It goes on because we have to look after the baby. The same way with analysis. Suppose this analytic conversion has results. She will have to live with them. It's not much better if the analysis doesn't have any results, because then, what are you spending all this money and time for? So, for her it's quite a frightening prospect; it's frightening to ... you can't very well have an analysis and decide that it's quite harmless, because it's not going to work. But if it *does* work, then she will have to live with the result. In certain situations, it can be like having to live with the baby that is generated, but even in analysis this kind of conversation can have an effect, but she will have to put up with the effect. In theory we expect the patient to get to know themselves better. In practice, if these theories are correct, then she will not only have to get to know herself better, but she'll have to live with herself—for the rest of her life. But if she—like all people that come for analysis—are likely to spend their lives up to the present trying to be somebody else—from the small boy, small girl, who try to be good; they don't want to be naughty, so they try to be good—if they know what good is—but it does mean not being who they are, because they know they aren't good, they know that they are naughty, bad tempered, and all sorts of things ... Now, take this grown man or woman they have got a pretty good idea by this time that they are not satisfied with themselves. That's why they've come to an analyst, because they're dissatisfied. So, if this conversation is going to lead to their being themselves, then they can be frightened of that prospect.

T: A adds something that he thinks confirms what you've just said. He says that this client has difficulty with her husband, but has invested great hopes in her children. She takes care of them, because she expects them to take care of her afterwards, but, nevertheless, he says that this has already been worked out, in the session. She is very afraid when she notices that they are growing bigger and bigger.

Bion: An intuitive mother can't regard them as simply being physically bigger and bigger—because they have characters and personalities, thoughts of their own. Now, what does bigger and bigger mean? It might be nicer and nicer, but it might be becoming wickeder and wickeder, bigger and bigger criminals. It's frightening to feel that the children have got wills of their own—they can become whatever they like, or whatever they learn at school or elsewhere. For example, here, what do the children learn when they go to school? It's quite common nowadays—even not so long ago—it's quite common to be able to get cigarettes—when you're a young boy or girl at school. Nowadays, you can also, as you call, get bigger and bigger. You can nowadays—besides getting candy and things sweets,—you can get cigarettes, you can get marijuana, you can get heroin. So, the—shall we say—the six-year-old child has a good chance of getting bigger and bigger. You've got a much bigger choice than I had when I was a boy at school and, I dare say, the same thing can be true here of your school days and what is possible to the children today. So, this patient's anxiety about these children that are getting bigger and bigger can't be dismissed as being just a neurosis. So, what are you going to say to the patient? Who says that her children are growing bigger and bigger? If you say the sort of thing that I've just been saying you could be accused of scaring the wits out of her.

T: Of …?

Bion: You could be accused of scaring the patient, of telling her all these terrifying stories about heroin and marijuana and all that.

T: A would like to, perhaps, correct something. What he understands when she says that she is afraid of the children growing bigger and bigger is not their growing bigger and bigger, but that they are leaving her. That they can leave her alone.

Bion: But there are lots of ways of doing that. They don't have to leave the home physically; you can go on talking, I mean … I've seen this with parents who assume that their little boy and their little girl behave very nicely, they're well behaved, they're polite and so forth … they don't notice that those same children have left home. They are not nice children who, like nice parents, go and see an analyst. In fact, if they ever talked with their friends, their brothers and sisters at school, the probability is that their brothers and sisters would think that their parents were just crazy to spend their time coming to analysis. I mean, I know of analysts who have wanted their children to be analyzed, who sent them to analysis and they've become the laughing stock of their school. These other children don't do dull, stupid things like going to an analyst. They ride bicycles and all sorts of other things. So, to come back to this patient, she may be being optimistic in saying: "They will leave home." How does she know, they haven't left home already? Their bodies are still at home. I've known situations in which the parents are horrified to find that the child's bed hasn't been slept in. If the parents say: "Where have you been?" They don't say where. Now, here again, the problem is: what is to be said to this patient? I myself got the feeling … I think that I would say: "I can see that your anxieties maybe are quite well justified. That is a matter which I know nothing about, because I don't know your children, I don't know what goes on at school, etc … So, you may be right in being frightened that they will leave home. I am not so sure as to why you think that they will leave home in the future and why you think that they haven't left home now?" Now, I don't want to frighten the patient, but on the other hand, I don't want the patient to think that there's nothing to be frightened of. When we analyze a fear of being robbed or murdered—to take a more exaggerated example—one doesn't mean that if you get analyzed murderers and robbers cease to exist. So, when we try to use this statement about the fear of children leaving the home, by using it as a free association and then giving an interpretation, we don't mean that children don't leave home, or that they do, but that in addition to that, there is some unconscious fear to which we want to draw their attention. For example: that she herself is no longer a child. She has left home. There is no father or mother, because she is a parent.

Now, I'm afraid it's late, so we have to stop.

Supervision A25 commentary

Maria Bernadete Amêndola Contart de Assis

It is always a privilege to read supervision sessions held by Bion because they put us into contact with his living thought produced in the emotional heat of specific moments, and this lets us note the natural flow of his associations. At these moments we are face-to-face with his spontaneous thought, born of the encounter, and this was exactly the type of thought he himself found so important throughout his entire work. He invites each analyst to be open to the unusual in their relationships with analysands and to be creative on the basis of this experience.

In the supervision session discussed here Bion makes no reference to theoretical concepts or to any type of technical teaching that relies upon either definitions or discussion. Nevertheless, his questions and comments related to the clinical material presented enable readers to identify some of his main contributions to psychoanalytic technique. During the entire supervision session one can note *the importance Bion gives to doubting, questioning, and the mystery* present in the analytic encounter. One can note how he shifts his viewpoint from the patient's psychodynamics to the observation of the emotional experience of both analyst and analysand. When the participants in the supervision session talk about the patient's "difficulties," Bion changes his perspective and talks about the panic that the analyst feels. This change in focus toward what analysts experience in their offices is noticeable during the entire supervision session. Here we see Bion the revolutionary, in that he is able to turn over, or turn "upside down," concepts that, by being apparently "consistent" and constantly repeated, run the risk of becoming meaningless and stale. He takes these concepts and airs them out, throws new light on them and thinks them through from new points of view. One can see him leading the participants in the group to think for themselves in the analyst's relationship with the analysand, an attitude that configures a moment of deconstruction of long-established ideas.

Grotstein (2007) describes this legacy of Bion in the following words:

> Bion pulled the positivistic psychoanalysis of Freud and Klein into the new, uncharted realms of *uncertainty:* from the strictures and prison of verbal language to a realm beyond and before the language. Here one experiences the dread of O, the Absolute Truth about an Ultimate, infinite, ineffable, always evolving uncertain and impersonal Reality that supplants the putative dread of the positivistic drives. We are born as fateful prisoners to the quality of the maternal—and parental—container that (who) initially contains our raw dread of O. (Grotstein, 2007, p. 44)

This displacement of the gaze should be noted as one reads this supervision session, since it is an endless source of development in psychoanalytic theory and technique. Right at the beginning we can see an example of this. The analyst who presents the case says of the patient: "She showed herself to him as feeling very destructive towards the people around her and her environment" Bion immediately asks, "Did *she* say that or ...". His question is apparently simple and seemingly a request for clarification, but it is immediately posed as a question, in his attitude of constant questioning that keeps us open to all possibilities, instead of quickly closing us into a single restricted point of view. If we take this as a type of "technical recommendation"[1] we have Bion's suggestion to always ask before saying something about a patient, such as "Who said that?" "Who did they say it to?" "How did they say it?" "When did they say it?" and so forth. Investigate, he seems to say, put yourself in the place of the one who is asking, not in the place someone who is answering. Put yourself in the place of a builder of ideas during the encounter with the patient rather than in the place of someone who already has pre-established or pre-constituted concepts. These are the "recommendations" implicit in his first question.

To be in the session in an attitude of constant observation and questioning, letting oneself be led by the unknown, is an implicit "recommendation" corresponding to Freud's recommendation (1912/1971), when he talks about the dangers of the analysts' position of looking for something instead of letting themselves be surprised. In Freud's words:

> Cases which are devoted from the first to scientific purposes and are treated accordingly suffer in their outcome; while the most successful cases are those in which one proceeds, as it were, without any purpose in view, allows oneself to be taken by surprise by any new turn in them, and always meets them with an open mind, free from presuppositions. (Freud, 1971, p. 114)

We read in Bion (1977):

> For consider: if his mind is preoccupied with what is or is not said, or with what he does or does not hope, it must mean that he cannot allow the experience to obtrude, particularly that aspect of it which is more than sound of the patient's voice or the sight of his postures. What sounds the patient makes, or what spectacle he presents, relates to O only in so far as O has evolved into the K domain. (Bion, 1977, p. 41)

Next in this supervision session, after the analyst describes his impressions about the analysand, Bion says: "I don't know if the patient is like this or like that." Then he goes on to talk about the fact that the experience of an evocative and provocative analytic encounter is exciting and terrifying *for both* analyst and analysand. In this way he relocates the analyst from the place of someone who sees, hears and interprets, to that of someone who, before all, *feels*. He says:

> At the same time, a type of conversation that takes place between us and the analysand is very provocative, very evocative, and can become an exciting emotional experience. Therefore, analytic work produces tension. It is prone to be a situation where the patient may feel angry or hostile or in love and so forth. [...] The same

> thing applies to the analyst: the analytic session can be extremely irritating. And it can also be extremely attractive.

Further ahead he says, "So, insofar as both people, the analyst and the analysand, try to cooperate and try to do this work, it's a trying relationship—for both people". Here we can also see the ideas expressed in Bion's article entitled "Making the best of a bad job" (1979):

> When two personalities meet, an emotional storm is created. If they make sufficient contact to be aware of each other or even sufficient to be unaware of each other, an emotional state is produced by the conjunction of these two individuals, and the resulting disturbance is hardly likely to be regarded as necessarily an improvement on the state of affairs had they never met at all. But since they have met, and since this emotional storm has occurred, the two parties to this storm may decide to 'make the best of a bad job'. (Bion, 1979, p. 136)

Here we can see an analytic encounter that takes into account all the depth of what goes on with the analyst during his work. Where is he touched? What fantasies, fears, and anxieties are stirred up in the analyst during a session of psychoanalysis? Bion calls attention to the fact that, submerged in all the experience that takes place in such an encounter, the analyst has the function of saying something audible to the way things the analyst, from the beginning to the end of the session. During the supervision session here, Bion stressed several times the intensity of the emotions that the analyst experiences. For example, it may seem obvious that the analyst might want to see a patient four sessions a week. The fear or resistance toward this number of sessions might be seen as a type of prerogative of the patient. Bion deconstructs this when he says,

> If she wants to have four sessions a week, then perhaps the analyst doesn't want to—or if the analyst saw her four times a week, the analyst mightn't want to have anything to do with a patient like that, he mightn't like her. That's the trouble of having two people in the same room at the same time who can have quite strong feelings.

Further ahead in the same paragraph he adds that, "So, [either person], or both of them, may not be able to stand the analytic conversation."

He categorically states that the analytic situation can be frightening for both. The analyst is clearly placed in an emotional field, not only in the sense of the constitution of the field, but even more radically, as someone who suffers the emotion produced in the encounter and who has the function of doing something with this experience. The analyst must do something significant for the analysand.

Considerations like these provide containing and naming for what analysts go through in their offices. Anyone who dares be an analyst knows quite well the pertinence and truth in statements like this. All these elements, like the unpredictable, the unusual, the mysterious, the depressing, the exciting or the frightening, are regularly present in an analyst's office. And once they are named they can be integrated theoretically, and they broaden the analyst's technical capacity. Just as an analysand may have an emotional experience of holding when she feels understood by the analyst, the analyst himself may also have this experience when he is understood by a supervisor, that is, when his experience can be named and signified. The analyst talks about the analysand's emotions and difficulties, while Bion talks about the emotions and difficulties of the analyst. By moving the focus he deconstructs, rearranges, and holds.

After this presentation of the clinical material during the supervision session, Bion makes a further intervention full of questions like:

> Can we stop a moment? What's your impression about this, now? Would you like to have this patient or not? Does this patient want to have the analyst or not? Do you think the patient would want to come to you? What's your impression about that?

We can see Bion casting "a beam of intense darkness" (Grotstein, 2007/2010) on the clinical material. We learn with Freud (and radicalize with Bion) that in order to see better one must darken the field of what is already known. In each session we renew the state of readiness for an encounter, and this demands detachment from everything we already know. What is new is the main stimulus. To throw oneself into the incalculable of the encounter with the other becomes a "recommendation." I remember a beautiful part of an interview by Elizabeth Roudinesco with the philosopher Jacques Derrida, who says:

> The other, the arrival of the other, is always incalculable. [...] Once its beginning is accepted, one is therefore open to what the other

> has to say and to the happening that will affect us. Therefore, this affect is that by which one defines life. At this moment one must organize oneself to invent the advent of a discourse that can apprehend [this other]. (Derrida & Roudinesco, 2001/2004, p. 76)

In Bion one can see the constant invention of a discourse that is alive and spontaneous. One sees a break with what is established; one sees the condition for broadening one's thinking about the being who is the analyst. Bion calls attention to the risks of overuse and familiarity, which can imprison us by tying us up in saturated, already known concepts that lead to repetitions and automatisms that belong to the field of non-life. To avoid this he invites us to a rigorous discipline in the exercise of freedom where renunciation of what is sensorial and the introduction of a "beam of intense darkness" open up paths to intuition. Bion, who served in the war, certainly knew the dangers of being a prisoner and generously showed us paths to freedom. This attitude is present in the supervision session we are studying.

I would like to bring up another point about this supervision session, namely, Bion's reflection on the potential effects—and risks—of an analysis.

> So, for her it's quite a frightening prospect [...]; it's frightening. [...] You can't very well have an analysis and decide that it's quite harmless—because it's not going to work. But if it *does* work, then she will have to live with the result. In certain situations it can be like having to live with the baby that is generated. But even in analysis this kind of conversation can have an effect, but she will have to put up with the effect. In theory we expect the patients to get to know themselves better; in practice, if these theories are correct, then she will not only have to get to know herself better but she'll have to live with herself—for the rest of her life.

The thought here is radicalized and one can therefore see better. The analogy he makes with the experience of having children leads the reflection to the extreme, that is, thoughts produced in analysis have the potential to generate new aspects that are as grandiose and permanent as having children. The presence of this in the Oedipus myth is evident: once the truth is known, nothing is to be gained from blinding oneself. Oedipus will have to live forever with this knowledge of himself.

The risk of the search for truth was underlined by Bion on many different occasions, and this supervision gives us an example. In it we frequently hear the word "frightening" in his discourse. To be oneself, to appropriate one's own personal history and become responsible for it can be terrifying. This brings us back to the idea I referred to at the beginning of this article. Grotstein (2007) says that Bion goes far beyond the conflicts that the drives can impose on man. He introduces the experience of the terror of being alive. Bion put it this way:

> Now they [the patients] have got a pretty good idea by this time that they are not satisfied with themselves. That's why they've come to an analyst, because they're dissatisfied. So, if this conversation is going to lead to their being themselves, then they can be frightened of that prospect.

This type of reflection brings in a wider dimension of the holding attitude of the analyst. It puts him into contact not with patients' "resistances" to bringing to light their conflicts or memories, but with a deeper and more crucial question yet, which is the fear of the results of analysis.

His change in perspective is interesting. It is as if our gaze is redirected from past to future. In other words, the concept of resistance implies a fear that something from the past will be revealed, while the fear of becoming oneself projects into the future, toward the condition (or non-condition) of bearing a knowledge of oneself and a responsibility for this knowledge which has "been born." This is not *revelation,* but *birth.* The unconscious we are talking about is not the repressed but the infinite, with full potential to be born. Ogden (2005) refers to this in the following terms:

> Psychoanalysis—significantly shaped by Bion over the past quarter century—has come to place great value on the analyst's and the analysand's capacity not to know. In this state of mind, one is capable of marveling at the mystery, the utter unpredictability, and the power of the unconscious which can be felt, but never known. The unconscious is an immanence, not an oracle." (Ogden, 2005, p. 25)

Here we can see a further characteristic of Bion's work, that of pointing toward the future, to the expansion of the ability to think not about what has passed, but about what is in the present with a view to expanding the ability to apprehend what is to come.

In my reading of the supervision session I would especially highlight the reconstruction of pre-established concepts. A good example of this is when Bion reflects on the fear the patient has of her children growing up. On this point he says that the patient's anxiety about the children's growing up "can't be dismissed as being just a neurosis". Here there is a questioning about anxieties that are intrinsic to life and to the experience of being a mother and they therefore cannot be considered pathological. Fear is inherent to having children, in being alive. In the same way, the emotions lived by the analyst in the session are intrinsic to the encounter. When the analyst gives meaning to an emotional experience of the analysand, the analyst cooperates with the analysand so that the latter may be awake to the emotional experience implied in living, thus broadening her capacity to dream about it. Ogden is an author who uses Bionian ideas very effectively. In his words Ogden (2005):

> Being alive to one's experience is, as I conceive of it, synonymous with being able to dream one's lived emotional experience. I am using the term *dreaming* here in a way that is informed by Bion's (1962a) work. To the extent that one is capable of dreaming one's experience, one is able to generate an emotional response to it, learn from it, and be changed by it. (Ogden, 2005, p. 23)

> The aim of psychoanalysis from this perspective is not primarily that of facilitating the resolution of unconscious conflict, but facilitating the growth of the container–contained. In other words, the analyst's task is to create conditions in the analytic setting that will allow for the mutual growth of the container (the capacity for dreaming) and the contained (thoughts/feelings derived from lived experience). (Odgen, 2005, p. 104)

This "recommendation" is far from being merely an effort to eliminate conflicts. The medical model is not present here. The point is that the analyst is in intimate contact (copulation) and generates transforming knowledge (children) the patient will live with for the rest of her life. According to Chuster and colleagues (2011), using the model of medical specialties, it could be said that we find in Bion an analyst "obstetrician," that is, one who promotes birth.

At the end of the supervision, Bion refers to the patient's fear that her children will leave home, with the question: "Therefore, returning to the topic of this patient, she can be optimistic when she says: 'They will leave home'. How does she know they haven't left home already?" The question points to the search that the woman is afraid of at that moment in the session. He suggests that it is the fear that she herself is no longer a child, and that being a mother, there is orphan-ness. There is neither father nor mother. There is she, the mother, generator of children (in the broadest sense of the term).

I would like to finish my comments inspired on this final phrase by Bion, using it for a reflection on what his theory brought up in us analysts. Based on his theoretical and clinical considerations we have the opportunity to realize that we become father/mother in each session, with each patient, in the sense that we generate feelings and ideas with our analysands. In each session, following the recommendations of being without memory, without desire, and without understanding (Bion, 1977), we are orphans of previously constructed theories and we are invited by him to realize that we are no longer children looking for precepts to be followed. We are alone, and invited to be ourselves (in *at-one-ment*) and to create in the sessions with our analysands. As Ogden says (2005): "It is the analyst's responsibility to reinvent psychoanalysis for each patient and continue to reinvent it during the course of the analysis" (p. 22).

Note

1. Here I use the term "recommendation" as a reference to Freud's article entitled "Recommendations to physicians practicing psychoanalysis" (1912/1976).

References

Bion, W. R. (1977). Attention and interpretation. In: *Seven Servants* (pp. 1–130). New York, NY: Jason Aronson.

Bion, W. R. (1987). Making the best of a bad job. In: C. Mawson (Ed.), *The Complete Works of W. R. Bion, Vol X* (pp. 136–145). London: Karnac, 2014.

Chuster, A., Conte, J. C., Walz, J., Walz, M. B., Beck, S. M., Castro, J., Antunes, C., Kloeckner, A. e, & Fracasso, C. K. (2011). *O Objeto psicanalítico: fundamentos de uma mudança de paradigma na Psicanálise.* Porto Alegre: Editora do Autor.

Derrida, J., & Roudinesco, E. (2004). *De que amanhã … Diálogo*. Rio de Janeiro: Jorge Zahar, 2001.

Freud, S. (1971). Recommendations to physicians practising psychoanalysis. In: *Sigmund Freud The Complete Psychological Works*. Vol. XII. London: Hogarth.

Grotstein, J. S. (2007). *A Beam of Intense Darkness, Wilfred Bions' Legacy to Psychoanalysis*. London: Karnac.

Ogden, T. H. (2005). *This Art of Psychoanalysis: Dreaming Undreamt Dreams and Interrupted Cries*. New York, NY: The New Library of Psychoanalysis.

CHAPTER FOUR

Supervision A30

In the text that follows, T stands for Translator; A stands for Analyst; P1, P2, and P3 stand for participants in the audience.

T: The patient has been in analysis for about four years and for the past two years has been sleeping a lot on the couch during the session. The analyst is writing an article about this to present at the Society and today he is bringing an extract of some of his work. After the client began sleeping during the sessions the analyst felt a great difficulty in establishing contact with him, because he interrupted what was being said to him, by the analyst, about his sleep by falling asleep! The patient acknowledged expecting a great deal from the analysis that had not yet been forthcoming and the analyst thought that the sleep was a response to not yet having found the idealized solution to his problems that the patient had hoped to find in the analysis.

Bion: Has anybody got any questions they want to ask? I have one question, which I would like to ask, at once. I would like to ask the analyst: what made him think that the patient had gone to sleep?

T: He (the analyst) said that he could notice it by the body expressions of the client, the sort of relaxation of the muscles and that he sometimes snored.

Bion: Anything else?

T: About the fact of noticing he's asleep, he has no other observations to bring to us. But the analyst does remember something that he would like to add; that while they were exploring this situation—the analyst and the analysand—it was decided that the client try sitting in the chair, so that it would be more difficult to sleep. Nevertheless, he fell asleep all the same!! The analyst developed the impression that the sleep was inevitable—that he couldn't avoid going to sleep.

P1: Just before falling asleep, what happened? What was the subject being discussed, or what was occurring between the client and the analyst just before he fell asleep? What was the main point of the material?

T: The client had complained, when he first came for analysis, of having difficulty in staying awake, or paying attention to his work. He was very ambitious, he wanted to extract all he could from his work, and he said that he took great pains and worked hard at whatever he did. This great expectation of working, he brought to analysis, and he believed that analysis would allow him to overcome his problem, stay awake and fulfill his work ambitions.

Bion: Here we've got an opportunity to discuss this matter, because here in this group this isn't an analysis. So I can now ask another question equally: how do you know he's awake? You've told me something about how you know he's asleep; now I want to ask another question: how do you know he's awake? Mind you, I'm not going to ask you easy questions. I am not saying they are easy questions, at all. Though, if they were easy, there would be no point about talking about it here.

Can anybody venture any suggestion?

T: He's (P2) asking what the client actually told his analyst, what his stated goals were in seeking an analysis? What did he, in fact, tell the analyst about his hopes for the analysis?

T: A says that the analysand told him in these words: he felt inhibitions in his work and "ambition" (sic.) in his relationships with women. He was married, but he felt a great difficulty in establishing contact with his wife and other women.

T: He's (A) trying to answer your question of how he could know that this client was awake and he says that he had the impression that his client couldn't tolerate the frustration of not having his analyst fulfill his ambitions and live up to his expectations. This, despite the fact that they had discussed quite a great deal about the analysand's difficulty in accepting what analysis really had to offer, that he had idealized analysis, and then was frustrated in not finding what he had expected. Despite the analyst's attempts to clarify and interpret this, the client always brought the same question up again and again and insisted on his fantasies. In this way, A felt that these discussions had a dream-like quality.

Bion: Which fantasies?

T: The fantasies of expecting to find a cure, or solving his problem in analysis, to gain power, to regain his … to get rid of his inhibition to work—to be able to work again, once more.

Bion: Why did he think that the analyst could do that?

[P2]: Did he show himself as aggressive in words or any kind of behavior? When he felt frustrated or disappointed, did he become angry? Was it then that he fell asleep?

Bion: How has his analyst frustrated him?

A: When he (A) didn't fulfill the patient's expectations, didn't get into the client's dream—didn't become a part of the client's dreams.

P1: Did the client say anything about dreaming, or the act of sleeping?

A: No, no.

Bion: I don't see how the analyst has frustrated him. The analyst, I take it, has made himself available. He said that he'd be in that office, in that consulting room in certain hours and that's where he was. So in what way can he say that the analyst frustrates him?

T: The client had very explicit expectations. He (A) confirms that they talked explicitly about what he didn't find, what he was looking for—that he didn't receive what he was expecting.

Bion: Yes, but how is that the analyst's fault? If he can't find what he's looking for, why doesn't he go and look for it somewhere else?

T: A says that this was something that they had discussed and worked on in the analysis. The analyst had asked the client why he was there. Sometimes the question of looking for a religion was also approached.

He (A) had the feeling that—after a certain time—the client was able to understand some aspects of the reality of the analytical situation, that it could be a positive situation—it could be a situation that would help him as client, but then envy appeared. He couldn't tolerate the feeling that analysis could effectively make him ... do him some good.

His expression was very explicit. He used to say to his analyst, for example: "I can't tolerate that you know something, that I don't know." Then the sleep intervened; and at this phase he slept a lot.

Bion: I still don't see what the difficulty is, because if he can't tolerate that, why does he come there?

T: This is a matter that A wanted to bring up here, because he frequently had a feeling that his work as an analyst with this patient was meaningless. He has now had many years of experience, as an analyst, yet, with this client, A is constantly worried if he should continue seeing him or not. But despite these worries, A nevertheless observed that the client always came, that he always came on time.

Bion: What is his grievance? That the analyst is there or that the analyst isn't there? What is the analyst supposed to do? Is he supposed to be there, or is he supposed to be not there? What is frustrating him, your presence or your absence?

T: Sometimes A raised these points, which were quite close to the ones that you mentioned here. For example: A showed the patient many times that the patient already knew the answers to many questions that he asked of the analyst. A felt that the purpose of these questions was to avoid something.

Bion: There's still the problem to why does the analysand come to the analyst? If he says he's frustrated, is he frustrated because the analyst is there, or is he frustrated because the analyst isn't there?

T: Whenever the question of why the client continued going to analysis was discussed, the client mentioned that he was feeling better, that he was profiting from his analysis.

Bion: Right.

T: Although his explicit declarations and reactions to the work …

Bion: Whose?

T: The client's … were always negative; he was in conflict, unhappy, not satisfied. [Here, T is telling her impressions.]

T: I couldn't understand. I thought I had translated wrong. A said that the patient thought the analytical situation was helpful—although most of the time, he expressed negative feelings towards the analyst. He also had the impression in the last encounters …

Bion: Who had the impression?

T: The analyst had the impression in the last encounters with the client that his expression was one of acceptance—of a more realistic way of seeing, with more respect for the analytical activity.

Bion: How did he show that?

T: Pardon?

Bion: How did he show that?

T: He said that it's difficult to say, because it's a feeling he has when he compares how the client behaved before to the way the client was now overtly speaking about him.

Bion: Well, if the analyst finds it difficult and the analyst has had a lot of experience, as he told us, well, what does he expect the patient to find?

T: I'm having difficulty in translating and A asked if perhaps you could help, Dr. Bion, in following up this point.

Bion: The point that I would like to have more elucidation about is: what is this state of mind, in which he is in when he says he's awake? And what is this state of mind, in which he is in when he says that he is asleep? Where does he think he is when he's awake?

T: Are you asking this question to A?

Bion: To anybody, anybody! We can bring our combined wisdom to bear on this problem.

T: P2 wants to know, when the patient is wide awake, where would he be? Would he be in your consulting room, in his own home, in the cemetery, now, or before? P2 would like to know how does this client use free association?

Bion: He doesn't. The idea is that he gets free associations confused with psychoanalytical ideas.**[1] A psychoanalyst can take what the patient says, or does, as a free association and then, he can try to interpret it—but that's got nothing to do with the patient. Where has the patient gotten this idea that the analyst is a psychoanalyst? Where did he get it from?

T: P2 asks A, does the patient want him to be a psychoanalyst?

P2: I'm asking A, the patient says that he wants you to be a psychoanalyst. He said that. And you said to your client that you are a psychoanalyst.

P3: Who said that?

P2: Now?

Bion: Yes!

T: The patient had read about Freud, he was curious about the subject, then he came to the Institute of Psychoanalysis and they sent him to A—to be psychoanalyzed. But from all the readings, he gathered that through analysis he would be able to put into practice all his ambitions of work, production, and women.

Bion: Well, I could only say: does he read and believe everything that he hears or reads? Again, it seems to me to be a peculiar state of mind in which he is apparently awake with all his wits about him. Where does he get this idea from? If it is from books, does he believe everything that he sees in books? Does he believe everything that he is told by institutes? If not, why does he make an exception in this case? I find myself getting back to the same question. What is this peculiar state of mind in which he is supposed to be awake to have all his wits about him?

P2: I'd like to think that I'm following you even if the state of mind could be: happiness, or sadness, or anger or something like that—an affective state of mind.

Bion: No, I think that the trouble is: we talk about these things, like going to sleep and waking up, over and over again and when it comes to psychoanalysis we have a chance of knowing what, if anything, these words mean. Therefore, I say: what does the analyst experience, which makes him think that the patient is awake? What does the analyst experience that makes him think that the patient is asleep? According to the language, articulated language, it appears to be quite simple: he's asleep, he's awake! Now, when we have a look at it close to, then one wonders: what are these different words referring to?

T: A, P1, and P2 are discussing, he makes reference to your question, what would he, the analyst, be feeling that makes him consider that the client is awake or not. Then, A answers that he has the feeling that the patient can't bear certain aspects of reality, that perhaps he would like to reach a state in which he could be both: wakeful and asleep.

Bion: Yes, I quite agree, all that is theory! But what I'm asking is: *what are the facts?* I'm not bothering about the theory! I've heard so many theories—that I'm sick to death of them. This is a very old story. Freud was most impressed because Charcot said: "Facts. Observe what is factual, observation." [Ver Stander Edition Vol. 1 Orbituário de Charcot] All the scientists, always, have attached great importance to observation. So, I likewise, say: what do we observe? Now, you've given a description about this. The patient snores and so on … But there's still the question as to: what is sleep? I could do this, I could say to the patient: "Where were you last night? What did you see?" I could get the answer: "Nowhere. I went to bed. I went to sleep." It's so simple! It doesn't answer my question. I'd still want to know: where he went and what he saw. Now I'm pretty sure that after a time the patient would say: "Ah, you mean what did I dream." I'd say: "No, I don't." He didn't go to sleep because sleep is nowhere.[2] What I want to know is: where he was and what he saw there. The same thing if he is what he calls awake. If this is true, if he has got all his senses about him, then where did he get this idea from, that there's somebody, or something, called a psychoanalyst, who will help him? What is this analyst—that he knows about—who could help him: whether he's awake or asleep! According to his behavior, it sounds as if he thought that the person called a psychoanalyst could help him even if he was present in body and absent in mind. I would want to know what he saw and heard when he was awake and know what he saw and heard when he was asleep. Of course, there's still the problem: what is … an ordinary human being to do when this patient is awake or asleep? Let's take this position, in which he apparently has gone to sleep. Alright now, what do you do then? If you were the analyst, what would you do?

T: A had said to him: "You seem to be asleep. You look as if you were asleep."

Bion: Did you say it in an ordinary tone of voice, or any other? These are practical problems, which every analyst has to be prepared for. That's the difficulty. What language do you talk to a person who behaves as if, and presumably he is, asleep? If you wake him, as we say, then he'd be in a different state of mind. Then, you are up against the problem of: what state of mind is he in, when he's awake? I don't think that any of these questions will ever be answered, except by the psychoanalyst. I think that if *we* don't answer them, no one else will.

T: A has the impression that the language of sleep must be the dream.

Bion: Well, would you advocate the analyst going to sleep?

T: Yes, A was afraid of that.

Bion: If that is the case, then one could say: it would be much easier to understand! If this was a physical disease, it could be contagious or infectious. But it isn't a physical disease, not that we know of. But I think that you are right, that one would be liable to feel that if the patient went to sleep, you'd do the same! But this is also true if the patient keeps awake, because you can get patients who come and behave in the same way, hour after hour, day after day, week after week, for months. The patient will come and say: "I am absolutely awful. I am sick to death of myself." They go on saying that. As far as I can make out, they are prepared to say it hour after hour, without the slightest difficulty. The analyst, I think, has to pay attention to that, maybe for six months, maybe for longer. So, the question as to what state of mind this patient is in when he's awake and what state of mind he's in when he's asleep is quite an important one.

I'm afraid we have to leave it now, for the present anyway—but it doesn't end the problem!

Notes

1. The translator understands that Bion is affirming that the patient is confusing free association with ideas or psychoanalytical theories.
2. Bion makes a joke here, punning on the word, "go," which not only is used to refer to *falling* asleep, but usually refers to movement towards a physical destination. Sleep is not a place, but a state of mind (Junqueira, 2015, personal communication).

Supervision 30 commentary

Antônio Sapienza

I will address my comments to three issues raised in the supervisory discussion in the working group, illustrating the dynamics of the supervision and the functions of the supervisor. Bion's initial approach consists in viewing the manifest conflict described in terms of *body language*. In this way, he emphasizes the difference between the dynamic situation of psychoanalytic supervision and that of psychoanalytic group therapy. He asks the presenting analyst a series of questions designed to penetrate beyond the conventions of ordinary assumptions: (a) "what makes you think that the patient has gone to bed?"; (b) "How do you know that the patient is awake?"; (c) "Why does the patient believe that the analyst can cure him?"; (d) "What is the analyst's fault?"; (e) "What is it that disturbs and thwarts the patient? The presence or absence of the analyst?"; and finally (f) "What are the clinical facts?" Bion concludes by saying: "When the subject is psychoanalysis, we have the chance to know what the words *sleep* and *wake up* mean." That formulation highlights the oscillation between two states of consciousness: "sleep" ←→ "awake."

Bion then subtly proposes to amplify the examination of *macroscopic conflict* using his reverie and capacity for containment to explore the theme "sleep" ←→ "awake" at a more profound *microscopic level.*

His investigation seeks to pass through resistances in order to arrive at points of catastrophic change. In so doing, he illuminates the relationship and even equivalency of the resulting turbulence and mental anguish with that of psychic "*growing pains.*" At stake in this clinical encounter are regressive issues that cannot be managed or resolved simply by a change of setting, such as face-to-face meetings that alternate with the sporadic use of the couch. The discussion that then ensues between Bion, the presenting analyst, and the group illustrates the difference between "explanation" and "exploration" as it relates to an analytical model of the mind, with the working group seeking to cultivate a fertile conjunction of ideas that can facilitate mental growth. In dialogue with the presenting analyst, Bion demonstrates his capacity for "dream-work-alpha" through which he enables the group—and presumably will eventually allow the patient—to move from lethargy towards experience and recognition of primitive anxieties. For example, Bion comments, "The patient may be physically present and mentally absent. Therefore, with what tone of voice will you wake him?"

Finally, as the group suffers a kind of mental fragmentation as Bion's provocative questions and responses come into benign confrontation with its members, there is the mobilization of emotional forces and the emergence of a progressive knowledge of *embryonic* factors related to the transition between the states "sleep" ←→ "awake." Here we also need to recognize and appreciate the role of Bion as "guardian of the supervisory setting," as he considers the importance of the *timing* and resultant elaboration of group work, signaling the end of the meeting contained by the available time. "I'm afraid we have to leave it now, for the present anyway—but it doesn't end the problem!"

Having introduced and discussed these three elements, I will now offer some further thoughts on the oscillation between the two states of consciousness: "sleeping" ←→ "awake." Bion might have denoted these states of mind and the oscillating relationship between them with their respective characters by the inscriptions: *S* (sleep) and *W* (awake). Within the sessions described in the supervision, the challenge presented to the analyst would be to focus attention on the dialogue with the patient in such a way as to facilitate the conditions that could allow an awakened state of consciousness (W) in the analysand.

In my original comments on this supervision, written in September of 2005, I began by emphasizing that one might consider the *neuropsychiatric conditions* as a possible *scientific vertex.* This would confirm or rule out possible phenomenological disorders (drugs, amentia, etc.) that might be the source of somatic conditions, such as stupor, catalepsy, narcolepsy, and lethargy.

However, from a more *psychoanalytic vertex*, there is from the very beginning of the presentation a presumptive layer in the material that indicates a loss of vitality of the patient described as a "boredom with life." Throughout the evolution of the supervision, Bion clarifies the possible progression that might result if the analyst is able to penetrate this smooth surface, which he compares to a mass of still waters, unveiling beneath it many violent streams of emotional turbulence.

On that occasion, I have proposed two analogies from the "aesthetic vertex." The first is from the film *Mulholland Drive* (2001) (the film title was beautifully translated to Portuguese as *City of Dreams)*, by the director David Lynch. This is a surrealistic thriller that presents complex plots, in which the protagonists live out states of mind in a restless trance, enveloped by predominantly violent and confused situations. The second analogy is drawn from Umberto Eco's novel *The Island of the Day Before.* The resonances produced by these two associated sources, may permit the analyst to establish possible correlations and begin to approximate a verbal language with which to approach the description of undifferentiated states of consciousness. The analogizing use of works of art may offer analysts the tools of communication, needed to understand the more bizarre layers of pre-verbal and non-verbal communications.

Bion emphasizes that in every clinical session what the analyst must bring to bear in order to more deeply understand the patient includes the following: (a) the *analyst's background,* including the experience of personal analysis, which will condition the use of rational and imaginative conjectures; (b) the cultivation of the capacity for *disciplined observation and a kind of analytic listening that is without memory, desire or theoretical preconceptions.* Outside of the session, the use of a grid of personnel construction (with the support of the "Grid," initially proposed by Bion in 1971) may serve as an additional, critical "holding device" needed to provide additional support for the exercise of a trained psychoanalytic intuition. This may even require the development and use of a *negative grid*, in order to help understand and think about the realm of minus K (–K).

Thus, Bion appeals to the analyst to cultivate habits of mind to reach *states of primitive mind*, in which archaeological trauma and residues of primitive disaster are buried. Detailed examination of these catastrophic levels requires patience, perseverance, and benign tolerance, so that catastrophic change can eventually be recognized, transformed, and can serve as the basis for creative change. The capacity to engage in this process will, of course, depend upon the emotional resources of each analytic couple. The analyst and his/her negative capability and condition of rêverie will be put to the test when attempting to contact the intimations of interrupted dreams that may appear as "conglomerates" and "exacerbations" connected to states of hallucinosis, similar to wild thoughts that radiate from the primitive mind.

In this supervision, and throughout his writings, Bion has bequeathed to us the tools with which to begin to explore the territory of *"psychotic refuges"* and *"impasses"* in analysis. As we do so, we will find that we must better acquaint ourselves with sudden *"reversals of perspective,"* when negative links prevail, leading to endless impasses and compulsions to continued repetition. These phenomena are associated with a psychic rigidity reinforced by strong defensive measures, supporting the maintenance of the illusion of a "perfect" mental world that is destructive to psychic growth. Under such conditions, the hidden psychotic parts of the personality will be safeguarded against knowledge and truth and will remain encysted. The understanding of this psychic configuration will require analysts to carefully expand their knowledge of mental constructions in which *negative links*—(–K, –L, –H)—prevail as *opponents* to the passions of knowledge (K), love (L), and hate (H).[1]

Note

1. Readers of this commentary and supervision who wish to examine these ideas further are directed to the following classical texts of Bion: (a) "On hallucination", Chapter Six of *Second Thoughts* (1958); (b) *Taming Wild Thoughts* [II] (1997); (c) *Transformations: Change from Learning to Growth* (1965), Chapter Ten; and to specific passages noted in the index of the latter book under the entries Hyperbole, Hallucination, and Hallucinosis.

References

Bion, W. R. (1958). On hallucination. In: *The Complete Works of W. R. Bion*. Vol. 6.—*Second Thoughts* (1958), (pp. 112–130). London: Karnac, 2014.
Bion, W. R. (1965). Transformations: Change from learning to growth. In: *The Complete Works of W. R. Bion*. Vol. 5. (pp. 240–257). London: Karnac, 2014.

Bion, W. R. (1997). Taming wild thoughts [II]. In: *The Complete Works of W. R. Bion*. Vol. 10. (pp. 169–199). London: Karnac, 2014.
Eco, U. (2006). *The Island of the Day Before*. USA: Mariner Books.
Lynch, D. (Dir.). (2001). *Mulholland Drive*. USA: Touchstone pictures.

CHAPTER FIVE

Supervision A10

In the text that follows, T stands for Translator and A stands for the presenting analyst.

T: Instead of beginning with a case, A would like to raise a theoretical point. We know that there are different vertices from which to observe the human experience and these vertices don't necessarily take into account the existence of something like a mind. For example, the theories of Pavlov and Skinner, which can deal either with behavior as it is observed or with reflexes at the neurophysiological level ignore the mind. This doesn't mean they don't believe the mind exists, but that they don't need it to do their work. Their views are in opposition to our model in which it is necessary for us to believe that the mind, or something like a mind, exists. And, therefore, because we, the analysts, are submerged in experiences in which we need the model of the mind, we may forget that this model of a mind is built by a mind itself. So perhaps although it is a question to be solved, whether or not a mind exists, we do not necessarily use this as a point of departure to our work. In recognizing this as a model, as a model with its peculiar characteristics, it wouldn't make it easier for us to work with it. For example, A has noticed that usually many analysts think that the mind is inside the skull but it seems to him that what is inside the skull is the brain and not the mind.

Bion: Hum … the problem has excited attention for many hundreds of years at least, so we get a lot of words like: soul, super soul, spirit, and more recently Freud talks about the id, ego, superego, these are more modern linguistic terms. I think that the attempt to map out those areas and to say where the id boundaries are, or the ego's or the superego's and so on, is very unsatisfactory. But linguistically, it is possible to make these definitions. Now, the rules of grammar are very useful for verbal communication, but the rules of grammar are not obeyed by the mind, nor are the rules of physics obeyed by the universe. This little scrap of the universe, this little bit of earth that orbits around the sun, some of the laws of geophysics appear to conform to the actual phenomenon, which we witness on the earth. But all those laws are really laws of the mind. They're the sort of things which human beings can understand and human beings are a very small portion of animate life. So, in spite of the fact that we think we are very important, in fact there is no evidence to support that whatsoever. It's our opinion that we are homo-sapiens. But whether we are wise or not is another matter all together. For example, is the human society obviously superior to, or better than, the society of bees or ants and so on? Now, as analysts we do have a chance of having a very close contact with what we, for the sake of convenience, call a mind. If you were to call out to your dog, your dog might come to you. If a stranger called out your dog's name, he wouldn't. Why not? Can that be explained by the laws of the sound waves in air and so on? Modulations of tone and so forth? No, it can't. It still wouldn't explain why the dog would answer one set of sounds and not another. Now, with regard to the mind, there's no sense that I know of which would detect its presence: it's got no smell, no taste, no color, and so forth, but if you bring two minds together then the difference between the two might give us a clue, because I say: "The difference. The difference between what?" I don't know about the fact of the existence of a mind, or soul or spirit, whatever you like to call it, but it would be very convenient for the purposes of our discussion to suppose that we can talk about it and discuss it, if we give it a name. Of course, it's an extremely limited scope, because even if you take this world, it's an insignificant structure and the creatures that walk about on it, crawl about on it, are even smaller still. Now recently the space probes have been sent out to find evidence of life in another very tiny area, namely: the solar system, which we consider to be a very large space, then perhaps we could be such insignificant creatures; and to be able to explore the solar system is virtually exploring nothing. In fact, one might need to have an astronomer here to give us a sense of scale at all. If we take even the system of our particular spiral nebula which appears to be rotating. If it is rotating one ought to be seeing across. But we can't see where the center is, even if it's located by astronomical mathematics in the position of Sagittarius, one can't see across; it's obscured by cosmic dust. But roughly speaking, mathematically, the diameter of this particular spiral appears to be something like ten to the eighth million light years, which is quite a distance when you consider what a light year is. And now, to make things more complicated, they've discovered what they call a black hole, and they've now discovered two black holes. Now, in these particular areas apparently the laws of physics don't apply. So that is sticking to the concrete and we are talking now about what we are pleased to believe is the soul or the spirit or the mind. It's striking that if one asks a quite simple question: what is the definition of the difference between the animate and the inanimate? There isn't a definition. You'd think that there ought to be a definition with the difference between me and this.

But there isn't. So much for the scientific method. So, to come back to our particular area, I think all that one could say is that the nearest to certainty that we're ever likely to get is only a probability. I want to define for a moment this idea of probability. For a thing to be what we call certain there has to be evidence. When there's not enough evidence for a certainty, then we have to fall back on probabilities. That which is probable is only something for which there is not enough evidence to know; and yet, as a psychoanalyst, we follow Freud's idea of a scientific approach to the mind. I think it's an interesting ambition but I don't know that science is going to carry us very far. I think it's quite a good idea that we should aspire to being scientific but I would like to suggest that the peculiarity of being scientific is to have a prejudice in favor of the truth. However, we have company in this because there are plenty of people who are not psychoanalysts, like musicians.

T: A would like to know what you think about this prejudice people have about the mind. Is it inside the brain, skull, or is it the same thing?

Bion: Hum ... no. I think that that is fallacious. Hum ... because it's ignoring the fact that there's been again a prejudice in favor of the diaphragm as being the location of the spirit or soul. It's quite reasonable, it's quite plausible because it goes up and down and when it goes up and down you're usually feeling angry or frightened so it could be caused by [here Bion makes some panting sounds] this thing going up and down. But so is the spleen. The diaphragm goes up and down and it seems to be mixed up with the breath. Well, perhaps the breath is spirit. It's gaseous, it's not solid. But the spleen is believed, even now, to have something to do with the blood and the blood also circulates and seems to be very closely connected with life. If the blood ceases circulating we seem to have to stop thinking because we're dead. Or if the reticular endothelial system gets out of order, again, there is trouble in the production of blood cells. So there's a lot to be said for thinking that the soul resides in the spleen. Now, what about the heart? People will say that so and so has no heart, no human feeling. So, again, there's a certain plausibility in *this* location. All this centers on the assumption that there is such a thing as a soul or a spirit. It's curious how durable that idea is, how robust it is. It goes on lasting through the centuries and there's even a lot of evidence that people believe that ... when somebody is dead and buried, they need the sort of equipment that is needed by living people. They live in heaven or hell. They are provided with funeral furniture and even paganism is quite up-to-date today. So, religion is having to move with the times, as we say. It has to be up-to-date. Even psychoanalysts have to up-to-date. Still, there's belief in a soul or a spirit. I don't know what the evidence is. I don't know why we think that some pieces of music are the sounds that we don't want to hear again and other pieces of music endure. Hamlet, Macbeth, even terrible plays like *Timon of Athens* still are read. Do you think that there are any case histories, psychoanalytic case histories to be read in ten years time? I doubt it. But that seems to me to depend a great deal on whether anybody can get closer to what, for wanting a better word, one has to call the spirit of man. Is there any case history that is likely to be read in the way that Shakespeare's case history is read? Or Racine, Moliere? It's one of the reasons why I think that we, as analysts, will need to find some method of communication. If we could, then we might be able to communicate with ourselves. I might be able to know that I've got wisdom up here [Bion indicates his head] but if I've got a pain in my foot, I can't communicate with my foot. So, although I may be able to think somewhere up here, I can't really augment my experience or wisdom by listening to the knowledge or wisdom or experience of my hypochondria, the things which are below the level of my "chondria." Even as it is, hypochondriac or hypochondria is spoken of as if it is some sort of inferior thing. The same thing with psychosis: we tend to feel that it is inferior to be what we call psychotic. But I suspect that the compliment is returned by our psychosis. It doesn't want to know very much about our so called intelligence and anything between the two falls into the ban of the excluded middle, the girdle, girdle type hypothesis or the mathematicians Brawer or Hating, both of whom have been concerned with intuitionism. But I don't know if I have answered at all what you were asking.

T: A would like to give special emphasis to a certain point, although he feels it has been answered. He's seen things which give him the impression that the profound belief that the mind needs a place to be located—a place like, for example the brain, or the diaphragm, or the heart—that this calls our attention to these areas in the body. But it's only then that they're propitious areas for people to make the projection of things like: thinking that the mind is there. And that the human experience, using the metaphor, goes even beyond using a phrase that can be said: "I have a heart full of things—I have a head full of things" and that this can even bring about a headache.

Bion: I think a lot more experience has to be obtained about migraine, which is a peculiar sort of headache, which is closely linked with patterns which appear to be observable by the eyes during a migraineous attack. What would you think was the significance of this localization?

T: With a little bit more of scientific understanding, men become ashamed of having attributed to certain areas of the body, like the heart and the diaphragm, the chief locus of what is fundamental. Gradually the nervous system—chiefly the cortex—is known as an area of integration and it now becomes an area that is quite liable to receive these attributions, mythological attributions, which acquire scientific basis, analogical basis. And we are so under the spell of this mythology that sometimes it's very difficult to separate a brain and mind and, if it's so, sometimes it would be the same thing as if we'd remained with behaviourism or skinnerism or any other such theory.

T: A says that the brain has even importance for the mind as if ... like the spleen has importance for the mind. We have to make this distinction in order to function as psychoanalysts, but that the mind shouldn't be made a prisoner of such a concept.

Bion: But it always is! As soon as you get a theory, shall we say a psychoanalytic theory, as soon as you think you'll see something very clearly, it becomes a system and one feels: thus far and no further. I don't want anybody to disturb my ideas about psychoanalysis. So, in this way, I don't want to make space for a development; but in so far as I am a good analyst, I make it possible for my patients to do much better than me. So every time I am successful with a patient, I become more and more out of date.

T: Out of date?

Bion: Yes. So, in a sense, if we are dealing with something which develops, it's still developing. If the spirit of man is capable of development, is capable of progression beyond savagery, brutality, rape, murder, robbery, we ought to make room in which this developing thing had a chance of developing. At some time the baby has to leave the mother's inside because there isn't room in which to grow. But I think the same thing applies to the mind. I still think that there is one, and I think that it is still developing and it has to have enough space in which to grow within the system in which it lives at present. So that it can break out of that system. But of course, people are frightened of that: "Doctor, I'm going mad" or "I'm going to have a breakdown" and so on. They want to help you to stop that pregnant idea from becoming mature.

Well, we will have to stop now.

Supervision A10 commentary

Luiz Carlos Uchôa Junqueira Filho

In this supervision, Bion is confronted, not with a clinical stimulus, but a theoretical stimulus: the "case" of psychoanalysis itself, and the fact that as a fundamental premise (or model) the patient, who is the subject of analysis, "possesses a mind." As an additional datum, there arises within the group the observation that this model, which posits a mind, is built by the mind itself, in a sort of specular procedure.

All of us who attended Bion's lectures and supervision sessions know that his "method" consisted in the search for metaphors, myths, and new vertices of observation in search of expanded abstractions, which encompass and elucidate a wide range of real human situations. This is how he "reacted" in this supervision to the belief that human beings possess a mind. He began to question the evidence of the seemingly unquestionable assumption that minds exist, noting that the mind should not be confounded with the brain and that its function was producing thoughts which, phenomenologically, he himself would name "imaginative conjectures," but which we, operationally, could name *reverie*.

In his first set of associations/constructions, Bion considers that the assignment of names to phenomena and things, the rules of grammar, or the laws of physics are all "human fabrications," thus giving us to understand, as he repeatedly states in his texts, that they do not necessarily guarantee a correspondence to the reality of things-in-themselves. Moreover, he hints that perhaps these might be mere "shorthand conventions among friends" a kind of "corporate action" designed to facilitate communication within the human species. In this sense, Bion suggests that the label, Homo Sapiens ("Those who have knowledge"), might only be a vain self-designation.

Next, Bion refers to the essential epistemological difference between sensorial and psychic realities, stressing the difficulty for us to establish the existence of "the mind" as an entity, because it cannot be smelt, touched, seen, etc. Its existence is something that must be inferred from the differences between personalities, from experiences of love and hate, as well as from the surprising evidence that psychic pain, different from physical pain, is liable to be "transferred" from one being to another.

In an imaginative demonstration of his α-function, Bion evokes a "pilgrimage of human curiosity" in search of a possible location of the mind in some organ of the human body. His reverie improvises upon the meanings of the Greek word *hypokhondria.* According to its etymology, it refers to the region below the cartilage of the sternum associated with melancholia, therefore, with a spiritual depression, which, however, according to one's vertex of observation, may even have a positive connotation.

Bion, apparently, does not try to make any sophisticated distinction between mind, soul, and psyche. In *All My Sins Remembered* (1985) he writes:

> And now I was supposed to be part of the psychiatric service—dealing with the psyche. Not the soul exactly—that was the job of the Chaplain's Department—just the psyche if you know what I mean (because I don´t). (Bion, 1985, p. 47)

In order to stress the ontogenic relativism of fundamental human questions, Bion makes a "cosmic leap" showing the insignificance of our mental space in relation to the infinity of astronomical space. This perspective allows the suggestion that the essential metapsychological antinomy would be that between the finite and the infinite, rather than that between the conscious and the unconscious, as professed by Freud.

Bion then muses about the possible scientific status of psychoanalysis and how, in the absence of empirically, sense-based evidence for assumed psychic phenomena, we remain restricted to the field of "probabilities" rather than "certainties." This, in spite of the fact that we must always be in search of "the truth." When Bion mentions that we, analysts, share this lack of an empirical evidentiary base with other fields such as music, he anticipates the recent formulation by George Steiner (2011), who ends his beautiful book, *The Poetry of Thought*, by suggesting that more contemporary epistemologies are anchored in hybrid genres such as music, dance, mimesis, abstract, and figurative arts.

Deepening the question of the bodily rootedness and location of the mind, Bion suggests that the psychotic part of the personality would be more closely linked to intuition than to intelligence, quoting thus Heyting and Brouwer. As Pierre-Henri Castel (2008) explains to us in "Bion, epistèmologue", Bion deepened Freud's notion of "intuition" (*Einsicht*), that was based upon Poincaré's (1914) core concept, that of "intuition–invention," thereby allowing for the elaboration of the concept of "the selected fact." And yet, despite the power of this last formulation, there will always be a greater reservoir of beta-elements than the sum total of what any of us can transform via alpha-function into that which can be used to think with and think about.

The last point that Bion raises is the question of internal space, which the human being needs to "produce" in order to guarantee mental development. A potential obstacle to this process is that developing this space is only possible through the experience of catastrophic change, which always poses a threat of madness. In addition to reaffirming the belief in the existence of a mind, Bion stresses that, at the same time that the growth of the mind must occur within the living system in the present, it must also "break-out." That is, transcend the limits of that system in search of the new.

At a certain point of his trilogy *A Memoir of the Future,* Bion asks if catastrophic change would represent a *break-out, a break-in,* a *break-up*, a *break-down*, or a *break-through.* Perhaps we must admit that mental growth would be a multi-faceted process encompassing all the implicit connotations of the verb *to break,* namely, a break, a fissure, a pause, an infraction, a penetration, a vanquish, and so on.

In this spirit, I will conclude by saying that although these have been *my* associations in response to this supervision of Bion's, each reader will have the opportunity to develop their own in a never ending spiral of creativity and new development.

References

Bion, W. R. (1985). *All My Sins Remembered*. Abingdon: Fleetwood Press.

Bion, W. R. (1991). *A Memoir of the Future*. London: Karnac.

Castel, P. H. (2008). Bion epistèmologue, envoi to *La preuve & autres texts*. Paris: Editions d'Ithaque.

Poincaré, H. (1914). *Science and Method*. London: Thomas Nelson and Sons.

Steiner, G. (2011). *The Poetry of Thought*. New York, NY: New Directions Books.

CHAPTER SIX

Supervision A3

In the text that follows, T stands for Translator; P1 stands for a participant in the audience.

T: Here is the situation I would like to begin by describing and having your thoughts about. During the session of the day before, there was a plant in my office with many leaves. One leaf was dry, wrinkled and looked ill. After the patient left, I removed this leaf from the plant. The next day, the patient noticed this and asked me, "Where is the leaf?" I answered, "You are trying to discover if I can take in and listen to what you tell me and hold it inside of me rather than having what you tell me turn into feelings and actions that I cannot hold and keep inside."

Well, I felt that my answer was sort of evasive. I *had* taken out the leaf and he could notice that it was no longer there. So in this sense, I felt, that perhaps my answer was a lie.

Bion: The only important point about that, I think, is: has one given the patient a correct interpretation? In other words, has one interpreted correctly *the facts*, which are available to you in the session? Now, sometimes, when you give an interpretation, which you think is correct, you feel: "Yes, that it is so" to yourself. Now, the patient may also feel: "Yes, that is so" he may say: "Yes" or, he may take no notice and go straight on. Now, I think that it is usually possible to tell when the patient appears to take no notice and goes straight on, that he has in fact changed, is now talking about something else. It depends a good deal on what he says, but,—if it's just what I have described—then, the interpretation is as correct as any interpretation is ever likely to be, because the subject is closed and he goes on to the next straight away.

Now, in the situation that you're describing, it's one of these situations, which—when you have given the interpretation—you can feel: "No, it's not correct." It's like you're drawing a design—you can see what you've drawn, the lines and so on—and you can see it's not good, it's wrong. You may not know how to do it better, but you know that that is wrong—you try to do a better one. But, the same thing is true in an analysis, only we don't see the interpretation that we've just given written down—it's too quick, it's said in the air, leaves no marks! So, you can only feel "that wasn't correct."

The patient may agree: "Yes, that's right!" but you can hear from his tone of voice, that it hasn't really meant very much—either because the interpretation wasn't heard, or because, in fact, the interpretation was wrong and the patient is just being quite polite. But that is a matter of *feeling* in the room. Now, the fact that you feel guilty is like any of these other facts: that you feel frightened, or anxious, or troubled about, whether the patient is going to do something stupid and so on … All that doesn't really matter! It's like, as I said, the military officer who realizes that the situation is desperate, but he isn't supposed to show it, he's not supposed to run away. So, what you feel—whether it is frightened or guilty or fond of the patient—is a matter of no importance, whatever. What the analyst feels in a session, or thinks, is of no importance. The only thing that is important in analysis is: what the patient thinks and feels.

So, however, whatever you're feeling—whether you're feeling ill, or as I say guilty, or sick, or a headache—are of no importance at all, because in the session, you have got that work to do. However you feel—whether you're feeling ill, physically ill, or mentally disturbed, or anxious, those are matters which you can go and see your doctor about, or your analyst about—that's nothing to do with the patient at all. So, the point that you mentioned isn't of importance—the only thing that is of importance is: that you should give the next interpretation correctly—if you can and so on … But, if you are, as I say, feeling guilty or frightened, then you tell your analyst and there, you hope that he will analyze it and so on …

Of course, if you are in my position, you've got no analyst to go to—you just have to put up with it. If I have a toothache I still have to give the correct interpretations. I have to go and see the dentist sometime. It's no good saying: "I'm sorry, I've got a toothache" to the patient, that's not his business. So, the main thing is: to recognize that, in your office, when you are seeing a patient, what is important is *his* pain, *his* feeling of guilt, or *his* feeling of fear, or *his* idea. Those are the only things that matter. So, what you are talking about there is an interruption of your dialogue. You and the patient have got some work to do.

I could put it like this: that your conscience is like a small child, who comes into the room and interrupts—it's an interruption. If I'm analyzing somebody, if the conditions existed for me to analyze you and you told me this story I could say something of this sort: "Our conversation has been interrupted, somebody has interfered with the intercourse between me and you."

T: I didn't understand correctly, you would say this as an interpretation?

Bion: I would say, I have said it to patients. I've had a patient who's saying: "Yes, I was going down the road and I want to tell you about this fact that … hum … hum … well, I mean to say … I forget what I mean now …" Let us say: "you have been interrupted." I'd say: "You were saying you were walking down the road, you were telling me something and we've been interrupted and I don't know what the story was." At other times the patient says: "I was going down the road and hum … a car came and it knocked down another person who was on the road … my little boy came back from school and he got very bad grades." Now, that is different. I could say to the patient: "You were telling me a story about walking down the road, a car came and knocked down the patient; I never heard what happened. What happened was, just now, you, instead of telling me the rest of the story, did that. [Here, Bion either made a gesture of separating or bringing together the two stories.]

This is a different story, this boy got a bad grade in school, but that doesn't join on here. These seem to be two different stories. I don't know the beginning of that one, I don't know the end of this one. You were talking to me and suddenly that happened. So, you've derailed, you've de-routed. You were unable to continue your way and got onto a different way. If you were walking, I would say: you were going down the street and suddenly you got moved onto a different street." Now that's a different kind of interruption, but it is a peculiar sort of disturbance—you can show the patient it's happening in the office. Now, sometimes the analyst can be deceived about this—well, very frequently, in fact—but I want to point out a peculiar kind of interference. Instead of interpreting what my senses tell me about what is going on in the room …

Sometimes one hears an interpretation of this sort: "… you're telling me that you're walking down the road; I think that this is an oedipal situation." That is a situation in which the analyst has been interrupted—he has been interrupted by his psychoanalytic conscience. Instead of interpreting what is going on—which has got a basis in fact that you're talking about—what you can hear and see, which the patient can also confirm—because it is what you hear and see. You've been interrupted by a psychoanalytic statement. The patient can't do anything about it because, the patient doesn't know what an oedipal situation is, or what this has got to do with walking down the road. But it's very easy for psychoanalytically educated people to be interrupted in their observation of the patient. The real point all the time is: is this an accurate observation? Have I put it into words which the patient can understand? That's the only point when you are the analyst who is analyzing a patient.

I hope that answered your questions!

T: P1 would like now to present a case, although we have only thirty minutes.

T: She (P1) would like to bring up the following question: It pertains to the special relationship which she has been experiencing with one of her clients—a woman client. She brings us a characteristic of that special relationship which she feels between herself and the client and the client towards herself—it is a kind of defiance, concerning the emergence of love and proof of love … a hope of fulfillment accompanied by despair, because hate is also present. So she selected material from a session and because she thinks this illustrates the situation quite clearly, she would like to bring it to us.

T: It was a session that happened yesterday, where the analyst came late. The client comes in, she lies on the couch, her first words are: "My life is so confused that when I get here …" and she interrupts. She makes a pause: "I feel confused when there is a multitude of people wanting the same thing as I." She makes a pause and she continues: "The places I have been visiting to look for work, are so filled up with people, that I end up giving up."

Bion: Yes.

T: There's too much competition.

Bion: Who thinks it's a special relationship?

T: She, P1 says, she herself feels this on the basis of former material. What she's going to bring after this initial introduction, pertains to the impression that the patient is competing with her, because she was late—because of her own personal life matters.

Bion: There are two different stories here. One of them is that there's a special relationship. The other one is: that it is not special at all. There are lots of people, or things, which are competing—it is not so special that you could say that the two people are married to each other, for life. The marriage is much more like a psychoanalytic marriage, which is only a temporary affair. The analyst sees other patients and has other things to do in consequence sometimes is late—which shows that the analyst has been doing or seeing somebody else. The patient also knows that they have other things to do, besides coming for analysis—other people to see and talk to. So, the analyst knows that he or she is not going to marry the patient and say: "We will live together for life." The patient knows that they aren't saying: "I want to be analyzed by you, forever." The patient, too, wants to get cured; that means to say to go, be able to go away, do other things.

So, is it a relationship which is exactly like every other relationship? No, it isn't! It is a peculiar relationship, it is a special relationship and that's why we use—if we want to talk about it—long words like psychoanalysis; call it "a psychoanalysis." It is a special relationship. There are feelings of *love* and *hate*, but, there are also other relationships, in which the analyst and the analysand have feelings of love and hate.

The analytic relationship is peculiar; it is therefore special in that sense. The analyst doesn't talk to everybody, make personal remarks, as he does, when he or she talks to a patient.

It is quite important, because you can get a very mistaken state of affairs, I think, in which—I've known two people, both of whom have been analyzed—they go on interpreting each other's behavior. But analytic conversation is, in my opinion, quite useful for purposes of psychoanalysis—it is not suitable for marriage, it's not useful in a shop. In other words, the analytic conversation, with these peculiar personal remarks which are made—which we call interpretations—is better confined to situations in which, the *minimum necessary conditions* exist. So, from that point of view, in analysis, we try to have a minimum of the necessary conditions; all of it's important, the minimum necessary conditions! In marriage, the minimum necessary conditions for analysis don't exist, nor do the minimum necessary conditions for a marriage exist if it is interrupted … if the marriage relationship is interrupted by analysis. Similarly, if an analysis is interrupted by a love affair, or a hate affair, which would be more appropriate if you were fighting somebody or if you were courting somebody. Similarly, psychoanalysis is not really a confessional.

If a patient wants to confess his sins, he doesn't get absolution from the analyst. The analyst interprets these confessions. Otherwise, what ought to be a psychoanalytic session, has turned into a confessional, or a psychoanalytic session has turned into a sexual experience and so on … through the list—those are interferences. The guilt of the patient, his crimes, his faults, his mistakes, they're quite useful to know what they are, but, there are other things in life, besides the patient's crimes, mistakes. So, for the whole analysis to be taken up with a confession of these various crimes, faults, mistakes, means that not enough time is left available, for the discussion of a whole area of human thought and activity.

If it were physical medicine, the patient could say: "I've got a lump on my knee" and the doctor could examine it and look at it and so on and so forth … and that's all. But the doctor is not treating that lump in the knee. He has closed his view in this sort of way, and is looking at the patient through a microscope. What we ought to be doing is examining the patient, examining that patient's chest or, if the patient was finding difficulty with these muscles here, [Bion indicates his facial muscles] and it were treated as if that was the only trouble.

The analyst needs to be open to the whole personality. So, with the story that's told, say: "All right, you've got a lump in your knee. I'll need to examine you. Will you get undressed, so that I can examine the whole of your body." Similarly, with the mind: "Can you tell me as much as you can about yourself, because I want to examine the whole of your mind. It's quite important that you've told me your infidelities, your sins, your crimes and so on—we'll bear that in mind—but I want to know something else, too."

Now, I wouldn't say this to the patient but if the patient has come to see me, then it's rather an obvious point. But, very often, what is obvious is easy to miss: that patient still exists. Therefore, they must have done something right between the time they were born and now, or they'd have been dead long ago. So, as well as their crimes and sins and mistakes and so on … I'd like to hear what they had done right, because I'd still like to know, so would they, how it is that they are still alive. After all, if somebody lives to the age of, shall we say, three or thirty, or sixty, they must know how to go on living in this world. So, I'd like to know about that; because, if they've managed to live to thirty, then they may live another thirty years. If they knew what they did right, between naught and thirty, then, they might know how to behave between thirty and sixty, or between thirty and ninety.

Freud describes this as free-floating analysis, I think—some phrase like that. For the analyst, it means that one's mind is wide open, as far as it is possible—you don't want to have a kind of one-track mind. It needs to be wide open, so that, when the patient says something, he does that. But, again, if he can do that there, again, he can be ready to do that here. In other words, if possible, one should be sufficiently flexible, to entertain new ideas or new impressions.

So, it's perfectly true that it can be a special relationship, but never mind, it's wide open, too. The patient may not like that, because the patient then thinks: "Oh well, there are lots of people I want to see and do, but so does the analyst. The analyst isn't really devoted to me." It's always a special history—a special relationship in this way. After all, why does the analysand come to you? Why not to all the other possible people: dentist, doctor, psychoanalyst, other psychoanalyst and so on … Why to you? It's no good asking them that, because they probably don't know. They probably don't know, how they got to you—except that a friend said that he went, or something like that. But those are rationalizations.

Sorry, we've got to the end of the time here.

Supervision A3 commentary

Maria Cecília Andreucci Pereira Gomes

> *How does the person know of blushing so invisible,*
> *noise so inaudible, pain so impalpable that its intensity, pure intensity,*
> *is so intense that it cannot be tolerated but must be destroyed even if it*
> *involves the murder of the 'anatomical' individual?*
>
> —Bion, 1991, pp. 51–52

Among the different paths that I could take to present these ideas on Bion's supervision A3, I chose first to base myself on the way I feel, live, and try to apply to my clinical practice the principles I have learned from Bion over the years.

In 1978 I was in formation at the São Paulo Psychoanalytic Society and I still clearly remember when Bion came, by invitation, to give a series of conferences. I remember the strong impression he made on me, even independently of the value of his theories. I was a young candidate in the first year at the institute and I took some improvised clinical material to a supervision session, and I was glad that Bion had asked that the supervision not be recorded.

I still remember that presentation, about a very unstable patient who had attempted suicide several times. There was a reaction in the group when I said that the patient had moved me emotionally and stirred up enormous pain, fear, and compassion with his missed sessions, depression, level of anxiety, violence, despair, and guilt. An older colleague in the group, a training analyst from a different society, said something like: So if the analyst was moved, she felt, and the analyst died.

In contrast, Bion went back to talking about the patient and showed his capacity for containment by making me feel accepted, understood, and respected. And he stimulated my curiosity to investigate together with him.

He responded to the training analyst's comment in approximately the following words: "No one here knows better than the analyst herself about what went on in the session." From that moment on, at least for me, that man was no longer "the mysterious Bion", but a master suggesting that I examine my experience and inexperience with him and open myself up to the opportunity of broadening my understanding. I forgot about the rest of the group and became completely absorbed in what Bion was saying. This emotional experience that took place so many years ago had a profound effect on me and I still remember it.

It is on the basis of this brief introduction that I begin my comments here with the curiosity that Bion's theories have always stirred up in me. But not only his theories were important. His personality also moved me emotionally. At one point during a discussion in Los Angeles, he expressed himself in no uncertain terms when answering a question by someone in the room: "Our fear maybe just as great as the client's." And Bion answered,

> "It certainly is. The only hope is that we may be capable of standing the stresses of it—nothing can demonstrate that except trying it. In analysis the important thing is not what the analyst or analysand can do, but what the couple can do; there should be something the couple can do where the biological unity is two, not one." (Bion, 1978, p. 44)

This curiosity about Bion made me go farther back in time to listen to the "voice of memory" that he, when an adult, still carried in the child-in-him. In his book *The Long Weekend* (Bion, 2014, p. 14) he describes a number of episodes from those earlier times. Here are some examples:

> I went into this question thoroughly—and others, like "Is golden syrup really gold?"—with my mother, and later with my father, but without being satisfied by either. I concluded that my mother didn't really know; though she tried very hard and she seemed as puzzled as I was. It was more complicated with my father; he would start but seemed to tire when I did not understand the explanation.

> > "In a sunny room I showed my father a vase of some yellow flowers, for him to admire the skill with which I had arranged them.
> > "Yes", he said, "very good".
> > "But do look, Daddy."
> >
> > "I'm not lying, Daddy. I did it all myself."
> > That stopped him in his tracks. He was upset. "Why did you say that?"
> > "What, Daddy?"
> > "I never expected you to be lying".
> > "Well, I wasn't", I replied, becoming afraid that Arf Arfer would appear. Arf Arfer was very frightening".[1] (Bion, 2014, p. 14)

At that age, Bion remembered, he never directed questions to his parents. The superior race did not behave that way.

> "He is only four"—said my mother. "Perhaps it will be different when he goes to school in England; a lot can happen in four years." (Bion, 2014, p. 26)

> > A long two years of "Shadows of the evening steal across the sky"; my mother felt it. I felt it.
> > My mother would caress my head with what seemed a new tenderness. …
> > "Mo-ther, you aren't sad, are you?"
> > "Of course not! Why should I be sad?"
> > "Well, why should she be sad? I couldn't think. It was ridiculous. Sad? Of course not". But she was. (Bion, 2014, p. 28)

> The infant knows what it is to have raging emotions—things to which we give crude names, like fear, depression, love, hate—but it doesn't know what to call them; by the time it has mastered articulate speech it has forgotten what it feels like to be an infant. So we, who have reached this stage of being capable of articulating speech, have almost forgotten what it feels like to be human. We spend too many impressionable years in learning how to be just like everybody else—not how to be ourselves. (Bion, 1980, p. 13)

Bion says in supervision A3 that:

> The most important thing to recognise is that in your office, when you are with a patient, the only important thing is their pain, their guilt feelings, their feelings of fear or their ideas. These are the only things that matter.

The main aspect of Bion's clinical work is the phenomenology that goes on in the session. By this he means the elements that make up the session, the emotional climate there, the impressions about it, the patient's emotional state of health, his thoughts and feelings, and desires. He gives special emphasis to the analyst's need to have contact with his own mental state and to deal with it.

Bion's clinical investigation into internal psychic processes of the analytic dyad is based on theories whose sources are the patient's personal experiences and the knowledge acquired through psychoanalysis. This involves abstractions of concepts taken from philosophy, mathematics, logic, history, art, and religion. Through them he constructs models, or myths, in his effort to establish approximations of the psychic reality of the patient. He proposes that psychoanalysis could also be understood and applied through vertices of mathematics, science, aesthetics, art, religious, and mystical experiences.

With his broad culture and acute intuition he respects patients by using accessible language that will have a strong impact on them, in order to put them into contact with the activity of their own minds. Bion was much more aware of external reality than Klein was, perhaps due to his own childhood history and to his later work with groups. He attempted to understand what the real mother and her capacity for reverie are like, and also what the real father is like.

For Bion, the analytic situation is essentially a binding process, a permanent interaction between two personalities—similar to the bond between a child and its mother—and the reciprocal effects of one over the other.

Since he held that analysis can take place from different vertices, Bion opened up space for the use of three dimensions of "analytic attitude": the dimension of dominating the senses*, the dimension of myth** and the dimension of passion***.[2]

According to Bion there are two basic principles in operation here. They function like compasses to guide analyst and patient in the chaos they must encounter and traverse, including rapid transformations that involve strong emotional experiences. These principles are: (1) the search for the truth and, (2) mental growth.

In supervision A3, Bion says:

> The situation you are describing is a moment such as when you give a correct interpretation [but you may] feel something like, "No, that's not right". It's like when you draw something—you can see what you drew, the lines and everything else—and you can see that it didn't turn out well, that it's wrong. You might not know how to do any better, but you know that that one is wrong—you try to do a better one.

I can see Bion's fundamental premises in this excerpt, which indicate the importance of the analyst being truly in contact with both himself and the patient. He should know when he was wrong and know how to accept the fact that he was wrong, then try to reformulate and, in general, deal with his own personal narcissism.

For Bion the mind can only develop through exposure to the truth, including processes through which the truth evolves and through which the mind can become blocked. In supervision A3 he says:

> The same thing happens in analysis but we can't see the interpretation we just gave, written on paper—it's too fast, it's said in the air, it leaves no marks! Therefore you can only agree that, "Yes, that is correct".
>
> Listening to your own tone of voice you can note that what [the patient] said didn't mean very much—either because the interpretation was not heard or because, in fact, it was wrong. But this is a matter of feeling in the consulting room.

In this short statement Bion refers not only to the characteristic movement of emotional analytic experience in an emotional climate of consistency and containing. He also shows how the analyst's mind operates like a sounding board, with its ability to distinguish among the patient's different emotional nuances, including feelings, reactions, and transformations related to the analyst's formulation. He can appreciate how difficult it is to move from chaos to form, that is, from the paranoid-schizoid position to the depressive position. It is a process which implies painful feelings that call for changes in the patient. Bion called them "catastrophic changes"

Bion supposed that this linearity was a rationalisation of a feeling of persecution, a "paranoid constellation" constructed by the mind as a defence to keep depression from flooding the personality.

Another important aspect in Bion's clinical practice was his position that one can only understand an emotional constellation after it begins to cause new patterns to emerge. With the presence of a different pattern, a new angle opens up in the perception of the personality; the analysand is able to "realise" that her earlier perception system was distorted. With this approach, Bion is referring to the need for discriminative distance.

A patient of mine, with prevalence of the psychotic area in her personality, once told me that, when she felt great anxiety and despair, she could not see what I was saying to her at that moment. She hatefully stated: "You don't know what it is like to be in the eye of the storm."

According to Bion it is only when a new emotional organisation can arise within the disorganisation, or when a new emotional constellation or a new pattern appears, that the truth can emerge and with it an awakening of hope. (J. Symington & N. Symington, 1997).

Another aspect of Bion's clinical practice is the following about what went on in the session: He considered it a very important step when an analyst is able to observe a change from a previous pattern to a new pattern in the patient, for example, when the patient is changing from avoidance of mental pain to being able to face it. But Bion also said that he cannot see the reason why this happens.

It is important to note that Bion's thought differs from Freud's on this point. The acceptance of mental pain is contrary to the search for the pleasure principle, and this is the central point in Bion's theory of development.

Bion once said that development consists of a change in motivational category, from a wish for immediate pleasure and the avoidance of mental pain, to a category that implies the emergence of the truth and the wish for emotional growth. For Freud, pleasure could only be renounced by postponing it in favour of a modification of reality where an alternative objective is in view, namely, a "quantum" of pleasure later on. (J. Symington & N. Symington, 1997).

In supervision A3 Bion's split, or cut, seems to be an attempt to introduce the possibility of changing the compulsion to repeat the same pattern. He adds another dimension to the analytic process, namely, that analysis should not be restricted solely to the unconscious level. The conscious level may also be focused on, as the communication between these two levels of the mind of the analysand (and that of the analyst) proceeds.

Following Bion, we might make use of an analogy to refer to the unconscious as if it was a little child that comes to the analyst's office and interrupts the dialogue. One might say: our conversation was interrupted.

In this supervision Bion refers back to the analyst suggesting that in specific moments he might say to the patient that he would be walking in one street and all of a sudden he heads to another one. I understand what Bion means that the analyst might use this analogy to make the patient aware of what is going on in the analyst's office. He emphasizes that sometimes the analyst might be wrong, but pointing out this kind of shift or interference is important.

Bion also asked, "Why doesn't a person know something that is going on inside them?" This was another significant point in Bion's investigations, which he seems to have begun when he was still a child, in India.

It was a personality trait of his. Ever since his childhood he was curious about emotional experience. When his mother was depressed he would ask, "Why?" "What for?" "Mother, you aren't sad, are you?" (Bion, 1982, p. 21) as we have seen from the quotes presented above.

Bion postulates that the essence of the bonds (links) between human beings are of three types: Love (±L), Hatred (±H), and Knowledge (±K). Emotional activities that are blocked always remain active, and the personality is thus afraid of the reaction. Bion also holds that fear is a passivity and passivities are consequences of activities.

Bond K, like Bonds L and H, is fundamental, because it values the way patients relate to their truths, falsities, falsifications, and lies in an analytic relationship. However, the patient only acquires understanding through Bond K, which is intellectualised knowledge, but in this case there is no true emotional growth.

According to Bion, this reversion occurs in order to flee from painful realisations. It would be very different for a person to have intellectualized knowledge about themselves, instead of experiencing it in relationship with an analyst. In Bion's own words, "even in the domain of mental curiosity, of wanting to know something about the universe in which we live, that hole can be blocked by premature and precocious answers" (Bion, 1978, p. 22).

As I see it, when the first analyst presented the fragment of a clinical case of a different patient, and when the second analyst presented the material for supervision, they prematurely filled-in the "hole of non-knowledge" with saturated interpretations, thus blocking the investigation. In regard to the clinical fragment, the first analyst reacted toward the patient's associations in a surprising way, pulling out "the sick branch of the fern" after the session. This gesture stirred up something in the patient's mind and the following session could serve to bring up conjectures in our discussion group.

In the supervision the second analyst presented the following character traits of the patient's personality: "special relationship with many challenges, love, hatred, despair".

The analyst arrived late for the session due to personal problems. With her interrupted thoughts the patient characteristically talks about confusion, disorganisation, lack of a place for her.

Based on previous sessions, the analyst takes the following direction to say something to the patient implying that the confusion was a defence against feelings of competition (rivalry and envy) toward her, the analyst.

This would seem to be saturated knowledge, because the question is: What did the patient really want to communicate with those interrupted sentences? Did the patient feel rejected because the analyst arrived late? Did she feel persecuted, abandoned, hateful? What was the prevailing emotional constellation at that moment when the analyst interfered? Was she "accusing" the patient of competing "because" she, the analyst, had arrived late, thus establishing with this interpretation a causal relationship that paralyzed the investigation? Or, could it be that, with the interpretation, the analyst was defending herself from her own internal world, from some paranoid constellation of her own? As we also saw in the clinical fragment, the first analyst abruptly pulled out "the sick branch" after this had been mentioned by the patient.

In answer to a question asked at one of Bion's (1980) "Conferences in New York" he said he saw some points in Kleinian theory in a different light, as Klein holds that patients have omnipotent fantasies through which they split their personalities and project them into the breast.

Bion, at that conference, stated that it is not so certain that such fantasies are only omnipotent, because he himself had been in situations where patients had stirred up feelings in him. He suggested that such feelings may be a difficulty in the analyst's mind, but this may or may not be true. Patients can do something to the analyst and the analyst can do something to the patient. "It is not only an omnipotent fantasy" warned Bion. He opened up an array of different areas of human communication to investigation, from the simplest to the most developed, and held that they are often two-way roads in the relationships between analyst and patient.

He also warns us in these conferences regarding the need for tolerance and patience on the part of analysts until the possibility arises for a pattern, or a selected fact, to emerge, which he then communicates to the patient using a formula that the analysand will be able to receive.

Bion held that in certain minds, with the constant oscillation between the psychotic and non-psychotic poles of the mind, the psychotic part becomes stronger and may prevail. This part hates to learn and consequently attacks the bonds. In these cases there may be a blockage or a regression in mental growth. These forces, which work against growth, can exist either in individual beings or in groups, and manifest themselves by the negative (–L,–H,–K).

For Bion there is only one way for an analyst to help a patient develop greater tolerance for mental pain and follow the path of love for the truth. This road is based on the analyst's capacity for containing, allied to the consistency of her personality, her capacity for reverie and her ability to feel genuine compassion. Only in this way, therefore, can an analyst generate hope, which can open up new feelings and new meanings.

These are the conditions that make analysis a "special relationship", so well treated by Bion in supervision A3, when he stated that: "There are two different stories here. One of them is that there is a special relationship. The other is that there is absolutely nothing special about it".

In *Four Discussions with W. R. Bion* he says that "What matters is whether the person can have enough respect for the reality, for facts, to allow himself to observe them" (Bion, 1978, p. 31). In other words, many things depend on the patient's being able to take the experience to the end or not.

This approach of Bion's is also treated in supervision A3, where he highlights the analyst's capacity to observe and investigate, not only pathological aspects of the patient, but also the patient's vital aspects. In the supervision he said:

> But very often what is obvious and very easy to miss is that the patient exists. Therefore they must have done something right between their birth and now, or they would have died a long time ago … . Therefore, besides crimes, sins and mistakes, etc., I would like to hear about what they did right. Because I would still wonder, and they would too, how they can still be alive.

He also emphasises in these discussions the fact that the analyst has a personality, which is not incompatible with the attempt to hold to the truth and speak in a true way. This is quite mysterious—"the analyst is trying to help the patient to dare to be himself, to dare to have enough respect for his personality to be that person".

> The analytic experience, in spite of all the appearance of comfort … —is in fact a stormy, emotional experience for the two people. If you are an officer in a battle you are supposed to be sane enough to be scared but you are supposed also to be capable of thinking. (Bion, 1980, p. 14)

To summarize the main thrust of Bion's work, we could say that the fundamental problem is whether or to what extent human beings will reconcile themselves to the fact that truth matters. We can believe in all-sorts of things because it pleases us to do so, but this does not mean that the universe will conform and adapt itself to our particular beliefs or capacities. Applying this to psychoanalytic theories, Bion constantly is reminding us that in practice, we are never faced with the broad generalizations stated in our theories, but rather with particular and specific instances. It is these that matter, for they are the real life of the particular moment and the only thing worth paying attention to.

Notes

1. Arf Arfer, a fictional character Bion created in his childhood mind, that was terrifying and persecutory, and based on the transformations of which adults are capable.
2. *The elements in psychoanalysis can be perceived sensorially, that is, by seeing, listening, etc.
   **Personal, non-sensorial working through by the analyst himself.
   ***Emotion felt intensely and warmly, but without violence, between the mind of the analyst and that of the patient.

References

Bion, W. R. (1978). *Four Discussions with W. R. Bion*. Pertshire: Clunie Press.
Bion, W. R. (1980). *Bion in New York and São Paulo*. London: Clunie Press.
Bion, W. R. (1982). *The Long Week-end 1897–1919: Part of a Life*. Abington: Fleetwood Press.
Bion, W. R. (1991). *A Memoir of the Future*. London: Karnac.
Bion, W. R. (2014). *The Long Weekend 1897–1919: Part of Life* (Vol. 1). London: Karnac.
Symington, J., & Symington, N. (1997). *The Clinical Thinking of Wilfred Bion*. London: Routledge.

CHAPTER SEVEN

Supervision A45

In the text that follows, T stands for Translator; A stands for Analyst; P1 stands for a participant in the audience.

T: This is the case of a lady who was presented to you three years ago. She came to analysis in 1971 with the complaint: "I have a sensation that I'm falling into a hole, a very deep hole, out of which I won't be able to come out."

Bion: [interrupting, asks] Who says that? The analyst?

A: The patient.

Bion: Oh, the patient! I see. Yes.

T: [continuing the patient's complaint and reason for seeking analysis] "Then there's a very strong scream, or a very strong handshake, and I recover my consciousness." She was thirty-six years old, at the time. She was not very well dressed, was inelegant, very tall, and we could, approximately, describe her as a masculine type of woman.

A wants to bring today's session, to talk about it and remind us that in the former supervision Dr. Bion had suggested the problem of double language: the verbal one and the language of illness.

T: For the last three months this lady—after spending five years lying down on the couch—started to sit up on the couch. She sits on the couch like that. [The analyst shows the position in which the analysand sat.] After a deep sigh, today, she said: "I can't stand it any longer. I'm going crazy and the craziness is ... that I can't talk anymore with crazy people. My mother is crazy, because she can't bear any change in life." Then, the patient describes a sequence of complaints such as: the loss of a lodger, the loss of a maid, problems with her maid, illness of a son, illness of a brother. Then she says it is her mother who voices all those complaints on the phone. She tells her mother: "Stop it!" And the mother answers: "Daughter, every day is a different day." The patient then adds that "I feel very anxious, because the two people that hold me on to this world are you and my son." She has an eight-year-old son. Then, she looks at the analyst, fixedly into his eyes and says: "How can I stand it? My husband cut some of the money he gives me and suggested that I interrupt the analysis."

Bion: It seems to me to summarize that, that one could say: one of the few facts which is, unmistakable, is: people die, but the illnesses *don't*, not even mental illnesses. So, this patient can be somebody who is herself a mother and has the load of keeping babies alive—babies of all ages. But in a sense, one can say: the things that are really immortal are *illnesses*. If the patient dies, that doesn't matter very much, because the illness just goes to another patient. That's one of the frightening things about plagues—like the Black Death, as we call it in England—tuberculoses and plenty of others. They are *immortal*. They can always find a fresh person or character to live on! The same thing with regard to mental illnesses. If this patient grows up and becomes a mother, then the mother can grow down and become a baby; but she can be a much worse baby than her baby was—her baby which has now turned into a mother. What is the position of the analyst? What does the analyst do when he hears two stories: one which is told him verbally by the patient and another which is told him physically, if he uses his eyes. We can do the same thing here: we can listen to what we are told and we can see what the analyst has just acted for us. Which story shall we listen to? The one that our eyes tell us, or the one that our ears tell us? We can imagine in a way—this thing that I've suggested before—namely: we can use the analyst to be our senses for us. So, he can bring us the information. He can be our senses, which make available to us this experience. Now, what is our interpretation of what our senses, or the analyst—who's taking the part of our senses here—tell us? Has anybody got any suggestions about this? We can make suggestions that the analyst could pass on, to the patient, if he wanted to. Have we got any suggestions, so far?

T: P1 wanted to put a question to A. Why did you bring up this case that you are bringing now? He asks him. Was it because of difficulty in the case? Were you thinking that it was complicated? What was your criterion for selecting it? Answering the first question, A replies that he doesn't have any easy cases. In this case, what he is studying are, for example, the transformations, the changes that her physical appearance undergoes. In six years, she changed into a feminine woman. She managed to get thinner, dress in an elegant way. She had a complaint about a variation in the rhythm of her heartbeat and was in the care of cardiologists. They diagnosed an emotional arrhythmia. She suffered from some sort of emotional stagnation, that accompanied her physical development.

Bion: What I could say to the analyst—or what I could say to my own senses—if I were analyzing the patient, would be: go back to the heart, ask it what it saw. Now, it is no good talking like that, because it isn't common sense and I don't know that A could do anything. I don't know that I could do anything, not in … not in this state of mind, not in the state of mind in which, I am when I'm awake and my senses are about.

T: My senses are?

Bion: Active. But, if I could do what is known as going to sleep and if I could get it as a state of mind, in which I am when I'm asleep—not the state of mind which I am when I'm awake—then I might ask my heart: "Where have you been? What have you seen?" But the trouble is: I am awake. I have been taught an awful lot of anatomy and physiology, all that, which really makes it impossible to ask my heart what it saw, or where it went to when I was asleep in bed. Now, even if my heart—or whatever it is, I don't know—leads me to have pictorial images, something which I call *dreams*, even then, I have to translate or interpret these dreams, when I'm in a quite different state of mind, when I'm wide awake. What I say, in the way of interpretations, is typically what a person who is awake, says in daylight. In this way, I think that it is easier to say—as Freud says—that you can interpret dreams, or that you should try to interpret dreams. Even then, it's doubtful if he can tell us a very great deal, if you consider, for example, what he says in the Seventh Chapter in the *Interpretation of Dreams*, if you look it up! There are lots of dreams which Freud talks about, but which he dismisses—as you know—as not properly interpreted. So, the problem is still: what we see and hear when, we are in the state of mind when we are asleep, and what we see and hear when we are in the state of mind in which we are when we are awake. Can this activity—which we call psychoanalysis—bring us any nearer to a state of harmonizing, or marrying both states of mind? Could we achieve … do we, in any case, live long enough, in order to achieve that degree of *synthesis*, in which we can be married to ourselves? Let's say: if myself could be said to be my heart and supposing my heart has a different rhythm from myself—in the ordinary sense of the term—in this self, within this state of mind? The physicians don't tell us much. They say: you can go off, get an electrocardiogram, but then, somebody's got to interpret the electrocardiogram. But is that any good? When what you really need to interpret is what your heart is telling you? If you take a poet like Sir Philip Sidney, he can say: "My true love has my heart and I have his. There never was a better bargain driven."

Bion: But what about us? Can we say that what we call our heart and our minds, are really working in harmony? Because if our hearts and minds are working in harmony, then they might be able to tell us much more than if it's only our minds, or only our hearts. In short, if we knew ourselves, then we might know a bit more about a self that wasn't us—like the patient that comes to us for help.

T: P1 would like to ask, how can you feel this self in this client—who we are discussing now?

Bion: I don't think you can. I think it takes time. I think it is a very great nuisance, indeed, that the psychiatrists, psychoanalysts, doctors, surgeons, that we all believe that we know a great deal—so we do, although certainly not as much as we *don't* know. Now, nobody can be such a good or knowledgeable colleague, for the analyst, as the *patient!* Nobody!

T: Using a model, which you already used, about the vasodilation … enlargement of the blood vessals, if in this case, one could use the model in another direction, in which there is a constriction of the vessels, so that it impels more blood into the heart.

Bion: Well, one could continue that model, for example: if a thrombus forms, then the body—whatever that is—knows how to find a diversion.

Bion: If your blood can't go from here to here, then, it will be … the body will produce a collateral circulation. That means we have to be on terms, in which we have *respect* for our bodies. Analytic theory, really, presupposes respect for the individual; it's considered that psychoanalysts ought to have a respect for the human mind, but having a respect for the human individual means: the total individual, his body and mind. It's really useful to talk about a body and a mind. There isn't such a thing. They are convenient methods of talking about something that we call, a self which is both: body and mind. The first, foremost lesson, we really need to learn is: how to respect the individual, particularly *oneself*. It's no good, for example: drowning our alimentary canal with alcohol, because it doesn't stop with the alimentary canal. So, what could be wine—what could be something which is stimulating both to the body and mind, the person—becomes a poison. The *quantity* makes it toxic. What about psychoanalysis? Is it harmful, or is it harmless? Have you ever come across a patient, who's had *too* much analysis for his health? Is it possible to have too much analytic training? Is it possible that we have so much respect for the human mind, that we forget the human body? Although we can have too much respect for the body to be good for the mind. I've known situations, for example, at Oxford University when I was an undergraduate, in which, the athletes were so physically fit that they were hardly in a condition to think: they were intoxicated with physical health! Conversely, one can be intoxicated with mental health! I feel sometimes—in looking at these matters close to—that: there is no fool so difficult to treat, as a really intelligent one.

Now, leaving these sorts of general considerations alone for a moment, what about this story that we've just been told? What about the story, which in this instance we, this body, is told by our senses, namely: the analyst. The patient seems to talk, seems to say things, but the patient seems, also, to be able to depict things; the patient doesn't simply assault our ears by what she says, but also our sight: by what we can see.

T: Well, considering, Dr. Bion, what we've been discussing about the division of the body and mind, could one think—concerning the patient—when she presents improvement in her physical appearance, care for the body, her state, her mental health, if she, in this position, would still need a husband to take care of her?

Bion: It's a curious fact. We don't know how it's arisen, it does seem inescapable: the human unit is a couple! It takes two to make one. If you're a man, you can't really be a complete man, without a wife; if you're a wife, the wife can't be a complete woman, without a man. Now, supposing the man has got a mind of his own, thoughts of his own, feelings of his own, supposing that is also equally true about the woman; she has thoughts of her own, she has feelings of her own, she has a will of her own: how are we to harmonize those two? Or, how are those two to harmonize themselves? To give a ridiculous answer—for the sake of contrast—one could fall back on children's stories: they married and they lived happily every after. Or would it be more accurate to say: they married and that is when their troubles started, that is when they began to solve these troubles. Now, in fact, this introduction of analysis is like introducing physical medicine, or surgery, as a sort of way of making it easier for the human being to live or exist. If we were religious, one could say: "Well, you need to go through the ceremony of marriage, you need to undergo the ritual and the procedures of getting God's blessing." It's simply a couple of examples of the sort of theories there are about how we are to try to make life bearable, when we know what we do know, about the universe we live in. Of course, with this particular instance, the aim is more modest, because we want to help the patient to live with him or herself—because there's nothing that we can do about that; the patient is him or herself, even if we don't know who that is, or even if the person concerned doesn't really know who him or herself is. So, really, our profession has to try to introduce the patient to him or herself. In the case that we are just hearing about now, this self tells us two different stories: one of them, is concerned with what the patient calls the mother, another of them, is concerned with this thing, you just showed us. [Dr. Bion makes some gestures, concerning posture.]

Now, those two selves aren't married, but when the patient talks about his or her mother, or father, he's really talking about his ancestors. He isn't simply talking about the ovum and the spermatozoon; he's talking about two people who produced those germ cells—but I want to suggest that in fact, she can't talk about herself, without recognizing that: herself is also her ancestors and her children's children. That is the debate; that is the drama at which the analyst is looking. So, it's hardly surprising if the analyst—who's trying to tell us what he sees—has a very difficult job. But he also has a very difficult job, if he is like a theatrical producer, who has to say to the actors on the stage: "No, no! That isn't the way to do it!" and so on … It's rather like that.

Supervision A45 commentary

Antônio Carlos Eva

In recent years, we've been increasingly aware that the contribution that comes from the unique personality of the analyst is essential for the effective practice of psychoanalysis. In this supervision, Bion not only makes some explicit theoretical proposals about how he understands the meaning of "the personality," but he also attempts to transform the group discussion into an illustration of how analytic listening depends upon one's own personality so that the participants in the discussion can find themselves commenting on the material presented, at each moment in a personal and private way. In this way, the group may develop thoughts and ideas about the patient and the material presented and experience an example of how each individual analyst's personality may engage with the person who is undergoing analysis.

It is important, I think, to differentiate the on-going clinical analysis in the consulting room from this exchange of ideas in a group in response to a stimulus that comes from analytical practice. This presentation is an opportunity for us to confront how a specific analyst responded to a patient and offers us a version of what he did and the results it produced, so we can think starting from that.

Bion's initial observations remove us from the naïve assumption that we can "objectively" comment on what is being presented without "getting our feet wet." It is easy to notice that the one who "gets his feet wet" most of all is Bion himself, when he generalizes about human nature based upon the singular particularities of the analysand in the session. It seems to me that even though Bion invites us to participate in a free flowing exchange of ideas in which each person is able to use his own subjectivity and imagination, all of which deserves respect from the beginning to the end, it is Bion himself who ends up being the author of most of the comments. This does not invalidate the existence of an emotional experience in the group that happens outside of "common sense." The topics addressed are neither common nor trite. And yet, it is fitting here to wonder about the operation in this session of the basic assumption of dependency, which seems to me to drastically interfere as an obstacle to the formation of a workgroup in this setting. Perhaps it is this resistance to the workgroup that inhibits the free use of the participants' imaginative capacity.

The fact that even Bion, who was such an effective group leader, capable of creating a way of seeing life that was acute and alive, had difficulty in helping in the formation of this workgroup, is a testament to how difficult that process can be. Nevertheless, we may take advantage of his comments in search of collaboration. As we examine them, each in his own way, what we will have before us is an example of human individuality and subjectivity, both of which are very dear to Bion: No two human beings are alike, starting with our fingerprints, let alone our souls.

Let me focus upon two moments in the supervision that impressed me the most because of their direct and close connection with the human personality.

From the very start, Bion proposes to the group that in the reported case we are able to distinguish two sources of stimuli stemming from the presenter. One of them is verbal through which he tells us of a psychoanalytical occurrence. The other is triggered by a gesture directed to the *visual perception* of those present. It is the union and synthesis of these two elements (one verbal and the other visual) that allow us access to the rich perception of what was lived and potentially can help us to discover, at the moment, who we are with. If this idea of synthesis prevails, we will have to abandon the proposition that there is a verbal and accessible consciousness and an unconscious "under it" that expresses itself indirectly and that needs interpretative translation.

We must admit that this is an important, even revolutionary perspective on what we call "personality."

This hypothesis of the complex and simultaneous apprehension of a dual set of stimuli requires that the psychoanalyst abandon the predominant or exclusive focus on verbal consciousness as the only source of analytic data. In the case reported, the verbal source will be amalgamated with the sensorial visual source. This complexity expands and enables the apprehension of the moment in which the emotional experience occurs.

In my view, parenthetically, it is unfortunate that Bion's proposal to use in the group these topics previously gathered, did not come to fruition. This, in spite of the idea contained in his words that this dual focus could offer a source of complex stimulation that could be used, directly or not, with the client depending on the choice of the analyst.

The second point that I would like to address reflects Bion's thesis that these two sources of stimuli, when in harmony, are conducive to a "marriage" of two states of mind. The first is when we sleep and they present themselves, for example, as a dream. We must wonder when we are awake, what happens in the experience of the analyst so that he can receive the two sources and then create a surprising answer that goes beyond the sum of the two amalgamated stimuli?

In my own experience, I often notice "new" ideas that occur to me, either in verbal form, or in the form of an image (often visual) and to which I must attend. At first glance, they may appear independent and distant from the stimuli accrued, but with patience, unsaturation, and a fundamental faith in the associative analytic process, they allow the opening of new, radically surprising paths, for they reflect and resonate with the present, emerging emotional experience.

I would like to emphasize the revolutionary impact that this formulation offers to psychoanalytical work, in regard to the apprehension of what is "coming," what is being produced in the analyst, and what may be "published" in the form of a comment to the patient within the session.

With Bion, I am assuming that two people in the presence of each other are, as in the analytic situation, in continuous and mutual influence and so it is not possible for one of them not to live the emotional experience of the encounter. *Learning from Experience* (1962) offers us the foundation for this particular perspective and way of thinking about psychoanalysis. It is worth emphasizing that in relation to older formulations of the analytic process, this vertex constitutes a significant departure from the model of an analyst who observes the analysand without being profoundly involved in what is observed. The rupture of the objective observation model disqualifies the consequent objective interpretation of "the other before me."

These two models of bi-personal relation allow us to shift from one model to the other depending on our capacity to contain or not contain what we are confronted with in the session.

It's not without reason that in the last years our psychoanalytical formation has been focusing essentially on the analyst's capacity of perception and thought. That, in the next step, forces us to question the models of psychoanalytical psychopathology pointed solely towards the individual and the intrapsychic.

I would like to end this commentary by pointing out that the junction and synthesis of the two sources raises a current and quite complex problem; it causes us to wonder how, in the state of being awake and dealing with this complexity, each one of us perceives our selves. I associate this to the obligation of the analyst, who, in the emotional experience in the consulting room, must abandon to the extent possible memory, desire, and comprehension.

I would like to further add, the observation made by Bion in his comment that the mental unity is a couple: two are needed to make one human. These two may be initially thought of as two individuals and yet from the psychoanalytical perspective we end up thinking of these two as mental functions contained in an individual working in harmony with himself and with another.

Reference

Bion, W. R. (1962). *Learning From Experience*. London: Heinemann.

CHAPTER EIGHT

Supervision S28

This is a double-length supervision. In other words, the same case will be discussed for one hundred minutes instead of fifty. In the text that follows, T stands for Translator; A stands for Analyst; P1, P2, and P3 stand for participants in the audience.

A: The patient I shall present is blind and twenty-six years old—she was not born blind. The problem was that she had cancer and her eyes were operated on abroad when she was eighteen. Five years before she began analysis, she had a metastasis of the cancer to the medulla and she lost all sensitivity in both arms. So, she had to learn to deal with visual blindness and with losing touch—touch in her arms.

Bion: The patient that we are talking about is one who has cancer …

A: The blind girl. When she was eighteen, she had cancer in her eyes. At twenty-three, she was operated on and she lost all the touch in the arms. She started analysis eighteen months ago. This is one session in which there was some kind of limitation, that I felt dealt with senses and thinking. So, I wrote it down and I have the dialogue with me.

A: She started the session quite happy and smiling, telling me she felt wonderful.

Bion: Her age now is …?

A: Twenty-six.

Bion: Twenty-six. Yes.

A: The last operation was two years ago. She said … [At this point one of the participants says something. Unfortunately, the voice is too low to be heard. One gathers that it is some sort of doubt about her first signs of illness—as the analyst is heard then to be saying …] … A thing that began in her eyes. Then five years later in the medulla and after she was operated on, she lost the touch in her arms. Eighteen, twenty-three, and now twenty-six. And she begins the session by saying: "Well, I feel wonderful in the summer days … oh no, it isn't summer, it's really cold outside."

Well, what occurred to me, at the moment, was that there was something behind this bit of comment—something that reflected her inner feelings, her state of mind. So, I responded to her like this: "I see that you feel quite well today and that you would like me to share in your feeling better—in this state of yours …"

Bion: Could we just pause a moment and consider one or two points about this. I'd like to check up with you, as to whether the impression that I've gotten is correct or not. I would be inclined to assume that, probably, this patient has got very little time to live. That, what one might guess, would be a fatal condition and the anatomical or physiological ending is one about which there is not much doubt. One could say—generally of course—that: if anybody is alive, then they are dying. It, usually, isn't an immediately obvious or pressing problem. But, with this patient, one would think that the facts of an imminent disaster of one kind or the other—of paralysis or rhythm or life, life itself, should seem to be quite an immediate possibility. That's really … it's more or less the reasonable medical judgment about it. So, any idea of what is so often called "cure," it is really more than usually irrelevant.

However, it is possible that she may have good reasons for coming for analysis and you yourself can have good reasons for analyzing her—such as those you've mentioned. You don't know at all, of course, in what other aspects, too, it might be possible to turn very adverse circumstances into good account. I'm not sure whether I'm mistaken or not, but I think that Freud himself thought about dreams, for example: there's nothing, nothing particularly valuable or good about dreams, but that it is possible to make good account of these somewhat adverse and tiresome experiences. So, in a sense, this could, again, be said to be another situation in which, terms like cure are quite irrelevant, but conceivably, the adverse circumstances could be turned into good account after talk. In some ways, it seems to me that that is the view of analysis, which is often lost sight of. We may be quite wrong about it, but we spend time and money on a way of using an opportunity, which we believe to be worthwhile. It could be a kind of way of thinking, which makes it possible to make the best use of the universe in which we live. However, let's see what happens.

A: Well, after I told her that she seemed that she was willing to let me share in that state of mind of hers, she said: "I brought a present for you and here it is." It was a piece of chewing gum. So, I told her: "That it is not only a question of you feeling good, that it's something good that you have and that you'd like to share with me, using at this moment all of your capacities."

Bion: I'd like to say in view of what you've already been saying, that it's possibly easier for this patient to do this with regard to a real person, than to admit that—whether she likes it or not, she is having to admit that—she is having to make available her central nervous system to be chewed up by a very hostile object insider her, as if she could afford to make a present of that. But, following up that train of thought, one wonders what's a good use of the situation, which, as far as we know—whether she likes it or not—is what is happening to her. The thing on which her life itself depends, is getting chewed up. So, if this is right: that she's offering one this chewing gum to chew on and if it is right, that she feels that there is a sort of internal thing, which is chewing on her, what is one to say to the patient? This is a situation in which it may not be obvious, that you just give the patient the … whatever you think is the interpretation … one would like to say to the patient the "correct" interpretation. However, I've interrupted you in the course of this, just to show the sort of effects this story is creating on me. I'm not suggesting that I know what the interpretation would be.

Well, let's see how it develops and see really what can emerge. It might be helpful.

P1: What she said brought something to my mind …

A: About the chewing gum …

P1: Yes, the chewing gum. It seems to me that she was asking if you could take into your body something, or some feeling, that was occurring inside her body. If you can cope with it, she'll be all right.

Bion: See, what it suggests to me is the possibility that an analyst might be able to interpret what is being told to him—not simply for the purposes of giving an interpretation—but an analyst might be able to diagnose a cancer more quickly than any traditional surgeon or expert. Supposing that these free associations had had some counterpart—I don't know when, twenty years ago, before there ever was an operation—whether it would have been possible to say to the surgeon: "This patient of yours, who's coming to me for analysis, has, I think, got an illness which is going to turn into cancer. I think this patient ought to be physically operated on." In other words, one would be saying that, thanks to psychoanalysis, perhaps one can diagnose cancer earlier than anybody, or anything else, that we know.

It seems, certainly at the present time, one would be very frightened to do that. I should hate to say: I have a fifteen year or eighteen-year-old girl, who I think is going to have a cancer and it is in the region of the medulla and I advised her she needs this operation. One wonders whether one can ever be so personally scientific about our subjects, that one can say to this surgeon: "You should be operating on this patient and the area on which you should be operating is such and such …"

I don't, myself, feel that this is all together fanciful and from that point of view one can be talking here about the patient, which may be the origin of a surgical operation a thousand years hence. We can, in this way, be laying the foundations of a type of medical diagnosis, which doesn't even exist yet. That may easily be a very important point, which is not of much importance to you or to her. It may be important about a future development.

P3: So, we ought to be physicians *and* psychoanalysts. An issue that certain psychoanalytic societies claim is essential; that one should be a physician to become a psychoanalyst.

Bion: See, even today, I don't think we do our public any service by allowing ourselves to be ... to agree that we are very inferior or uneducated people, because we may already be better trained than the vast majority of people, who are theoretically far in advance of us. In short, ignorant and stupid as we may be—maybe—I don't think there's any reason, why we should permit ourselves to believe that we are as inferior or stupid as other people might like to believe. It's very difficult when we are trained to know our weaknesses, in this point or the other, and so on ... In fact, indeed, by the end of training, both people have been told of every possible defect [Dr. Bion says this in a laughing tone] that they can have. But, it may just as well be important to salvage from all this mass of failings and so forth in ourselves—that there may be some redeeming features.

I may say I tried by telling the general practitioner what was the matter with this patient and that the patient would be liable to die shortly. It was a complete failure. I did ultimately get a letter back to say: "Dear Dr. Bion, I'm sorry to say you were entirely wrong about this patient. He died of pneumonia." But in fact, the patient had died ... not exactly of pneumonia, but a paralysis of the intercostal muscles,***[1] which I predicted and would probably have been doubted. So, what I heard was that I was entirely correct: the patient had died exactly as I expected. However, that may be sort of looking through the future, as to what would happen if we tried to warn people.

T: P1 says that this reminds him of something he was once told by a physician who works with diabetics. He's also an analyst—he only analyses people with diabetes. The physician was talking with a patient of his about a big lamp that had shattered. There was a great blow and it broke into many small bright pieces. All of a sudden, the patient had an eye hemorrhage. The diagnosis of the physician was that the discussion of the lamp had been an anticipation, like a dream that Freud once mentioned in the *Interpretation of Dreams*, about the development of cancer ... It was a dream in which a man is being bitten by a snake...

Bion: (Returning to the current case discussion) ... Well, how did it go? She ...

A: So, she said that, referring to the first part of it, she started: "Well, I said that it was a summer day, because of the sun, it was very warm. Nevertheless, there was a very cold wind." So, I said to her that ...

Bion: Who said this: that there's a very cold wind, she or ...?

A: She did. Well, I said: "There was a summer day, because the sun was hot, but there was a very cold wind inside her." But, I told her that perhaps her body was accusing her for having a pleasurable sensation. But I felt that at this moment, she needed to share some kind of explanation with me—to share that sensation with me. That she needed to explain it mentally, to be able to share it with me. She couldn't just feel it, that she needed some kind of explanation. She said: "Today is just like a day in Germany, when I was quite different from who I am today!! Even yesterday, I was very angry because I could not look at the football game at my sister's and I remembered the details of being in Frankfurt."

Bion: Why Frankfurt?

A: That was where she was operated on. There was a football game going on and that reminded her of her days in Frankfurt.

Bion: Yes. Of course! It's tempting to say, in view of what you've already said, that she can feel in the summer of her life, this very cold wind is blowing. It sounds more like the wind of death! The temperature of the coast of winter. Even if the facts were told, they'd be more important than this football match, perhaps more important than her operation.

Bion: What was her ... this memory of Frankfurt? What does she say about it?

A: She can feel it, when she was looking at the game, it became more difficult to remember. The harder she tried to remember, the harder it became to remember. The only thing she could remember was lots of cars parked on top of the sidewalk of the hotel, where they stayed—she and her sister—and that the name of the hotel was Vera—her sister's name. She said, "I can't remember anything more." That was the only thing she could remember.

Bion: This name Vera, can be very significant. Why should she mention it? What matters in analysis is: what this word means. She used the name, so it must be significant. What impression did you get about that?

A: As far as I can remember, I didn't pay much attention to it, because she said—during the dialogue—she was just listening to the game at Vera's house. At the end she said: "The name of the hotel is Vera." So, I didn't, at that moment, connect it with anything.

Bion: Well, it depends if it turns up again in one form or another …

A: I think I'll be able to pay more attention from now on, than I did.

Bion: The trouble about just paying attention, especially if you pay more attention to one point, is that you're liable to pay less attention to others. That is why, in a sense, I feel that: *memory* and *desire* have this curious effect!! Because, they draw something in front of you—one has the idea and then one can't see what the truth is. Even in analysis, one can start trying to remember what the patient said. But while you are trying to remember what the patient said, you're missing what the patient is saying.

This is one of the troubles about analysis: the more tired you are, the more you bother with things like trying to remember some theory, or something the patient said and so on … instead of being open to what is going on. For example, over this matter of *Vera*: I don't know whether you think it would be typical, but it occurs to me that it might also be *spring*. Just spring, summer, and this cold weather, all at once. The cold might be anything from birth to death, emerging from the warmth of the womb.

P1: In Portuguese, spring is pri-ma-ve-ra, which is cousin Vera.

Bion: Yes, yes!! What can we say to the patient?

P2: It might be some hostility towards her sister, because her sister is …

P3: Cousin.

P2: Yes, cousin. Well, it could be that her sister is with the cousin who lives farther away, a type of person … showing up some kind of rivalry, conflict of rivalry or envy, towards her sister, talking about prima-Vera.

Bion: It could certainly be an envy of her sister's body, which her sister lives in.

A: He's (P2) saying that she mentioned that yesterday she was angry because she couldn't see the game on TV, but rather started remembering the details of Frankfurt: that it could be aspects of her anger, that is there behind what she says at the beginning. That was all the rivalry, meaning that, in a very bad sense, she doesn't see well at all.

Bion: Even with thought. It is a game or behind it is there … could it be a kind of murderous game, a sort of not football, but a war itself. However, the point in this: this is a thing that people can only *feel* in the room with the patient. That's the great advantage if the patient will actually come to the session and if the analyst will actually come to the session. Personally, I attach much more importance to the *practice* of analysis, than to learning up all these theories—for which there isn't any shortage of supplies—so many, that one could be absolutely vague in psychoanalytic theories. Still to use the popular expression: "You can't see the forest for the trees."

A: How can we connect with someone who is a professor, like Kant, who teaches a theory that is really useful?

Bion: Well, one does feel a kind of need to communicate naturally. That's why I quote sometimes the passage from *The Memoires of Max Planck*, in which he points out, he makes this discovery, which we are pretty familiar with, that comes to him as a great shock, that you can't teach anybody anything—one's opponents are never converted. Change occurs only over time. Opponents die and the newer, young ones take their place.

Now, it seems to me that if you're in the advantageous position of the professor, you can try to have children, that can keep their minds open. While one is teaching them things, you may always be able to teach them things, which cause them to learn more things. In other words, so long as you are teaching something; not which makes you feel: "Now, we can go to sleep. Now we know all the answers. Now, they can wake up and start learning."

What subject are you teaching your students? [This is a question that Dr. Bion asks P1]

P1: Introduction to Freud's works.

Bion: Well, as far as Freud, who was a revolutionary thinker, the revolutionary thinker Freud has now been turned into something now *standard* ... "The speaker of truth and of certainty." [The last part of this sentence is said in laughing tone]

At least these are the standards which I have seen waved and flickered at me and others in Los Angeles. It seems to me that there are those who are very often bearing the standards of Freud and Anna Freud ... a kind of: "You can go thus far and no further."

A: How does this relate to your work?

Bion: It all appears really to be: "thus far and now we start moving"! Freud and all, that was the starting point, not the end of the matter.

A: Well, to go back to the case, after she mentioned remembering her days in Frankfurt ... I told her that it was impossible for her, at this moment, to return to that situation—to her state—when she lived in Frankfurt, because her body was not the same anymore ... Her present sensations are not the same and don't agree with the theory that she has about it. What I thought was: she was talking about seeing things, looking at things then and today she can't do it, there's a change in her body. But she can, all the same, feel pleasure or pain ... So, she's a different woman and in another way, at the same time, she's the same woman. Now, I didn't say it in this way, but I think that's how it is. She said to me: "Today my arms, they don't feel anymore. They have no possibility of experiencing anything."

Bion: This is a situation that she's describing. It can, in a way, be a situation with which she's familiar, namely: of not really being able to do things. Because, in order to do things, you have to have arms. The same thing goes on, applying to a whole lot of physical activities: like football, running, and so forth … All that is impossible to her, but you can say she is feeling though, as she felt, when she was an infant, but may have forgotten it and could travel about by her eyes. For example: I may not be able to move, but I can go from there or there, to over here. [At this point, Dr. Bion probably made gestures that reinforced his statement that we can move or travel about with our eyes] What about a blind woman? What can she see? Milton says, in *Paradise Lost* (Book III, lines 51–55):

> "So much the rather thou Celestial light
> Shine inward, and the mind through all her powers
> Irradiate, there plant eyes, all mist from thence
> Purge and disperse, that I may see and tell
> Of things invisible to mortal sight".

In other words, the real point is: if it's not possible to look out, then look in. There were a great number or reasons why he couldn't "look out." Milton's political party had just been defeated. The whole of the Protestant cause in England had failed. The Catholic royalty was restored. But that doesn't matter. The thing is that he found some method. In the same passage he talks about: haunting where the Muses haunt themselves.

T: Haunting …?

Bion: A ghost or a visit. He visits … in other words, he falls back on the capacity—poetic capacity—which gives him the mobility that he otherwise lacks. In short, he finds some method of continuing to operate. Now, the question with this patient is: has she found some method of continuing to live a full life—which is not a life of the physical senses or physical capacities like moving arms or legs and so forth?

It's not possible to believe, that a fetus can believe that it can't move it's arms or its legs or its eyes, or anything. And yet, can be mobile inside the womb. This isn't that situation anyway, but it's like a situation in which he has no capacity. However, the point about it is: what interpretation is to be said to this woman who, as far as we know, anatomically and physiologically, is just dying. In fact, what is she saying to you? What, according to her associations, is she able to do?

Well, let's see a bit more of what she said. You got to this point that she can't move her arms or she can't feel her arms anymore …

P1: When you said that through the eyes it's possible to move …

Bion: Yes …

P1: And the patient replied—your patient—that she could not feel … I was thinking the other way around, using her arms or body, instead of the eyes.

Bion: Yes. But there might be some substitute of that sort, but what is this aggressive situation, in which she loses her capacity for sight? Loses her capacity for movement, loses her capacity for moving her arms. So, let's say this: what is she saying she can do?

P3: Dream maybe?

A: She worked as a reporter in a newspaper, helping an important reporter—interviewing people, moving back and forth … But right now, I think that she really feels that she doesn't know it anymore. Something happened that she's losing her balance, her ability to stay upright. She throws up everything she eats, she suspects that her illness is getting worse in ways she does not yet understand. So, she, in the last two weeks, missed all the sessions. She couldn't come.

Bion: I see. She comes or she is brought by a …?

A: She's brought by a chauffeur. A chauffeur. He brings her in, sits her on a chair. She doesn't lie down. She did once, but she felt very uncomfortable lying down. So she kept on sitting up. She comes in and the chauffeur picks her up, after the session. He's the one who pays me personally, because she can't handle the money. She just can't hold things. She doesn't have any feeling in her fingers. She doesn't have the feeling of touch.

Bion: But now: she isn't coming at all?

A: In the last two weeks, no. I have doubts, how far does my responsibility go? Must I go and see her where she is? I don't know if she's in a hospital or elsewhere, because she asked me just before she started missing sessions, if I would go to see her. She was going to have an examination, a brain examination, and it would take a couple of days, or a week. I didn't say if I was going to see her or not.

Bion: Is it possible to see her? For you?

A: Yes. Yes. I have the possibility, it's just a question of … I don't know if she's at the hospital or at home. She didn't call me on the phone. She said that she was going to and I said: "Well, I'm at your disposal. If you wish to do so, please do it." She didn't call.

Bion: I think, in that case, you're losing time. If the patient can't do anything and if the analyst can, then I shouldn't hesitate about doing it. If you can do it, do it. So often it can be very difficult for the analyst to see a patient. One relies on the patient coming and so on … or being brought. If that can't be done, then one can't do it oneself, then there's nothing more to be said. But, I think that if you could, if you have the time or money, which makes it possible to do so, I shouldn't hesitate to go.

A: In this case, I think I have the possibility of seeing her.

Bion: Well, I think it's … one can only say that nobody can tell you how you feel, or what you feel able to do. But, I wouldn't hesitate to do it. [This passage is spoken in a very warm way.] You see, very often, one finds oneself in a position where everybody might say: "You're being a very foolish man … what makes you see a patient like that?" I've had it said to me about patients who are mentally affected, psychotics and so forth … And it's quite obvious, it's dangerous and is running a risk. Well, nobody can tell you how much risk you feel prepared to run, whether you can afford to do it, or not. How do you feel about seeing her? Knowing what you know about her now?

A: Umm, I feel that, right now, after eighteen, almost eighteen months of work, that I can see her freely. That I'm not compelled to. I don't think that she would take that visit, or these visits, as a result of her wish to control me. Because, at the beginning, she tried very much to control everything. She called in, tried several times to change hours it was a kind of very painful and difficult work. I said to her that I had my limitations, that she had hers, that we had to work together, because everyone in her house does everything she wants, like a …

Bion: Yes, like a center of attraction maybe, yes. And she tried very hard to make you into a kind of satellite. Very, very, very painful work to do this.

A: She suffered enormously to see what reality was, as far as my possibilities were concerned.

Bion: Who is she dependant upon now?

A: She depends on her mother and father.

Bion: On her parents?

A: Yes, she lives with them, she always did.

Bion: So, you would have to visit the parents home, or a hospital, or something of that sort?

A: Yes, yes. In fact, I couldn't tell her directly that today, Monday, because of this meeting, I was not going to be there to see her. The only thing I could do was to call her home and leave a message, because she was ill. She couldn't leave her bed to go to the phone to talk to me. So, I left the message that I was not going to be able to see her today.

Bion: Remember Ernest Jones, when he was dying, what he said about it? You don't remember that? Well, he was obviously dying and he knew it and he said that he hoped somebody would put the diagnosis into a sputnik and fire it up there. You'd think that he must have known what the diagnosis was. But he didn't. One wonders this, with this girl, if she knows what the diagnosis is—or whether she's just forgotten all that. But, what's the attitude of the parents, to you seeing her and so on?

A: She never mentions it. Apparently, I am a very special person for her—the only person, at least this is what she tells me—that she can talk to. Other people she can't.

Bion: Yes, it's quite possible.

A: I can believe her, why she says this.

Bion: That's why one feels that there can still be a kind of a reason for seeing her, but it depends entirely on how you feel.

T: When you remembered the Ernest Jones situation, were you comparing that to this patient?

Bion: Yes, simply that the patient is dying and it is interesting to know whether she retains any contact with the fact that she is dying, or whether she has forgotten that. Or what it is, one doesn't know, because Ernest Jones, after all, he was a very capable physician. He wouldn't have had the slightest difficulty in diagnosing the condition, if it had been somebody else.

P2: But why are you asking about this patient, who is in contact with the idea that she is dying and communicates this to the doctor all the time? Should the doctor go or not? What is the relation to this aspect?

Bion: Well, because, simply he is analyzing her, he seems to be an important person to the dying patient, that's all.

P2: But, isn't this a good thing to the patient, to keep in contact with her dying?

Bion: No, no. In fact, one just doesn't know whether she's in contact with that fact any longer or she loses contact with everything, except this one person who's her analyst.

T: This experience that you had with Ernest Jones, we had the same kind of experience with a friend of ours a radiologist, who had a cerebral tumor and remained conscious for a very long time and never came around to diagnosing it. The question is this: recently a colleague, an analyst—she was a friend of hers—had a cancer and for a very long time, she was deceived. She was an active woman. She became paralyzed in both legs, she had also cancer in the medulla. When somebody told her she had a cancer, she became quite tranquilized.

Bion: Yes, in a good sense or ...?

T: In a good sense, prepared herself for death.

Bion: Yes, she was allowed to know the truth.

T: The question is: to hide the truth in a moment like this is a medical recommendation, not to tell the patient at the time. When the woman knew what was happening, she became calm. Before that, she was very nervous and she was taking tranquilizers.

Bion: It's very profound this faith in keeping things hidden either on the grounds that the person is too old or to ill, or too young. There's always a good reason for not telling the truth. The difficulty is: the analytic belief that there's a lot to be said for saying what is true. We are always in the risk of seeing people saying: "It makes people so ill to tell them all these horrible things." But the examples that you give seem to be a demonstration of the fact that: if it's possible to tell the patient the truth, maybe it's the best thing to do. Ernest Jones obviously felt to be, what he's being told, to be true. But, it's a difficult matter when ... the patient has gone, because one doesn't want to push oneself into their troubles or difficulties. I don't know if there's any way in which it is possible just to make a simple inquiry. If you don't do that, it may sound as if you were completely indifferent.

T: Yes.

Bion: You can't very well write to her because she wouldn't see it, would she? Do you have an address to which you could write or ...?

A: I have a phone number. She called me on the phone, not the last two weeks, but before that, she did.

Bion: Yes.

A: The worst thing in this situation came up when she fell and hit her head on the floor. From that moment on she thought, felt, that her situation, her health, was just failing ... . In some of the last sessions, she mentioned, after the falling accident, that to come to analysis, was the only thing she could really do. Most of the time she was lying down. She couldn't stand up. But, somewhere, she obtained the strength to stand up and come. I can believe this when I see her—that this happened. I wouldn't at the beginning, because it looked to me at that moment, it might be a manipulation of hers, trying to control me, but right now, I think this is what is happening.

Bion: Of course, it can very well be so. I've known a patient who was obviously dying, suffering from a most unpleasant infection, through the development of a sort of parasitic growth. But she … misled everybody by her insistence on, in a very neurotic sort of hysterical way, that she was ill. This was an infection not properly treated. But, it was a horrible surge of infection, which was erupting, visibly. You could see it had broken through the skin and so forth … But, everybody knew it was fatal, but she kept on talking about it, as if it was a kind of weapon that could be used to attack the indifference and so forth … of the rest of the world.

It is also sometimes like that with the threat of suicide by a patient who does not know what we know and that is: how dangerous these threats of suicide are. Because, in fact, they *can* kill themselves, but they don't believe it. They believe it's a good weapon to use, but they don't really believe it could kill them, or that they could die.

A: What is more important the menace, the threat of suicide, or the suicidal impulse in itself?

Bion: The threat is only effective, because it's a threat, but psychoanalysts know how dangerous it is. So, it's a very good weapon to use in waging war against psychoanalysts. All you can do is: to point out the fact that they hope to frighten away. That they don't really believe that it's dangerous, as the analyst thinks it is. One may not be intimidated, but that doesn't mean that we don't know. However, is there some more you would like to say about this patient?

A: No, not especially.

P1: I have a question. What could be implied in this attitude of threatening suicide, either showing that they are in terrible pain or the other way, that the patient won't, at least, feel pain anyway ... That the patient is going through pain, or other things, or threatening.

P2: Meaning to share it?

P1: It is the way to let you know that *he* exists. For instance, if you feel pain, then he exists.

P3: This makes him afraid of something.

Bion: Physiological pain is so odd, because the intensity of the pain doesn't really indicate the intensiveness of the illness. Something's so incredibly physiologically painful, and it may be of no importance whatever. There's a mental pain for ... I think somewhat similar. There may be apparently very, very little mental pain, which is proportional to the seriousness of the condition. But your point about this is ...

P1: The use that the patient can make of it, the function.

P3: Which function really does it serve?

P1: It seems to me that instead of love, the patient uses hate with the meaning of love.

Bion: Yes. I was thinking of a child or the baby, who'll cry, and cry, and cry. The situation which is created for the parents by this baby who cannot be quieted. You can try drugging it, which is a very unsatisfactory situation in dealing with it. But I think one is very suspicious with a child who's really psychotic, who does that, who's able to disturb the entire family, very much indeed and completely exhaust the mother's capacity for caring for it. It seems to me to be one of these situations in which it is a kind of psychological monster. A monster, which cannot be dealt with by mental means, anymore than the monsters which can be dealt with by surgical means. There are, of course, certain monsters that everybody knows, in which the surgical intervention is worth trying. Has anybody ever analyzed a case in which the patient is one of a separated twin? [At this point, various people murmur "no"] Xiphopagus. I had an experience in dealing with identical twins, but not monsters.[2]

I don't quite know where a monster begins and where it ends. The identical twins, the space in between them, it runs like that.[3] But I certainly think you've got to consider, when you're treating identical twins, that you've got quite a remarkably different situation from say: twins. I've had both the monovular twin and the ordinary twin.[4] They're both difficult, but it's a different sort of difficulty.

Notes

1. Some nervous disease as Duchenne-Erb Paralysis, myelosclerosis leads to a paralysis of the intercostal muscles. The pneumonia that frequently occurs is due to a hypoventilation of the pulmonary tissue—an after effect of the intercostal muscle paralyzes.
2. Like for example: xiphopagus, parasitic monster, etc.
3. Here Dr. Bion must have made a gesture.
4. Identical twins are those which have the same placenta, thus derived from the same ovum—mono-ovular, mono-zygotic. Twins that are not identical, ordinary twins, are biovular.

Supervision S28 commentary

Arnaldo Chuster

The case presented to Bion is about a young woman, twenty-six-year-old, who is blind, with neoplastic disease in a stage diagnosed as terminal: a forthcoming total failure of treatments. During the supervision Bion questions: Which interpretation should be given to a woman who one knows is dying anatomically and physiologically? What is she saying? What do the associations say?

In my understanding it is a case that exposes the *limits* of the psychoanalytical field. What is the extent one should go? What are the boundaries?

We must try to pose those questions; otherwise there is no way to stay in the analytical field. We must know our limits; otherwise we are prone to be prey to memories, desires, and the need for comprehension. According to Bion they are the main three elements that obliterate our psychoanalytical capacities.

In Ancient Greek times the basic meaning of the word "limit" was *measure*. From this vertex one could say that every object has its own limit (or a measure). Therefore, it was considered a kind of tragedy when someone was going beyond his limits (Greek tragedies demonstrate this in many forms talking about Hubris—the Greek notion of sin). Measuring was in fact something essential to the understanding of what is a *good object*.

The origin of the word medicine comes from the Latin word "mederi." Therefore, to medicate means to give a proper "measure." If one reaches the right measure this achievement is equivalent to having a healthy mind and a body in good physical shape. In the same line, to have *wisdom* is equivalent to reaching temperance and modesty (both also derived from mederi). A wise man is someone who keeps everything in the right *measure*.

It is about this matter that I would like to focus on in Bion's paper, that which has to do with setting the analytical field through the search for measures: "Making the best of a bad job" (1979).[1] I will follow and mention in my current comments some ideas and parts of this article, where Bion proposes a lot of questions it seems to me very illustrative for the case presented.

There is an object in *transience* that reveals a vision of the world: a kind of *bad object* that is chewing inside the patient, that brings a cold wind blowing like the wind of death, a very hostile internal object or a kind of monster similar to that which is created by a baby crying for help when the parents cannot understand why the baby is crying.

One can consider that the patient cannot separate this internal object from the external world due to her physical condition, or is it the physical condition that cannot be separated from the psychological condition? Where does the mind begin and the body end or vice versa? Is the body a representation of the parents that cannot understand the baby? Or is it the mind of a kind of body in extinction?

One can notice that Bion's way of thinking is making a spiral, the elements that he is pointing out are interconnected, but they take distinct directions, in different levels: thinking is always expanding. It never stops to make questions. I think this is the understanding of *transference* that one can find in what is called "*the* late Bion."

The first feature one can draw attention to is the *terror* caused by such an object that Bion is describing. Every terror is a paranoid anxiety that paralyses the capacity of thinking. Therefore, it also paralyses the acting which is the consequence of thinking. Dealing with terror, to overcome it, leads us to contact with *reality*, which can be very painful and unpleasant and requires us to be *courageous*. If there is a *lack* of courage one can always appeal to forms of evasion: sleeping, to become unaware of the universe, becoming ignorant or idealizing. Those are all very common kinds of evasion which we are very used to.

But what is a daring or courageous analyst or what is analytical courageousness?

I think this can be described by the *three principles of life*_listed by Bion in 1979. He proposes they should substitute for the two principles of mental functioning described by Freud. They are:

1. Feelings.
2. Anticipatory thinking.
3. Thinking + feeling + Thinking (Prudence or foresight in action).

Those principles face the problem of idealization that usually is widespread and create complex expectations to the real role of the analyst. Idealizing can be also a vehicle for saturated conceptions; they create obstacles for the realization of the preconceptions in new conceptions.

The three principles have the advantage of not opposing pain to pleasure; an opposition that can be implicit in the two Freudian principles. Knowing truth, although painful, can be healthy and not destructive. To respect truth means also to respect life and vice versa.

The destiny of idealization is mentioned by Bion when he writes on the tendency to incarnate *omnipotence* in the role of a father or a mother, or a God or goddess. He said: Sometimes this is made easier by physical inheritance like beauty. Helen of Troy could mobilize great powers such as good looks; as we know through Homer: "Is this the face that launched a thousand ships and burned the topless towers of Ilium?"

The destiny of idealization is to produce disillusion that will open a space where the individual must equilibrate between hostility and understanding.

Understanding means to differentiate the Self from the object, internal world from the external world: "mental space." Bion wrote:

> I now turn to the problem of communication within the Self (I dislike terms that imply "the body" and "the mind", therefore I use Self to include what I call body or mind, and a "mental space" for further ideas which may be developed. The philosophical statement of this approach is Monism). When we are engaged in psychoanalysis in which observation must play an extremely important part as has always been recognized in a scientific inquiry—we should not

> be restricting our observation to too narrow a sphere. What then are we observing? The best answer that I know is provided by the formulation in Milton's introduction to the Third Book of *Paradise Lost* (Bion, 1979, p. 250):
>
> So much the rather thou Celestial light
> Shine inward, and the mind through all her powers
> Irradiate, there plant eyes, all mist from thence
> Purge and disperse, that I may see and tell
> Of things invisible to mortal sight.

In other words the main question is: if it is not possible to look outside, let us look inside. Let us take all the material as a dream.

In a case like this it is quite possible that the patient could use losses as a proof of the existence of an omnipotent object, in face of which the whole world is *helpless*. Therefore the analyst is included. What should we do if the problem is a physical one and leads to death?

Omnipotence/_helplessness is a very important *invariant* in the analytical field. It becomes manifest with another invariant of choice which is quantity *v's* quality of life. That is, the quality of life must be confronted to the extension of life. In the same direction essence and appearance need to be confronted.

The body can be brought in to redress the unpleasure of the mind; reciprocally, the mind can be brought in to redress the unpleasure of the body. The basic assumption of psychoanalysis is that the "function" of the mind can be used to correct the *fallacious solutions* ...

For instance, the fallacious solutions produced by idealization.

All those expressions used above are from the order that Bion called *combined words* like I-Thou (mentioned in the text of Martin Buber).

One can say that words have their own life; therefore they can die and be reborn. A metaphor which is considered dead can be brought to life just by connecting it to another. Something happens that transforms an idea into something beyond and more diverse than it was before. A thought is created together with language and circularity begins: language is thinking, language thinks for of us and we think through it.

Words can be just like a coin that is used so much that it loses its sign of value. Therefore, as analysts we must keep our words in good shape to be used in interpretations. There is no need to have an erudite vocabulary, but the analyst must know very well the words he is using.

Just like the musician must know very well the score in order to play the music.

Note

1. In: Bion, W. R. (1979). *Clinical Seminars and Four Papers*. F. Bion (Ed.), Abingdon: Fleetwood Press, 1987.

Reference

Bion, W. R. (1979). Making the best of a bad job. In: F. Bion (Ed.), *Clinical Seminars and Four Papers* (p. 247). Abingdon: Fleetwood Press, 1987.

CHAPTER NINE

Supervision D17

In the text that follows, T stands for Translator; A stands for Analyst; P1, P2, and P3 stand for participants in the audience.

A: Last week, when we were speaking about Dr. X's case, I remembered my patient … I told you about her. She is the patient who wants a child and can't have one.

Bion: This is one of the things, which I think is an advantage about talking about these matters all together, that they tend to tell you something about some other one.

A: Yes!

Bion: Because, there's always this resemblance between one human being and another human being, so that it can always tell you something about someone else.

A: This patient, she is not young anymore. She is perhaps thirty-seven, thirty-eight. She's not so old for having a child; but she's not so young either. All her life—she's been married for many, many years—she has been trying to have a child. She went to several doctors. She began analysis with me one year and four months ago after having been in analysis with Dr. X. She is also a very difficult patient—with a great deal of acting out, although I don't know if I can call this acting out.

Bion: Don't bother about that, because as time goes on, you may feel satisfied with some sort of name. It may be something which is already mentioned in the dictionary, or it may not; and when it becomes clearer, you can give it, or try to give it, a name. At any rate, discussing it here, like this, the advantage of that is: you aren't bound to say that you're going to call it that forever. It's just a hunch or an idea that you may have; but, you may not stick to it, or you may—one doesn't know.

A: She is very anxious; she shows that she is very anxious. She's not able, for instance, to lie on the couch all the time. She has to look sometimes at me. She moves about, a few times she sits up, but, in a very few sessions she can lie down and relax. Although not all the time.

Bion: I'd like to take up a point about this, straight off, which seems to me to be fairly common. That is: the patient has, apparently, tried everything. Apparently, according to the patient, the patient is married, the patient has had analysis, the patient has had all sorts of stuff; you needn't go into all that. When everything has failed, the patient expects the analyst to do something. Now, why?

Now, I'm not asking this question to be asked to the patient, or anything of that sort, but just to draw attention to this extraordinary fact that *when everything has failed, that is when you are supposed to help*. That is when an analyst is supposed to do something.

Now, the first thing that comes clear to me about this is this: this patient can't even have a verbal intercourse, so I'm not surprised that she can't have, what appears to me, to be a sexual intercourse. It's a matter of opinion, of course. It depends on what you, yourself, call a sexual intercourse. But, to me, it seems pretty clear that if this patient can't even have a verbal intercourse, then it's hardly surprising that she wouldn't be able to have a sexual intercourse. Or anyway, just to make it a bit clearer—I don't know if it does or not—I'll call it a passionate intercourse, meaning by that, something which is more than a merely physiological intercourse.

Now, I can quite believe that this patient can be married, that she can be convinced that she's just like a married couple, or she's just like an analytic patient: she comes and so forth … But, that isn't like *being* or *becoming*!! In a sense, one would say, if one thought as it were, if one's asked: "No, you aren't just like your mother and father, or you aren't just like mother and father, or you aren't just like daddy, but you may become, you may be becoming like that." Now, you can't very well say that to a woman, who is married and all that; but secretly to oneself, one can say she isn't married. She's just *like* a married woman, she's just *like* a parent of children, but she isn't a parent of children. She may become one, but she isn't one now.

Now, I just put it that way, because it happens over and over again. People are always coming, but on the face of it, there's nothing you can do for them, because they have done everything, they know everything. So, the question is then, in a sense: how are they meant to come to an analyst? So, one can bear this point in mind. By the time the patient has come to you, everything has been tried, according to her, and it's always been a failure. The wonder is: she can still bear to try analysis. So, that's the size of your problem.

A: She, herself, said something like that: "How can I dare to want to have analysis, even in order to have a child."

Bion: Yes! Well, it might be worth drawing her attention to this that, *that* is one problem, that there are two people in the room. So she could feel that she'd like to know how she dares to, but she'd also like to know how the analyst dares to be an analyst. Now, the analyst can't tell her that, but it's a sort of anxiety where she's got two people she's frightened of at the moment: herself and somebody who'll listen to her.

In fact, it has never really gone into, when people marry, because, when they marry, they have never really been married before. They may have played at fathers and mothers and so on … or they may have been *just like* married people. But they've never been married people to each other. So, they are two ignorant people who come together. That's why honeymoons and that kind of thing are, time and time again, miserable experiences!! Theoretically, people say: "Very happy time, very happy honeymoon!" But, that's nonsense! Because that depends on forgetting what a miserable experience it is. However, let's see a bit more of what she tries to do, of having a verbal intercourse. Of course, she doesn't even lie on the couch!

A: It's very few times she lies down and, when she does, it's very difficult really to have an analysis. In the beginning, in her first analysis she had a woman analyst, for nearly four years I think, then she had another analyst for some years, two or three—I don't know the time. Then, she went to Dr. X; she had perhaps two years with him and when he died, she came to me.

Bion: What did you say to her about this, when she told you this? Do you remember?

A: I don't remember.

Bion: I asked, because I think that one reason why it's useful to say to a patient: "Well, of course you've already tried analysis. However, if you want to try again, we can try. I have got a vacancy." And if you've decided, by this time, that you are willing to see her again, you can say: "Well, we can arrange another session, I can see you tomorrow, or the day after" or whatever it is. But, of course, you may also wish to be more cautious than that. You may wish to say: "Well, I don't know that I'm likely to have a time, if you'd like to call me up, or write to me at some time later—if you haven't got a phone. It may be a great nuisance to let me know and if I can help, I can tell you what help I've got available."

Now, that means that you are not committing yourself to this patient. Mind you, it may not make much difference, because patients have a way of paying no attention to what you say. And if they want to come to you, they will believe, honestly, that you have promised them a vacancy. But, I think it is a good thing to be quite clear in your own mind, if you have not promised them anything. But if they would like to try again and if they haven't got fixed by then, you'll see what that might be possible. That is a belief and that will give you a little bit of time to see how this patient goes.

If the patient still wants to come to you, that itself is something. You can form your own opinion whether it makes that patient someone who you might want to see more of or less. However, in this case, we needn't bother about that, because the point is: it's not quite the same, but, of course, there's the question about whether she wants to come and see you at the next appointment, or whether you want to see her at the next appointment.

A: I remember something she said about the first analyst, who was a woman. She said that in the end of those four years, she found that the relation with this woman was very difficult. I think she was linked to her very ... passionately. But, at the same time, she said that she was not so good as other analysts. She was trained as a therapist.

Bion: Your patient was?

A: Yes. And she was treating some children. She used to have supervision with an analyst, who was a medical doctor. Then, she began to have doubts about her own analyst who was not. It was for that, that she changed from the woman analyst to a man. She called him: "the doctor of little groups." Then, she studied medicine hoping to become a psychoanalyst. When she finished medicine, she began analysis with Dr. X for that. But then Dr. X died.

I was abroad then and she phoned a friend to ask me, if I could take her as a patient when I returned. I said to this friend: "She should try to speak with me, directly." She wrote to me and I answered her saying I could give her an interview when I came back to Brazil. I said the date I would return. I didn't say that I would have her or not. When I arrived, she rang me up and she asked for an interview. I saw her when she was on vacation. She came from her country house. I don't remember the interview, but I remember it lasted only a few minutes. She asked if we could begin. I don't know exactly what I said, but I made the appointment to begin the analysis. I was surprised, because I found that it was too quickly. She couldn't wait. I had the impression she couldn't wait. She had to have an analyst quickly. She was really very anxious. Also, one or two months before, her father had died. That was how she began analysis.

Bion: Starting with you?

A: Yes, then, she started with me. In the beginning, it was very, very difficult. I thought for a long time it was really very difficult. She was always in doubt if I would I be as good as Dr. Z, an analyst who worked abroad. She was always comparing: "I would like to go to (abroad)—my friend is there, another friend is in there. I would like to have an analyst from there ..."

Bion: She knows what it is like to come to you. She knows something about that, because she's actually come. But she has to compare this with what she didn't do. And what you don't do can always be what you like! Like any thought, or idea that the patient changes into an action. Then, you can compare the actual facts, which she then learns for the first time, and compare them with these other facts, which she doesn't know, because they haven't happened. Of how much better it would be if she were, or you were, in (abroad) and so on and so forth …

You can always, or at least, your patient can always tell how unsatisfactory the facts are, compared with what might have been had she done the another thing!

Now, there is a difficulty, because the worst treatment the analyst can give a patient is to die. So, a patient whose analyst dies—that analyst is hated by the patient for dying. Then, there's a difficulty: it's wrong to hate people who are dead and if she hates the person who's dead, then she's afraid that she caused the death. So, it comes back to this where she doesn't feel able to express hatred at all and if she tells her analyst what a bad analyst her analyst is, then, she's afraid that her analyst will go and die and that would get very awkward for her.

So, you get this curious business, in which you're compared with what might have happened, if she had done something else. In so far as you are a fact, a fact can't be as good as the ideal. Well, the question is, what can one say to a patient like this? How is this case made clear to the patient? Of course, you could try something like this: "Since you have been coming here, you know something of what it is like to come to me and how bad this is and how good it would have been if you'd been somebody else and if I had been somebody else. If you weren't here and I weren't here, how much better we should be. So, there's always this problem about the thing that you haven't done compared with what you have done." You could try putting that point to her, but it's simply a way of drawing attention to this fact, that the facts appear to be so much worse than … well, what one could call the facts. They are facts and facts are very limited compared with what would have happened, if it were an ideal situation, or a daydream situation.

Well, I don't know quite what will happen next, but … I would not expect this patient to be likely to be satisfied next anyway. But when everything has failed, so far, I don't see why she should be satisfied. I mean, what is a mere analysis, as I understand it, or as you understand it, or as you understand it, or as you understand it. [Here, Dr. Bion is pointing to different people.]

You can try to draw her attention to what is happening. You can say to the patient: "You now have facts about what happens to you if you actually come here. You can observe how dissatisfied you are with the facts and so on … how bad the facts are, compared with these other facts that might have been.

You can't tell until you say it and then, it isn't important that she have one kind of reaction or another. But, I would expect it to be more of the same thing. I would expect further discovery of what a bad analyst I was. That I would think, I would be pretty certain, mind you; if by any chance she decided I was a good analyst, I'd draw attention to that, say: "It's really rather surprising that I now appear good to you. So, it's as if, although you'd like to think that I'm a good analyst. I actually … apparently you think I am a good analyst as well."

Now, from what I've heard about this patient, I wouldn't expect her to feel better at this moment for my having said this, because I would expect her to feel extremely envious both of me, for having treated her so nicely, and of herself, for treating *me* so nicely. She'd be envious of both people.

She would be like two people: she would be the person who is envious both of herself, for being so lucky as to come to a good analyst, and of the analyst, for being so lucky to have a patient who thinks that he's a good analyst.

So, you get this peculiar thing where I would guess—that she would go on … caught between fears and feelings of guilt for having been responsible for not loving or not liking her analyst, or not appreciating the fact of being responsible for his death. So she'd be guilty about feeling: "What a bad analyst I was." She'd be guilty about feeling that I was a good analyst, because it's disloyal. So, I think that she'd almost certainly feel she couldn't do right, but she's also furious with the person with whom she had such a nasty experience who happens to be an analyst.

So, I don't think that the analyst should expect to keep getting much appreciation from this patient. After all, she *is* still alive, she *has* been married and if none of that is good enough, why should she expect anything so ordinary as a bit of a conversation between two people to be good enough. It is really almost unreasonable to believe that psychoanalysis is going, really, to cure, but it surprisingly does cure.

Surprisingly, it appears to be helpful! So, the patient will discover that it's worthwhile coming again, next time. She'd be angry about coming again next time. That's why I think that it will take you a long time … it depends on those things that have gone wrong with her: the analyst has died and so on … But, I wouldn't be at all surprised to find that you didn't really come into the picture very much as being helpful.

[Here, P1 asks a question, but the recording is inaudible and it cannot be transcribed. From Dr. Bion's comments, it apparently has something to do with generative intercourse as opposed to physiological sexual activity].

Bion: Compared to sexual intercourse, physiological intercourse is, really, quite easy and even children will succeed at masturbation and playing sexual games and so forth … but, they don't get through it what we know could be possible, namely: passionate desire. That may be possible for the analyst, but the patient thinks they know all about it. Very often, a man behaves as if he knew everything about the sexual matter, that he's out to prove it to everybody and a girl, likewise, is out to prove that she knows everything about sex, more than her mother ever knew. So, it's a bit of a shock when they find that they don't. It's a terrible admission to have to admit to whoever knows.

A: What you just described, it was more or less like that. Three months ago, she changed in a very curious way, because she attacked me and she used to say: "This is not analysis, you do not have to ask questions." She had definite thoughts about analysis—"analysis has to be like that, that and that."

Bion: Yes.

A: She used to say: "This is not analysis, what you are doing." If I asked something, if I observed something, she complained it was not a real interpretation.

Bion: What you could say about that is: "Well, what you are telling me is what you 'know' about analysis. What I know about analysis is about learning about what you don't know."

A: This is her knowledge of analysis?

Bion: According to her!

A: She used to look like a very strong person. She knows what's best, she knows about analysis, she knows about treatment and she's a good student and so on ... But, I noticed that this was so superficial that, in reality, everything she was bringing—it was not in the beginning that I noticed this. I noticed that she was never able to give her own opinion.

Bion: But, this question of who's the best, if that's all that analysis is, it's hardly worth bothering about. Now, the question is: how could you put this to this patient? How could you make it clear to her? Because, so many things would seem to be joining in with this sort of "who is on top game." Who is the best? So, I think that this is a game, that you have to tell her is going on—and nobody else can tell it really except yourself—so long as the patient comes to you. So that, you can feel, rightly or wrongly, I don't know, but you *can* feel what the interpretation is that feels right to you.

A: I could catch something of this and give an interpretation. One day when I heard what she was saying to me, she lay down and I said: "You don't like the way I am working" or something. I remember one day I said to her: "Look, you enter inside me and you think for me. It is as if I am not myself, because you say what I am."

Bion: Well, I would doubt that that would help her, so much as drawing her attention to the fact that she may be right and so forth ... But it would be useful if she gave you the evidence of what she's saying. If it is right, what she says to you, then you'd say: "Well, you haven't told me the evidence of how you have found this out" and see what would be her response to that. You could say: "Well, we still don't know what the evidence is. You are saying that because you feel this is so. That is enough for you without any evidence." I think, in fact, that you have to know what the evidence is.

A: I don't know, but I had the feeling she was doing this—when she used to say: "I want to think in your place." But then there was a step forward, because then I could say to her later on, when she used to say something that was coming from others, that she felt that they were doing to her, what she wanted to do to me: to think in my place and not let me be myself. As a result, she never understood really what she was feeling, but only what somebody else was feeling.

Bion: The trouble there is that it's quite a difficult point to put over to her and she would probably think you're just trying to be better than she. So, in a sense, it is simpler to say: "We need the evidence of the thing."

Now, this doesn't mean that you're agreeing that she's better or that she knows more about psychoanalysis, nor is she saying that you know more about psychoanalysis than her. All that it is, is that it seems in *your* opinion it would be useful to have some facts.

Now, the disadvantage of that situation would be: the patient may not be able to give you any facts. On the other hand, if you give an interpretation, then you get a situation in which the patient says something: you give an interpretation; then, you've got another interpretation … In this way, the gap gets wider and wider and the analyst is thought to be making more, and more, and more, theoretical interpretations … But, if you show that you don't mind her being a better analyst than you, but you want to know what the facts are, then she can decide to tell you what the facts are, or she'll have to change her ideas. She'll have to revise her opinion, if she can't find any facts that stood for them.

The trouble with a sophisticated patient like this is that: they've had a lot of experience. So, they probably know, not consciously, but somehow or another, how to be difficult. Now, if being difficult is all that is required in analysis, that's fine!! If being an awkward partner is all that's wanted in a sexual relation, that's fine!! But, if there's such a thing as a passionate intercourse, then it's not so good!! It's not good for her, just being able to do what any boy or girl can do in the way of making intercourse.

That sort of thing may be quite all right for a child. It may be quite all right to make it as difficult as possible for a father or mother. Now, this patient may still be able to know how to make even a verbal intercourse. Putting myself in her place, I can imagine thinking, "I see, you have a chair in the room and a couch in the room and I can … I can see that if you've got those things, you may want me to lie on the couch. Well, I'll stay in the chair. Nothing much has happened so far. I can try coming again another time and again, I can stop the very frightening things from happening, but it also means stopping analysis."

Now, one doesn't want to say to the patient that they must lie on the couch. They know that if they lie on the couch it might be more easy for you than sitting up, what with the analyst behind them, where it's easy for you to do your work. They can either make it easier for you, or more difficult. Now, this patient knows enough to know how to make it more difficult.

Again, the trouble is that the analyst has to do something—has to say something—and the patient knows this. So, one does try to make some helpful remark or whatever is possible. But it's, sometimes, very useful perhaps if you make some helpful remark, the patient will ... Sometimes she can say: "That's very helpful," and they'll say something more, or they won't say it's very helpful. But, they will show that it is by saying something, which is helpful themselves, which gives the analyst something to go on.

But, you have to be firm with this sort of patient, the kind of difficult patient who, as they find out what is helping them, then takes care to say something *less* helpful. So, as I say, you can find yourself drawn into this sort of fact, in which, you have to do more and more work, with less and less facts to go on. So, I think, in a way, you will learn after a time not to ignore all the facts as you learn them; but in the actual practice of being an analyst you know what are your *minimum working conditions* and you can know that if you don't have the *minimum conditions, your* minimum conditions, you can't do the work.

Now, even if you can't draw off a list of what your minimum conditions are, you can know them. You can know, for example: you have to have a chair—that's reasonable enough. It doesn't matter if there's a back to it, or something of this sort, you lay down. That you know four hours work or seven hours work or whatever it is, it is your idea of a professional life.

Well, sometimes a patient might say: "But, doctor, surely you could pick one more session, or you could see me at the weekend." But, of course, it's one thing if you don't mind having a chunk taken out of your long analytic time. But from your personal time? Only you know how much you have to do, as well as psychoanalysis, and nobody can tell you how you are to decide your precious time. You can gradually get to know how much you are prepared to spare in professional work and how much you can't spare, if you're needing more rest or recreation, for private affairs of your private life. That is something that only time shows you, but, I think that you have to be clear about this. So, with your patient you can make up your mind how much you are prepared to tolerate, how much allowance you can make for the patient.

Now, when you've got a patient who, if you make allowances, then they want more allowances, you make some more allowances and then make more allowances further. But, you have to feel pretty clear in your own mind, when you think there's now a reason for staying strict about the minimum conditions for your practicing analysis. You are not anybody else. It doesn't matter how anybody else does it, but it does matter what you do.

It's sometimes difficult to stick to that, because it seems so easy to handle it, to think that it's important to do nine hours, when you decide that eight is enough.

Well, if you haven't settled this yet, then you can pick up an idea about it, if one discusses this, whether one would practice this way or that way and so on …

Supervision D17 commentary

Ana Maria Stucchi Vannucchi

In my first reading of this supervision, I was immediately moved by some sentences especially the following ones: "she *tried* to have a baby" and "I will *try* to say something about it." Next, the analyst refers to the difficulty in talking to the patient, to the difficulty in finding the proper words, the patient's difficulty in lying down and relaxing. Bion says he shouldn't worry, since the analyst has to wait and after a while he will be able to find what to say to the patient: "it will become clearer, and you may give, or *try* to give it a name." Right after, he says: "apparently the patient *tried* everything ... when everything fails, the patient *expects* the analyst to do something, it's when everything fails that *supposedly* you have to help."

The *try* word was the one that moved me. I looked it up in the Dictionary of Portuguese Language (Holanda, 1975) and there I found numerous definitions for the verb *to try*. Definitions go everywhere from words that clearly include desire and means to obtain what is desired to words that place the verb in a broader situation, more distant from desiring, such as to put in practice, to attempt, to experiment, to risk or to be adventurous as is suggested by Camões' poem: "Have you watched that insane phantasy, the one of challenging the sea with a sail and an oar?" (Camões, 1954, p. 203). So I thought, I can *try* to make a comment. I am not a profound expert on Bion, but his ideas are very useful in my clinical work and in my life. As we are reminded by Parthenope Bion Talamo (1987, p. 65) in "Why we cannot be entitled as Bionians": "the main thing would be for us to have freedom to be ourselves." From this perspective, being myself would be approaching: "I am *trying* to be a psychoanalyst"! Here, *trying* appears as a navel in my reading of the text, such as the expression proposed by Freud (1900/1962, p. 111) "dreams' navel," a contact with the unknown, the impenetrable, on the other hand the contact with the mother's body, that supposes the birth's caesura. So then, *trying* means splitting certainties, a dive into the unknown?

Trying to become a psychoanalyst, *trying* to write a comment, to take a risk, to dare, to me implies on expecting an encounter with myself, with the patient, with the reader. How *to try* when there's no hope? How is hope related to desire? How to deal with such paradox? This might end up in divergence, but since we don't know, *we do try*.

This led me to the text "Notes on memory and desire" (Bion, 1986), that I find usefully prescriptive, in that Bion proposes achieving the discipline of attempting to listen without memories and desires. Then I thought, how to have hope with no desire? Is it possible for the analyst not to desire that the patient gets pregnant? On the other hand, would it be possible for him to treat her in psychoanalysis if he had this desire in the center of his attention? How to observe the experiences within the session and the expanding possibilities if he is imprisoned by this desire? From my point of view, these issues are all posed and need to be considered.

Trying reappears right after, now connected to daring: "she is still able to bear *trying* analysis." "She dares, but would like to know how the analyst dares to be an analyst" … "you have *tried* analysis, if you want to *try* it again, we can *try*".

The analyst feels anguished because the patient is "anxious" and is not comfortable neither with him nor he is with her. It all indicated that he would like to succeed, he would like her to succeed, he would like to be this person's analyst. If she can accept something from this analyst, could she get "pregnant", perhaps?

What I would like to highlight is, according to my point of view, how impossible it is to entirely dissociate hope from desire. In Bion's *Cogitations* (2000) I found a remark that points in this direction:

> Fears are opaque as hopes. Is hope different from desire? Yes; like knots, it desire + time ... Craving for fulfillment, unlike pursuit for fulfillment announces the existence of a vacancy (minus)- the knot resembles a vacancy. (Bion, 2000, p. 309)

I believe that this formulation allows me to illuminate the nucleus of "*trying*": a time-mitigated desire, contained and transformed in hope/expectation, as described by Hesiod (1996) in his *Work and Days*, while referring to Zeus' revenge against Prometheus and the humans sending them Pandora, who opens and let loose the jar/box filled with human sufferings, leaving only Hope (Expectation) as a remainder. The translator mentions that this term carries more than expectancy as a broad meaning (positive or negative). Thus, we connect *trying* to hope/expectation.

Bion says to the analyst: "a good thing to keep in mind is that you didn't *promise* anything .... you'll see what's possible". Again, this passage reminds me of Freud (1900/1962) and Irma's dream, Psychoanalysis opening dream: "I was conscious that my friend Otto's words—'she is better, but not quite well'—, or the tone in which he spoke them, annoyed me"... "I fancied I detected reproof in them, such as ... in the sense that I had *promised* the patient too much; and, whether rightly or wrongly, I attributed the supposed fact of Otto's siding against me". (Freud, 1900/1962, p. 106, italics for emphasis). "The dream acquitted me of the responsibility for Irma's condition, by showing that it was due to other factors- it produced a whole series of reasons" (p. 118), "the narrower subject of the dream which gave rise to the *wish to be innocent* of Irma's illness" (p. 120, italics for emphasis).

I believe that this observation made by Freud, allows us to consider the analyst able to deal with his *desires* that analysis be something useful for the patient's life. It seems to me that Bion, in this supervision, matches usefulness for the patient's life to the word *cure, which we usually consider negatively*: "It is almost irrational to believe that Psychoanalysis will really cure, but surprisingly cures and seems to be useful".

I believe that the idea of the usefulness of analysis in the patient's life is associated to the possibility of her perceiving herself, observing herself, coming across the *love feelings* (good analyst/good patient) and *hate feelings* (killing the analyst, bad analyst, bad patient), envy and guilt. Beyond that, I believe that such usefulness is related to the idea of "feeling it is worth coming back to the next session." It suggests, in my opinion, a preconception that an encounter will be possible. Hope? Would hope be a preconception? This term, hope, has been going round my mind during the whole time while I am writing this comment. Hope for an encounter that is useful for the analysand's life, but also for the analyst's life? Hope that life and encounter are both worthwhile?

The second point that moved me was the notion of *passion*, through the idea of "*passionate intercourse*." If the patient can't have a verbal intercourse, how can she have *passionate* intercourse? A passionate *intercourse* is more than *simply* a physiological sexual intercourse, that as a matter of fact, does not fertilize. The "*passionate* relationship" idea allows us to consider body and soul as an indissoluble unit and fertility as something that is not just physical, organic. The same applies to marriage also. Bion asks: "What does it mean to be married?" "You can secretly suppose that the patient is not married," since I believe that being married goes far beyond *what eyes see, ears hear and hands sign*. It implies a mental dimension, not quite simple to be reached.

The theme love and *passion* has come up here and there in our meetings. It lead me to re-read Plato's "Banquet", where we encounter very stimulating and modern formulations about this subject. While reading it again, many years after my philosophy studies, some points came to my attention, which previously went unnoticed. The narrator was Apollodorus and the banquet had occurred in Agathon's house, many years before when Apollodorus was still a child, which puts us in contact with memory issues and transformations in reconstructions of the past, as Apollodorus tells Glauco something that he heard from Phoenix, who heard from Aristodemus, a fervent admirer of Socrates and then reconfirmed by Socrates himself.

Upon the arrival to Agathon's house, there are many guests laying on long couches. Aristodemus is welcome and Socrates remains "thinking" outside the house. Everybody discusses on how much they are going to drink and decide that drinking shall be free and non-mandatory. Then Eryximachus suggests that they have a symposium in order to celebrate Love, a not very glorified god and everyone agrees. Many guests glorify love as a very ancient god, honored and powerful for the acquisition of truth and happiness among mankind, both in life and after death. "They exhort that one should equally love body and soul, and elect music, concerning harmony and rhythm as the science of love phenomena" (Plato, 1972, p. 26).

Then Aristophanes's discourse appears with the myth of Androgynous, which was also cited by Freud in "Beyond the pleasure principle" (1920/1955): "Everything about these primeval men was double: they had four hands and four feet, two faces, two privy parts, and so on. Eventually, Zeus decides to cut these men in two" (Freud, 1920/1955, p. 57).

It is then that love emerges, as the fruit of the human being's state of incompleteness and mutilation:

> each craving for his own missing half and seeking to be united, while getting involved with their hands and getting entwined one to the other. This led to such feeling, such heat and confusion and general inertia, that they were in danger of starving, as they wouldn't want to do anything away from each other. (Plato, 1972, p. 29)

This search for a complement seeks restoration of our "ancient nature," makes one only out of two and "cures" human nature of such suffering.

Socrates then starts asking Agathon some questions and refers to a priestess named Diotima as a "fictional resource," who would be understood in love matters. In this dialogue, "the neediness for love in relation to beauty and goodness" emerges, because if "one searches beauty this is because one doesn't own it." Socrates proposes that love isn't a god, but yet a "Daimon," a genie or spirit that is "in between gods and men": one that has the power to interpret and transmit to gods what comes from men, and to men what comes from gods, pleadings and sacrifices of some and commands and rewards from others.

And who are the parents of love?

In Plato's word, in the birthday of Aphrodite there was a feast of the gods, at which the god Poros or Plenty, who is the son of Metis or Discretion, was one of the guests. When the feast was over, Penia or Poverty, as the manner is on such occasions, came about the doors to beg. Now Plenty who was the worse for nectar, went into the garden of Zeus and fell into a heavy sleep, and Poverty considering her own straightened circumstances, plotted to have a child by him, and accordingly she lay down at his side and conceived love (Eros), who partly because he is naturally a lover of the beautiful, and because Aphrodite is herself beautiful, and also because he was born on her birthday, is her follower and attendant. And as his parentage is, so also are his fortunes.

In the first place he is always poor, and anything but tender and fair, as the many imagine him; and he is rough and squalid, and has no shoes, nor a house to dwell in; on the bare earth exposed he lies under the open heaven, in the streets, or at the doors of houses, taking his rest; and like his mother he is always in distress. Like his father too, whom he also partly resembles, he is always plotting against the fair and good; he is bold, enterprising, strong, a mighty hunter, always weaving some intrigue or other, keen in the pursuit of wisdom, fertile in resources; a philosopher at all times, terrible as an enchanter, sorcerer, sophist. He is by nature neither mortal nor immortal.

This myth seemed very interesting to me, because it allows us to think from a standpoint in which need is a characteristic element of feelings of love having courage, energy, and vitality as its counterpart. It's as if Plato/Socrates would propose that by means of a feeling of love one would "exalt" beyond the human condition of mortality, limitation, and ignorance, such as the philosopher, who also inhabits the intermediate territory between wisdom and ignorance.

Right after, Socrates mentions, always through Diotima (it is an interesting fact that Plato chose these words to be voiced by a woman!), that the conceiving and creation of a new life, resulting from love, both from body and soul, allows for man's mortal nature to project itself in the direction of "immortality," approaching towards the gods in a certain way: one wouldn't easily find a "human nature collaborator, even better than love" (Plato, 1972, p. 49).

So Alcibiades arrives, very drunk, "jealous, envious and violent," for having had his love rejected by Socrates. Such rejection is described in detail in his speech, which alternates praising of Socrates assets, revealing at the same time, deep pain and suffering for having been rejected. He accuses Socrates of not being capable of loving and only wanting to be loved, in this way displaying anger and resentment.

One can then say that love, according to Plato, puts us in contact with the most "noble and sublime" feelings, but at the same time with the most human and mundane feelings such jealousy, possessiveness, rivalry, hate, vengeance. Here we are faced with the paradoxical nature of love as a passage/transition between body and soul, love and hate, sensory and psychic, at the same time verifying that these words are very simple and restricted for the expression of human experiences. Poets are needed for a clearer and more significant expression.

Adélia Bezerra de Menezes (2002) sharply and sensitively finds an expression of such paradox in Camões`words:

> Love is a fire that burns unseen,
> A wound that aches yet isn't felt,
> An always discontent contentment,
> A pain that rages without hurting. (Menezes, 2002, p. 57)

Octavio Paz (1994, p. 185) also emphasizes the loving feeling's paradox relating it to the body which is "pleasure and death," and to "a blow that makes a persona out of each man and each woman," defining in this way the double flame—love and eroticism, which are both fed from sexuality's original energy.

> Love is indifferent to every transcendence: it starts and ends in itself. It's the appeal to a body and a soul, not to an idea: a person. This person is unique and free, so the lover has to win his/her will in order to obtain such person. Property and surrender are reciprocal acts. (p. 187)

In his *Elements of Psycho-Analysis*, Bion (1966) proposes that: "By passions I mean all that is comprised in L, H, K" (Bion, 1966, p. 20) He considers the *passion* domain as one of the dimensions of the psychoanalytic object, "the component derived from L, H and K ... the term to represent an emotion experienced with intensity and warmth though without any suggestion of violence" (p. 31). Then he says: "*Passion* is evidence that two minds are linked" (p. 32, italics for emphasis). What would a *"passionate love"* be, one that the patient hasn't experienced yet, but which "is possible for the analyst?" as suggested by Bion in this supervision?

I here remember a colleagues question: "what kind of love is this, the one we have for our patients?" I then ask: Can we then think about a *passionate* verbal intercourse, where a connections "magical moment" might happen? At this point, the analyst's word can be the bearer of affects and propitiate a *passionate* experience for both minds. This is what I think "at-one-ment" is. I believe that this mental state, the one of being in unison with another, is located in evolution (or passage, if we consider Guimarães Rosa) from K -> O, that is, from knowing to being: "the interpretation is an actual event in an evolution of O that is common to analyst and analysand" (Bion, 2006, p. 42).

If there's an encounter and the experience of being in unison with the other, fecundation and fertility may happen. So the patient could get "pregnant"? That's why, I believe, says Bion: "analysis is not knowledge". I think: I believe it is experience. It is really a paradox that a "mere analysis," or "something as ordinary as some talk between two people," might turn in certain moments into something so precious and essential in a person's life! Could we consider here Octavio Paz's idea of reciprocal surrender and property between analyst and analysand?

Another topic that was of interest to me is related to facts: "How *unsatisfactory* facts are, when compared to daydreams!" "A fact can never be as good as an ideal" or "how terrible facts can be when compared to facts that could have happened!" I believe that here Bion is calling one's attention to issues connected to the construction of Freud's reality principle (Freud, 1911/1958) and to the intrinsic pain inherent in this process, which is therefore needed for one's physical and psychic survival.

Freud refers to the artist and to the possibility of transforming his phantasies into realities:

> he can only achieve this, because other men feel the same dissatisfaction as he does with the renunciation demanded by reality, and because that dissatisfaction, which results from the replacement of the pleasure principle by the reality principle, is itself a part of reality. (Freud, 1911/1958, p. 224)

> The strangest characteristic of unconscious processes (repressed), to which no investigator can become accustomed without the exercise of great self-discipline, is due to their entire disregard of reality-testing. They equate reality of thought with external actuality, and wishes with their fulfilment—with the event—just as happens automatically under the dominance of the ancient pleasure principle. (Freud, 1911/1958, p. 225)

The whole subject linked to the dispute of "who's best," who knows how "to analyze" is based on the notion of *evidence*, and therefore on the observation of psychic facts experienced by the analytic pair. Bion observes that the analyst gets annoyed at the patient when she says: "you don't like the way I work." The analyst responds: "see, you get into me and think for me. I am not myself because you tell me who I am." Bion suggests that the analyst could search instead for *evidence*: "How did you find that out? or "What gave you this impression?" In this way, the possibility for observation could be developed within the analytic pair, offering the patient the possibility of observing herself.

I believe that in this passage Bion also calls the attention to the analyst's self-observation capacity and to the danger of giving "theoretical interpretations" not based in *evidence* that will only increase the distance between analyst and analysand: if the analyst has to get into the dispute of who's best, the possibility of investigation within the pair and self-observation will fatally become remote.

But, what are facts? In *Evidence*, Bion makes use of Bacon "Novum Organum", Kant (1781, cited by Giuffrida,1996, p. 2) "intuitions with no concepts are blind, concepts with no intuitions are hollow" and questions himself: "how can intuition be introduced in concepts and concepts in intuitions?" He then suggests: "a feeling is one of the few things which analysts have the luxury of being able to regard as a fact" (Bion, 1985, p. 136).

I think that this patient's feelings of helplessness, impotence, and disillusion are expressed by her omnipotence of wanting "to get pregnant without having a *passionate* sexual intercourse," of wanting to have analysis while being her analyst's analyst, in this way turning the encounter into something very "difficult." It seems that at this point, she cannot find another way of existing and relating apart from the "difficult" one. Alone, secluded, and inaccessible, but needy and helpless as well. Poverty and Plenty in Plato's words?

We can see that this situation exasperates the analyst, who can't find an acceptable manner to communicate it to the patient at this point. I ask myself as to what exactly is a difficult patient and as to whether there are easy patients: wouldn't "being an easy one" be difficult as well? Wouldn't difficulties be always present when communicating with oneself and with others?

Finally, the supervision ends with the "*minimal working conditions for the analyst*." I consider this to be a very current issue, since the analytical setting has been the subject of numerous discussions in our society.

In my opinion, one needs four to five weekly sessions for training analysis, so that the analytic pair is able to experience closeness in depth, as well as to become familiar with primitive mental states and any kind of feelings, that an analyst needs to observe in him/herself: "observation and contact with my mental experiences" (Nogueira, 2010, p. 6). This implies the analyst's caution with his/her own mind, as Bion seems to suggest in the supervision`s final portion.

Bion increases these *minimal working conditions* by approaching the analyst's personal needs, such as time, pay, rest, leisure, for example, which need to be taken into consideration so that a true analytic relationship is installed. It is interesting to observe that Bion emphasizes that these elements are personal and can't be "lent" to others: "It is no good that someone keeps telling you how you should look at things, or from where you look at them—no one will ever know, except you yourself" (Bion, 1985, p. 139).

References

Bion, W. R. (1966). *Elementos de Psicoanálisis*. Buenos Aires: Hormé. (Original work published in 1963. Original title: Elements of psycho-analysis).

Bion, W. R. (1985). Evidência. *Revista Brasileira de Psicanálise, 19*(1): 129–141. (Original work published in 1976. Original title: Evidence).

Bion, W. R. (1986). Notas sobre a memória e o desejo. *Jornal de Psicanálise, 19*: 33–35. (Original work published in 1967. Original title: Notes on memory and desire).

Bion, W. R. (2000). *Cogitações*. Rio de Janeiro: Imago. (Original work published in 1992. Original title: Cogitations).

Bion, W. R. (2006). *Atenção e interpretação.* Rio de Janeiro: Imago. (Original work published in: 1970. Original title: Attention and Interpretation).

Camões, L. de. (1954). Canto VI. In: L. de Camões, *Os lusíadas* (pp. 195–223). São Paulo: Melhoramentos.

Freud, S. (1955). Beyond the pleasure principle. In: S. Freud, *The Standard Edition of the Complete Psychological Works of Sigmund Freud* (J. Strachey, trans.), Vol. 18, pp. 1–64. London: Hogarth. (Original work published in 1920).

Freud, S. (1958). Formulations on the two principles of mental functioning. In: S. Freud, *The Standard Edition of the Complete Psychological Works of Sigmund Freud* (J. Strachey, trans.), Vol. 12, pp. 213–226. London: Hogarth. (Original work published in 1911).

Freud, S. (1962). The method of interpreting dreams: an analysis of a specimen dream. In: S. Freud, *The Standard Edition of the Complete Psychological Works of Sigmund Freud* (J. Strachey, trans.), Vol. 4, pp. 96–121. London: Hogarth. (Original work published in 1900).

Giuffrida, F. (1996). Reflexões sobre alguns aspectos da intuição [Reflections on some aspects of intuition]. São Paulo: SBPSP, 1996. p. 21. Trabalho apresentado em Reunião Científica, São Paulo.

Hesíodo. (1996). *Os trabalhos e os dias* [Works and days] (Mary Lafer, trans.). São Paulo: Iluminuras. (Original work published in VII century B.C. Original title: Erga kaí Hemérai).

Holanda, A. F. B. de (1975). *Novo Dicionário da Língua Portuguesa*. [New dictionary of the Portuguese language]. Rio de Janeiro: Nova Fronteira.

Lafer, M. (Trans.). (1990). *Os trabalhos e os dias* [Works and days]. São Paulo: Iluminuras. (Original work published in VII century B.C . Original title: Erga kaí Hemérai).

Menezes, A. B. (2002). A paixão na literatura [The passion in literature]. *Literatura e Sociedade*, 6: 40–62.

Nogueira, P. O. (2010). Frequência analítica: uma questão do analista e não do analisando [Analytical frequency: a question of the analyst and not of the analysand]. *Unpublished text.*

Nunes, B. (1969). O amor na obra de Guimarães Rosa. In: B. Nunes, *O dorso do tigre: ensaios* (pp. 143–171). São Paulo: Perspectiva.

Platão. (1972) *Diálogos—O banquete* (José Cavalcante de Souza, trans.). São Paulo: Ed. Abril. (Original work published in: 380 B.C. Original title: Sympósion).

Paz, O. (1994). *A dupla chama: amor e erotismo* [The duble flame: love and eroticism]. São Paulo: Ed. Siciliano. (Trabalho original publicado em:1914. Original title: La llama doble).

Talamo, P. B. (2000). Porque não podemos nos intitular bionianos? *Ide*, 3: 60–65. (Original work published in 1987. Original title: Perché non possiamo dirci bioniani).

CHAPTER TEN

Supervision A36

This case was presented to Bion by an Argentine analyst, whose native language was Spanish. The tape of the presentation reflects both a degree of language confusion—inconsistent English and "Spanglish"—and what was probably considerable anxiety on the part of the analyst that is a reflection of the case. Some of the confusion has been edited out for the comfort of the reader, but some is inevitable and left in, because coherence and clarity is impossible to determine from the transcript or the tape. In the text that follows, A stands for Analyst; T stands for Translator; P1 stands for a participant in the audience.

A: It's a woman patient; she's thirty-three years old, unmarried, and a psychologist. Two months before this session, she had an operation due to a sacro-coccygeal teratoma. This session is on Monday. She begins as follows:

> "How pretty you are today, doctor. Well, why is it so difficult for me to communicate to you the good and the bad? Yet, just here, this is the place where I can do it. I have been thinking about the fourth analytic hour.[1] Last Saturday, I went early to work and after work, I had lunch with a friend. After that, I went home to change clothes,

> then I went to X's home. I was laughing. I stayed chattering. I said to myself that I had spent a Saturday working. Sunday was the sixth anniversary of my father's death. I did not go to the cemetery.

Today, I got up at six-thirty, I studied and worked for the same man—besides, I was glad. I have difficulties with the fourth hour. Since June or July, they have not paid me what I am owed, and so I can not pay my bills. I had the surgery at the hospital—the patients and the social worker orders.[2] On account of this, I was thinking about whether or not to leave out or not leave out the fourth hour. I hope that my fees will be twice as much as they have been (emphatically).

At work, they have asked me for a study about risk. This is only a project. My own idea is to leave out one session due to my [financial] need. It may be that I will drop the session now and then take it on again. I do not mean—when I earn twenty millions a month—but when I get a steady salary; for, doctor, if I cannot, I cannot.

I am able to see how hard it is for me to receive and to be in debt to someone and I found out that one can get oneself cured here. This [possibility of being helped in analysis] is not just a desire or a fantasy. I can't explain it to you today as clearly as yesterday. Yesterday, I did the report alone, I studied, I understood. I could see things in the seminar, I could contribute.

On Thursday night I had a dream. It was at night, it was a theatre, where a chorus was singing. Did I tell you that I belonged to a chorus? What a ridiculous phase. We were going to prepare the Chorus of *The Cavalleria Rusticana*. I have a solo. The chorus was of five voices. In the dream, I arrived dressed in a college woman's apron, but smoking; with my apron and tie. I felt out of place, someone looked at me and I noticed the cigarette. I went back, left the cigarette, then a fire began. In a little table, at the bar, was X"—the patient's sister—"I do not know if she was standing or sitting. A figure appears. It was a tall man, light brown hair and greenish blue eyes, with a Russian look. Very colorful like a typical colorful character. I do not know if you remember Romeo and Juliet? He was dressed up in black, black trousers and he was a medical product propagandist, his name was … maybe George Breast?"

Bion: Can we just pause a moment? Do you mind being interrupted? You don't mind if any of us ask any questions, at any time?

A: Yes.

Bion: So, I suggest that, if any point is not clear to you, we just stop and ask the analyst to make it a bit clearer.

T: She said that that would be done and …

A: Yes.

Bion: When she said that she had a dream, did you think that that was correct, that it was a dream? She says that she had a dream. Now, what is your idea about it? Does it sound like a dream to you? Or if not a dream, what would you call it? Or, in fact, would you simply think: yes, it is a dream.

Anybody, any ideas?

Well, we haven't any responses, so we could go on.

A: "His name was George Breast or Braid. I don't know if I was a shy girl and 'X' introduced me to him. Did you remember 'X?' 'X' told him that I was no longer a child, but an adult, married. Afterwards, there was nothing to eat and I ran to some other park. It was twelve fifteen p.m., but it[3] was closed with an iron net of polyethylene. The iron was of cheap material. I knocked, but it did not work, because of this everything was all quiet. I thought it could be a morgue. What stood out—what was in color—was the figure of the man: Breast, Braid or Brecht. What can it be related to? Berthold Brecht was a German playwright—but I do not remember anything about him. 'Braid,' does not mean anything. 'To reduce?' No. 'To be all right?' No. That means alright. Is it 'to bring?' No. I do not remember. 'Breaking?' It does not tell me that it means break." The patient rises on her elbows for while, my skin …

Bion: She was lying on the couch?

A: Yes.

Bion: But she rose on her elbows?

A: Yes, like this.

[A gesture was probably made].

Bion: What do you think of that? I ask you these questions because … all of us—except the analyst—weren't there, so we are dependent on the analyst being able to describe the situation. But, at the same time, we can imagine that we were there. So, I could ask you, what are you observing? If you're in the room with the patient, what do you want to see? What do you want to hear? Has anybody got any suggestion to make us, to what we, as psychoanalysts, think we are going to observe?

P1: I knew this material previously and I don't know if it's useful that I speak … taking your first question, concerning if it was a dream … perhaps it could be another state, similar to a dream—some kind of semi-hallucinating state, some … I don't know how to say it, some hallucination, some kind of hallucination—perhaps that's the thing that happened, when she rises on the elbow.

Bion: The point is that we, as the analyst, have got to be prepared for anything. I can say: the mind or character or personality of the patient—I use those words, I use them, because it's the only language I really know. But, even using English—which I know better than any other language—I find it difficult to say what I think what,—I or we—would be looking at or observing. At the same time, I do consider that the basis of scientific observation is observing the facts, looking, listening. If it were a physical matter, one would say: "Alright, now take your clothes off, lie on the examination couch and I will examine you, physically." But we don't do that. I'm not sure that, therefore, our method of procedure is the correct one, but on the whole, I think that the psychoanalytic investigation technique, is the best technique I have come across. That does not mean the best possible technique; it only means the best that I know, or that we know. It does not mean that it is the best. However, since it is the one that we use, then we have to have all our senses open to what it is.

Now, Freud talks about what he calls, I think, *"free-floating attention."* As usual, these phrases don't mean much. After a time you begin to get the idea of what free-floating attention means. Similarly, I'll try to say things to you, I'll try to use the same language all the time, not because I think that English is the best, but because it's the best I know. It's the language that I talk most easily, but even then, I'm trying to talk about things, which are very difficult to describe, even in English—with it's vast vocabulary and with such words as I know.

If you were a painter, then you could draw me a picture of this patient rising on her elbows. *Leonardo* can draw a picture of St. Ann, the Virgin Mary, St. John. He can not have met the Virgin Mary; he can not have seen St. John; then, what was he drawing? Now, take this patient: what is the analyst trying to describe? Well, we want to know, can you draw me a picture of this patient's mind? This patient's character? Now, if you're very gifted, like Shakespeare, you can draw a picture of Hamlet, or Lady Macbeth, or the Weird Sisters in Macbeth, verbally. Now, Shakespeare—the English language was never the same again after Shakespeare, it became a different language. Who's going to write a case history? Who's going to draw, or paint in words, the soul, or character of this person? So, although it seems to be relatively simple to bring a case history, to read it to us here, in fact, it is very difficult and, in fact, I think that psychoanalysts will *have to become* artists, if they're going to tell somebody—like telling us here—what this experience was, that the analyst had with this character.

I could put it another way: the thing that we are wanting to help has a body—there's a body attached to it—in the same way, as I've got to live with hands attached to my mind. But, the idea is: we think there is a mind, or a character, or a personality. Now, you may have to try to do it in Spanish words. You might have to do it, in the way that somebody was able to draw a Don Quixote; so that, you and I, have an idea of Don Quixote. We haven't seen him, we haven't met him, we don't know him, but thanks to that artist, we can have a faint idea of what he's talking about. So, Don Quixote is known all through the civilized world a little bit—it's an extraordinary achievement and that is what we aspire to do. This paper—the paper that you're reading—is the nearest that we can get to telling somebody else—who wasn't there—what this thing was.

Now, there are lots of words, like *"a dream."* We all learn that and we learn other things like: father figures and so on … it becomes commonplace—it becomes part of our language; but, it's very doubtful whether those words and those theories help us to see this character. However, when we discuss it, like this, we can begin to feel: "Yes, I think I know what you mean"; so, we can feel—trying to be analysts—that we need to become artists, who could express what it is we have seen, what it is that we saw, the last time that we talked to a patient. It sounds simple, say: "Yes, I saw … there were a 'senhor,' whoever it is, or a 'dona,' whoever it is, at ten o'clock, on 3 April." It tells you nothing, because I wonder: who is "senhor" "x" or "dona" "x"? Who was it? What was his experience?

Similarly, if I had this patient, I wouldn't say this, but I could feel: "I don't want to hear about these dreams." I don't mind hearing about them, but what I would say is, or what I would like to say is: "Where were you last night? Where did you go? What did you see?" The patient might say nothing, or the patient might say: "Oh, well, you mean, I had a dream?" No, I don't mean that. I mean: "What did you see and where did you go?" I could put it another way and say: "Yes, alright then, you saw …" then, whatever this patient says—"you dreamt. But now, tell me, what did your heart see? What did your spleen see?"

There are countries, in which, the inhabitants, talk about the girlfriend or the boyfriend as "my heart and liver." Why heart and liver? Not brain? So, I could put it the other way and say: "No, I don't want to know what your eyes saw. Tell me what your heart saw, tell me what your spleen saw." Nowadays, the physiologist and anatomists …

[Some words were lost while the tape was changed over].

… blood. Even when I was learning anatomy, there used to be a joke: "the lecture on the spleen." "The spleen is a mysterious organ, we don't know what it does—that ends our lecture on the spleen." Today, much the same thing is true about the human person. You say: "Oh, yes, look at it there: the 'Standard Works of Freud' and the 'Standard Works of Melanie Klein,' the 'Standard Works of Abraham' and so on and so forth … through the list." When you have read all these books, do they remind you of people or not? Can you write a paper, which would remind somebody else of a human being? For example: can you read this paper or hear this description and say: "Ah, yes, I remember a person just like that," that's what I want you to do now I want you both to listen to the paper—we've all tried to do that—and also, at the same time, perhaps, remember, if we've ever met anybody like this and if so, if we were seeing this patient, what would be asked to the patient? I don't think I would want to stop the patient, if the patient said they'd had a dream, but, for myself, I would note a question: is this a dream? Is this, as you suggested, possibly a delusion? But, observing—whatever you can observe—when the patient comes into your office, then, amongst other things, the patient does that, like that, what is he doing?

[A gesture, or movement seems to have been made].

A: She was then saying something in front of me.

Bion: That's the advantage of being there. That is one of the advantages of practical analysis; you actually don't have to depend on what you've been told about this patient and so on ... You can actually see the person for yourself and this movement, it doesn't really mean very much. Now, the analyst can tell us, what sort of movement that was. But, note: that wasn't a dream. The patient was wide awake. Now, if she can see something, if she can do this, because she sees something in broad daylight, then again, you'd have to consider who, or what, is this patient. Now, there's a difficulty here, the first difficulty is: what do you see, what do you hear, what do your senses tell you? The next question is: when you know what your senses tell you, what does that information mean? For example: what we've just heard from the analyst. Now, there's another question: what shall we tell the patient?

I don't think that we would regard it as wise to say to the patient: "You are hallucinated!" or "You are deluded!" because that would not be a statement which the patient would understand; but, it could be a statement which the patient would *misunderstand* and if you said: "You are hallucinated!" the patient would get up and walk out and never come back. So, this question is also a difficult question. What would you say, or do, if you were there? You don't have to say what, because of this point that you are talking to somebody and we don't know what language the patient would understand or misunderstand. So, from that point of view, we have to wait, but not for too long, because if we waited too long, the patient would, again, walk out and wouldn't come back. That's why the practice of analysis is so difficult, much more, much more difficult than talking about—like I'm talking about it—or theorizing. That's why I would pay, or be much more impressed by somebody, who's actually practicing analysis, instead of somebody who's talking about analysis.

Now, are there any other questions that you'd like to ask the analyst who was there? The analyst can be our senses for us. We can't see this patient, but the analyst can do the seeing for us. So, are there any other questions that you'd like to ask the analyst? Or any questions that you'd like to suggest, that *she* should ask the analysand? Incidentally, this is another point still: that the best help the analyst can get, is not you, or me, not us, but *the patient*: that is always the way. The best help that the analyst can get, *always*, comes from the patient. So, for that reason, it's a good thing to make it possible for the patient to help us. That's why I say, it would be wrong to frighten the patient so much that they got up and walked out. We lose our best friend for the analytic experience.

I've known this problem—it's not an analytic problem only—it's quite a common problem, only we have to go into these things. I was once assisting Wilfred Trotter, who was, at the time, the finest brain surgeon in the world. He also wrote *The Instincts of the Herd, in Peace and War.* Now, his chief assistant was a brilliant technician. If a patient came in to see Trotter, perhaps not a very well educated patient, Trotter would say: "Well, what is your trouble?" "It's my kidneys, doctor," said the patient. Now, Trotter listens as if this is the wisest thing he's ever heard, pays great attention to this statement and the patient tells him more, and more, and more … So, by the end of half an hour, let's say, Trotter knows a very great deal about that patient. I've heard him behaving like that with a poor and uneducated person and do the same thing with King George the V. But the patients are all, after all, human beings; they're all suffering, we can tell something.

Now, the brilliant technician if he's told: "It's my kidneys, doctor!" would fly into a rage: "Your kidneys, nonsense. You don't know anything about your kidneys." The patient would stop talking, wouldn't say any more. The results of these two brilliant surgeons are very different. Trotter, who as I say, was a brilliant brain surgeon, could put on a skin graft and it would take. If his brilliant assistant did the same thing, with equal perfection, the skin graft wouldn't take. One was a brilliant and successful surgeon, the other was a brilliant and unsuccessful surgeon. The same thing applies to us. We have to make it possible for the patient to be able to talk to us. It isn't necessary for us to know an awful lot. It is useful to know as much as we can about anatomy, physiology, psychoanalysis and so on … but, the really central thing is for us to be able to learn.

I'm sorry to talk so much, but, will you now do some talking? Will you ask some questions?

> [The tape was switched off at this point, we then hear Dr. Bion continue].

… still you may not know what to ask. Anyhow, perhaps you could tell us some more.

A: Continue?

Bion: Yes, yes.

A: "I think you're afraid that I am … that in reducing a session, it would be as if I was putting a grade, a grade on analysis and you feel this … that it is a grade from me and not only as you say[4] … but it's just a break between two hours … (silence). Arh … I became happy because in the dream … I was told that I was no longer X but Z.[5] That I was no longer a child. I thought about you last weekend, for three or four hours. I felt that I could dream about being able to be separate from you, not restricted … I felt … where can I go? I left truthfully … which have a name …[6]

A then said to the patient: I believe that you feel … in order to feel better you have to … eliminate the fourth session … yourself because you are … feeling the frustration of the weekend and you want to put me in a closed place, full of these bad things and you want to run away from me."[7]

Patient: "People refer to me in two ways, some call me X, which is my own name. X has a cold connotation, an intellectual one. Others call me Z, which is more emotional, dramatic. The medical societies propagandize about who works on the medicine. I also thought of a painting called "The Devils." It is a moving picture we went to see with George, in X city. X city is about fifty kilometers from Y city. The film takes place in a convent. A priest appeared and he agreed to give up the priesthood and become a man and he married. In addition, Vanessa, the protagonist, prayed for poverty." She had a fantasy where she saw herself naked and she was in love with this priest. "That picture showed me." She was considered possessed by the devil and she was exorcised by introducing an object into her vagina.

"How terrible! George Break or Brecht appeared as a handsome affective man. He was not sinister. There is a colored picture of my father, he was red haired, but he was not tall. The name George is related with George"—the patient's ex-boyfriend that declared himself as a homosexual. "This dream is a message for me."

Bion: Just pause for a moment. Are there any questions about that? Or any observations you want to make?

P1: This commentary about the … what you said about the dream?

A: Yes.

[After a slight pause on the tape the analyst continues, but in Spanish, which was translated for Dr. Bion].

T: She (A) wants to know, what you think about the fact that, before she came to analysis, this teratoma never manifested itself and after starting analysis, it started suppurating and occasionally it did, until it ended in the operation …

Bion: What did you say was suppurating?

T: The teratoma.

Bion: Ah, yes.

T: It's a congenital teratoma she had and that had never manifested itself up to the moment she started analysis …

A: During the first holidays, vacations …

T: … it started to suppurate.

A: Before this operation she had …

T: Before the operation she had a tooth taken out that … because they were very …

[A word is not audible] and she (A) wants to know whether, if you think there's a relation between this teratoma and the dental problem?

Bion: There's always one relation and that is if the patient talks about the teratoma and the tooth, then she has related the tooth and the teratoma, because it is the same person who has brought these two ideas very close together, so they are related, always. Now, taking the more theoretical point, would the suppuration actually have anything to do with analysis? I don't know, but one can guess that if the patient begins to talk to the analyst, it must be because she has got more relaxed, she is prepared to say things to the analyst, although the analyst *is* listening. She wouldn't want to say things to the analyst if she thought the analyst wasn't listening, or was absent in mind. But, if she feels that the analyst *is* listening, then she might be afraid of saying anything; that, itself, could tell you something about the patient, as to why, when a patient can find somebody who'll hear what she has to say, why she or he has to stop saying it. But if …

[There is a pause on the tape, but from the context it seems Bion says that if the patient is relaxed enough to talk].

… to relax enough to dare to say whatever she thinks; then, it doesn't seem to be unreasonable to suppose that the body would also be relaxed. I don't see anything particularly obscure or mysterious about that. In fact, I can see, in a situation like that—where the patient thinks that the analyst would stay awake—and would listen to what she has to say, sometimes you get a patient who then goes to sleep. Now, because that is very inconvenient for us: the patient comes to see you, lies down on the couch—and before they've said a few sentences—they've gone to sleep and they stay in a profound sleep. It's difficult to wake them again within the session—because it's the end of the session. But, in fact, it indicates a certain ability to relax, an ability to go to sleep. Now, I don't see why thinking should be through the body; the body could be clenched up tight like that.

> [Through the tone of voice we get the impression that Dr. Bion assumes a certain position].

I could relax enough for a suppuration to start. Now, this, of course, is pure conjecture; it can't be regarded as scientific fact—but it may turn into scientific fact sometime; it may be possible to say: "Yes, that is so." At present, one can only say: "it could be." It's a conjecture.

I think that in scientific investigations—as the sort that we analysts do—there is a place for *imaginative* or *rational conjecture*—whatever the scientists may choose to say. In fact, I think that they themselves use it, much more than they realize—*inspired guesses* as it's called and so forth … But whether it is so, only time could tell. But certainly, I'm quite familiar with situations, in which, after quite a lot of work, the patient dares to be ill, the patient dares to feel … "I am afraid that I'm going mad, I am afraid I am mad." If they hadn't been tensed up tight all their life, they'd be familiar by this time with the fear that they were going mad. Most people have, at some time or another, been unaware of the fear that they are going mad, or that they would go mad, or that masturbation would cause them to go mad and so on … millions of these theories; but, if patients dare to have these theories, then it doesn't come as a great shock when they, suddenly, find that they're having them in analysis—as a result of analysis. Of course, that always causes trouble for the analyst, for the patient and so on ... but it's a thing I think we have to be used to, that it's a part of analytic progress that the patient can dare to become worse and know it. Of course, it's easy to say that analysis caused the teratoma to suppurate, but it isn't so—I don't think it is so. It may be that the analysis makes it possible for the patient, to be aware that there is a suppuration there, even to go to a surgeon for an operation. But if patients can have vestigial tails, if patients can have vestigial brachial testes, then they can also have vestigial minds. So, one must be prepared to see, feel, and hear in your own consulting room a vestigial mind, a mind which is a primordial.

Well, maybe we have to stop.

Notes

1. Editors' note: This hour had apparently been in question due to financial and other considerations.
2. Editors' note: This is a literal transcription of what was said, but its meaning is unclear.
3. Editors' note: it=?the food kiosk or café?
4. Editors' note: This is the analyst describing what the patient has said.
5. Editors' note: Apparently, X refers to a childhood name for the patient and Z a more adult designation.
6. Editors; note: This is a literal translation and transcription. It is not clear from the tape what is meant.
7. Editors' note: The analyst here is speaking rapidly, in English with a heavy, hard to understand Spanish accent. As with other presenters, Bion does not seek to "correct" the analyst's presentation, but listens to the experience of the presentation that is. For example, when other presenters mentioned a poem and began to translate it into English, Bion also asked to hear it in Portuguese, presumably to catch the music and flavor of its sound and the emotional meaning that that might convey.

Supervision A36[1] commentary

Paulo Cesar Sandler

The analyst introduces the case with sensuously apprehended, concrete, social data about the patient.[2] Epiphenomenal data taken at its face value may introduce bias, embodying mutual seduction, collusion, prejudiced social views, judgmental values, and other indications of unanalyzed countertransference (Green, 1993). Does this set, right from the start, the ethos of supervision A36? An exclusive use of epiphenomenal data would preclude the practice of "real psychoanalysis" (Bion, 1974, p. 114; 1977, pp. 303, 307; 1979, p. 509), dismissing the effects of the unconscious processes on what is just raw, low-level empirical data. In contrast, real analysis looks for what is *told*, which underlies or overlies what is plainly, concretely *said*:[3] the latter being the final products of the patient's transformations of beta elements (Bion, 1965, p. 25; Sandler, 2005, p. 800)—something materialised that needs to be "digested" or elaborated by the analyst, in order to be "immaterialized," if one achieves a good enough apprehension of Freud's concepts of manifest and latent contents, and Bion's concept of alpha function (Freud, 1900, 1914; Bion, 1962).

Epiphenomenal data may be useful when matched with observations of the patient's evolving immaterial data: free associations, dreams, slips of the tongue, unconscious phantasies, defences, etc.

If those matched data can be constantly conjoined with an intuitive, critical attention to variations in the behaviour of the patient in the "here and now" of the session (Bion, 1953, p. 25; 1957, p. 55; 1965, p. 18), the analytic couple achieves a living, experienced material for scientific comparison (Bion, 1977, p. 269). Manifest contents, what is *said* during an analysis, are under the sway of defence mechanisms. Analysis must look for the latent contents, "a new class of psychical material between the manifest content of dreams and the conclusions of our enquiry" (Freud, 1900, p. 277). The analyst may glimpse, albeit transiently, central aspects of what really is happening at that moment, in the analytic setting, embedded and, paradoxically, pervading the emotional climate and the relationship between patient and analyst (Sandler, 1997; 2011, p. 189); he (or she) may "dream the patient's material" or "the session" (Bion, 1962, pp. 53–54, item 3; Bion, 1992 [1959, p. 43]; a complete review can be seen in Sandler, 2005, pp. 219–230).

If raw data taken in isolation tell us little or nothing about the mental state of the patient, do they tell us something about the state of mind of the analyst? Yes, provided they are matched with what may emerge from the unknown (Bion, 1958–1979, p. 175). This case presentation begins with commonplace information, perhaps displaying a proclivity to overly rely upon memory, desire, and understanding: resistance against the unknown (Bion, 1965, p. 171; 1970; 1967a; 1967b; 1975; Freud, 1911; 1926, pp. 75–125). The analyst seems to be immobilized in what can be called an "already known realm." However, he (or she) also introduces a "scoop" worthy of a tabloid: the patient had an operation to remove a sacro-coccygeal teratoma.

Upon reading that, I found myself invaded by peculiar thoughts: "Teratomas in that area, if diagnosed early, usually lead to boring, but successful surgery … lay people are scared of such awful names, but …" I was prey to my memory, attempts to understand (previous medical education and practice) and desire (that this woman, whom I never knew, would survive). In noticing that transformations in hallucinosis (Bion, 1965, p. 133)[4] were at full bore in myself, I think that I was able to discipline my memory and desire-ridden transformations, and put a stop to my own flux of misunderstanding-bound thoughts (–K: Bion, 1962, p. 52). It is a case of "making the best of a bad situation" (Bion, 1976, p. 243). In hindsight, I supposed that these initial responses were an effect of a built-in invariant of supervision A36, transferred to the transcript and then to myself, as a reader. Sometimes transformations in hallucinosis may be conducive to transformations in K and transformations in O. Was the analyst unconsciously trying, via projective identifications, to provoke emotions in, rather than impart knowledge to, the supervisor and the audience? Is this the value of recorded case reports, that somehow a transcendent invariant (Bion, 1965, p. 1) is conserved and can be caught by future readers?

The patient complains about her studies and work, in an attempt to provoke emotions in the analyst and to reverse the perspective, as if the analyst were the most important person in the room (Bion, 1957; 1962, p. 24): "How pretty you are." This is done amidst disjointed, hyperbolic thoughts presented in a seemingly rational way, typical of transformations in hallucinosis: complaints mixed with rationalized explanations. There are "advertisements" of the patient's own skills, who next shows her curiosity about the extent of her analyst's knowledge, enticing the analyst to use memory ("are you reminded of Romeo and Juliet?"). She then mentions a "dream" with a character named George Breast.

Only now do I realize that there were two females present in that session, which allows for a second hypothesis: of a sexualized environment, indicated by (i) the reference to feelings of prettiness, attributed by the analyst to the patient; (ii) the complaint of rising early and working and studying "with the same man" and being explored by him—analytically, pierced by an obnoxious or abhorred man; (iii) the reference to a tragic, impossible love; (iv) the hypomanic mood, both in the analyst's report and in the behaviour attributed to the patient, beautifully compacted and illustrated in the Chorus of Mascagni's popular opera *Cavalleria Rusticana*, which I see as a free association of the analytic pair depicting the reality of the very session; and (v) the mutual, serialised impositions performed both by the patient and the analyst.

If an analyst catches this environment of crossed projective identifications and attributes those kinds of statements to the patient, as this analyst did, I hypothesize that the analyst was (unconsciously) displaying her own judgment about herself. An unspoken, but acted out idea underlies the report: "how pretty I am, presenting this pretty, emotion-stirring case to that pretty, distinguished supervisor." The choice of things, events or characters to be reported in clinical cases is under the sway of the analyst's unconscious system. When analysts write up clinical cases, they are taking a risk: mostly they write about themselves, albeit unwittingly (Bion, 1977, pp. 227–228).

Bion respectfully interrupts the report, looking for the analyst's agreement, and invites the audience to participate: "When she said that she had a dream, did you think that that was correct … Does it sound like a dream to you?" But the analyst flatly dismisses Bion's query. Nobody in the audience dares to speak. As a reader, forty years later, I suppose it was not a dream, but transformations in hallucinosis, obeying the rules for hallucinosis: serialised phantasies of superiority (Bion, 1965, pp. 133 & 144). The patient challenges the analyst's knowledge—"do you know … are you reminded"—by curiosity, arrogance, and stupidity (Bion, 1957). The analyst in turn needs to prove that she "knows everything" in order to keep her "status" as a "VIP." Bion renews his invitation, which again falls into the void, unchallenged by an irresponsible (?) or shy (?) audience.

Then the analyst constructs a rather long, complicated, and rationalized tale of pseudo-psychoanalytic innuendos. Bion interrupts again offering a chance to pay attention to empiric research: "She was lying on the couch? But she rose on her elbows?" The analyst answers affirmatively to both queries; Bion increases his observational pitch: "What do you think of that? What are you observing? Has anybody got any suggestion to make as to what we, as psychoanalysts, think we are going to observe?" But the analyst is eager to follow her course, building suspense worthy of a Hitchcock movie: "This dream is for me like a message"; the audience remains shy or unresponsive. The report now assumes a tone intended to prove the analyst's idea that the patient's illness is psychosomatic.

A participant, P1, interrupts. In an ambiguous tone, he or she suggests the presence of hallucination, based on the patient rising on her elbow. It seems to me that this participant wanted to show what he or she had "learned about Bion." At that time, many analysts were deeply impressed by Bion's descriptions of dealing with psychotic patients.

Bion interrupts with a series of comments about the analytic condition and posture—analysts must be "prepared for anything." In hindsight, I would add: supervisors too. He respects P1's comment but neither agrees nor disagrees. The analyst, who until now spoke very broken English, unexpectedly begins to speak Spanish. A translator comes to the fore. The analyst asks for Bion's opinion on her causal "psychosomatic" theory about the suppurating teratoma of her patient. Uttered as if it were a question, it displays her urge to obtain Bion's confirmation of her theory. Now the analyst dispenses with the services of the translator in her eagerness to prove her causal idea: "it started to suppurate." Resorting to two comparisons, Bion emphasizes the unavoidable drawbacks of using conversational language when making "scientific observations" of facts in the analytic setting: (i) Verbal forms in the English language can be compared with observations of the physical or material realm available to physicians, but in analysis, there are serious problems of communications caused by the use of technical terms: "We think there is a mind, or a character, or a personality"; (ii) As an alternative, Bion resorts to the model of authors—poets, playwrights, etc.—who can deal more successfully with words in order to depict transcendent, non-verbal aspects of the emotional states of humankind. He quotes Leonardo da Vinci's picture of the Virgin Mary, and verbal forms used by real authors, quoting characters in Shakespeare's plays, and also mentioning Cervantes. He does this in order to present the immaterial realm of psychoanalysis: Leonardo had never seen the Virgin Mary; no one "heard" Hamlet or Lady Macbeth; Cervantes did not touch Don Quixote. All of this is "like a dream," for artists are able to describe characters who remind the audience of someone they "already know"—so the audience, if made up of practising analysts, could recognise a given emotional experience or complex "constellations." Bion says:

> If you were a painter, then you could draw me a picture of this patient rising on her elbows ... Who's going to write a case history? Who's going to draw, or paint in words, the soul, or character of this person? So, although it seems to be relatively simple to bring a case history, to read it to us here, in fact, it is very difficult.

It seems that what Bion said next gives rise to one of many misunderstandings surrounding his work.

> I think that psychoanalysts will have to become artists, if they're going to tell somebody—like telling us here—what this experience was, that the analyst had with this character. I could put it another way: the thing that we are wanting to help has a body—there's a body attached to it—in the same way as I've got to live with hands attached to my mind ... We all learn that and we learn other things like: father figures and so on ... it becomes a commonplace, it becomes part of our language, but it's very

> doubtful whether those words and those theories help us to see this character.

Some among us overvalue one phrase at the expense of the rest, taking a part as if it were the whole.

Bion was not recommending anything[5], but some members of the psychoanalytic movement, already fascinated by artistic productions, enthroned concretely "artistic gifts" as if they were just what analysts needed. If self-attributed, it spells omnipotence. If attributed by the encircling social milieu, it spells idolization and shared hallucinosis. The concretized idea is that analysts should be artists, or writers, which fuels unanalysed omnipotent phantasies of the analyst. As far as I can see, Bion was just reminding us that body and mind are simply words: feeble models to approach an unreachable, ineffable, paradoxical reality, or the truth of the human mind's existence—material and psychic reality (Freud, 1900). Bion called it "Reality Sensuous and Psychic" in the same book in which he called for a "language of achievement" (Bion, 1970, pp. 26 & 125–126).

Then Bion firmly states the scientific, empirical status of psychoanalytical research:

> being there. That is one of the advantages of practical analysis; you actually don't have to depend on what you've been told about this patient ... You can actually see the person for yourself and this movement ... But note: that wasn't a dream. The patient was wide awake.

He dwells on many difficulties and needs when one is bound to make observations in the immaterial realm: the need to use our sensuous apparatus; to nourish a human respect towards patients who may misunderstand what we say:

> What shall we tell the patient? I don't think that we would regard it as wise to say to the patient: "You are hallucinating"! ... The best help the analyst can get, is not you, or me, not us, but the patient ... always ... it would be wrong to frighten the patient ... We lose our best friend for the analytic experience.

Was he warning the audience about not causing more pain to an already pained patient (Bion, 1963, p. 75)? The discharging of psychiatric labels by professionals—uttered or not—is a way to cause useless pain. Bion differentiates "hearsay" evidence from evidence derived from "being there"; talking *about* psychoanalysis from *being* or *becoming* an analyst.

Does the psychoanalytic establishment prefer the theoretician at the expense of the practising analyst? In supervision A36 one has, in a compact form, Bion's lifetime attempts to make explicit both limitations and possibilities of achieving psychoanalytic observations of the immaterial realm. Were his warnings heard? If not, it would not be surprising that fewer people look for analysis: the so-called "crisis of psychoanalysis."

I suggest two mutually exclusive hypotheses about supervision A36: (i) the analyst did not apprehend Bion's advice; (ii) she did apprehend it, albeit unconsciously, and attacked (hated) her own apprehension to the point of asking a question whose ethos runs contrary to what Bion said. For the analyst discharges a fully-fledged "psychosomatic theory" linking the teratoma with teeth, with no empirical evidence to back it up. Bion furnishes another technical, psychodynamic hint: he considers what the patient was telling the analyst—as distinct from what she overtly said:

> if the patient talks about the teratoma and the tooth, then she has related the tooth and the teratoma, because it is the same person who has brought these two ideas very close together ... after a time you begin to get the idea of what free-floating attention means ...

It seemed to me that the analyst was not listening to Bion, and the audience seemed not to accept Bion's renewed invitations.

Who may know now if the audience was apprehending what Bion said? In any case, Bion made another attempt to furnish a psychoanalytic vertex, fully considering the theoretical question put to him by the analyst. He emphasises the here-and-now, the reality of that specific session:

> taking the more theoretical point, would the suppuration actually have anything to do? I don't know, but one can guess that if the patient begins to talk to the analyst, it must be because she has got more relaxed, she is prepared to say things to the analyst, although the analyst is listening ... I don't see why thinking should be through the body; the body could be clenched up tight like that ... If they hadn't been tensed up tight all their life, they'd be familiar by this time with the fear that they were going mad. Most people

> have, at some time or another, been unaware of the fear that they are going mad, or that they would go mad, or that masturbation would cause them to go mad and so on ... millions of these theories ... if patients dare to have these theories, then it doesn't come as a great shock when they, suddenly, find that they're having them in analysis, as a result of analysis ... it's a part of analytic progress that the patient can dare to become worse and know it.

So Bion does not dismiss anything that the analyst says, but tries to use it psychoanalytically, bringing back common sense and the scientific ethos to the event, and as a consequence, showing that both must be part of any analytic session:

> I could relax enough for a suppuration to start ... . This, of course, is pure conjecture; it can't be regarded as scientific fact, but it may turn into scientific fact sometime ... *inspired guesses* ... But whether it is so, only time could tell.

Was Bion talking about intuition? One learns from experience—from one's errors—when one enjoys freedom to make imaginative or conjectural hypotheses, in stating untruth to the analyst in order to obtain approximations to truth (column 2 of The Grid; Bion, 1963): "By indirections find directions out."[6] The opposite situation would be the analyst hallucinating nonsensical serialised pseudo-theories, as distinct from making conjectures as a way to "pursue-truth-O" (Bion, 1970, p. 29):

> Of course, it's easy to say that analysis causes the teratoma to suppurate, but it isn't so, I don't think it is so ... It may be that the analysis makes it possible for the patient to be aware that there is a suppuration there, even to go to a surgeon for an operation.

Instead of breathing the rarefied air of pseudo-theorisation, the analyst may put his or her foot on firmer ground: "real analysis is real life" (Bion, 1977, p. 303). Is not analysis a procedure that allows one to make contact with reality as it is? Or "the whole of psychoanalysis [is] just a vast, towering Babel of paramnesias to fill the gap where our ignorance should be" (Bion, 1979, p. 540)? Visible in the sprouting of serialised pseudo-theories. Like any lie, it needs constant fixing.

Would it be timely, forty years later, to take a serious look at whether or not his warning was heard? Why is it that so few in the psychoanalytic movement remember that the term "unknown" is synonymous with "unconscious" (in Freud's German: *unbewußt*)? Too many would like to "understand" the unconscious, misreading Freud's maxim of dreams being "the royal road to a knowledge of the unconscious *activities of the mind*" (my emphasis) and misquoting it as "dreams are a royal road to a knowledge of the unconscious." In omitting a crucial part, they deny the ultimate unknowable ethos or "O" the origin (Bion, 1965, pp. 12–15, pp. 32–56; pp. 139–154; 1970, p. 26; Freud, 1900, p. 613; Sandler, 2005, p. 833). Bion's last warnings about this were written at the same time as supervision A36:

> The erudite can see that a description is by Freud, or Melanie Klein, but remain blind to the thing described. (Bion, 1975, p. 5)

> You heard that fellow Bion? Nobody has ever heard of him or of Psychoanalysis. He thinks it is real, but that his colleagues are engaged in an activity which is only a more or less ingenious manipulation of symbols. There is something in what he says. There is a failure to understand that any definition must deny a previous truth as well as carry an unsaturated component. (Bion, 1975, p. 92)

Notes

1. In approaching this supervision, I purposely avoided reading the whole transcript or listening to the tape in advance, so as to approximate as much as possible, the conditions experienced by the original audience. My thoughts were put onto paper as soon as they emerged. Apart from standard editing procedures, the comments were not changed afterwards. This methodology approximates Bion's own view of similar events (Bion, 1979, p. 577; 1958–1979, p. 377).
2. Gender, age, marital status, and profession.
3. The distinction that I am trying to draw between what is "told " and what is concretely "said" is the difference between what is more fully unconsciously conveyed of the **O** of the encounter ("told") *vs.* what is more rationally, consciously, and concretely communicated ("said"). The former is more complete and closer to being a "psychoanalytic object," while the latter is more restricted, a product of the secondary processes.

To "say" or to utter words, is nearer to the sensuous apparatus, to the external appearance, most times rationalized and disguised by the many mechanisms of defence of the ego. Conversely, to "tell" as for example, "to tell a tale," has the vector of O, the ultimate reality that must be intuited and used, but cannot be uttered or understood.

4. Hallucinosis: presence of hallucination in an otherwise in tact, non-psychotic personality.
5. On propaganda and psychoanalysis, see Bion, 1965, p. 36.
6. *Hamlet,* II i.

References

Bion, W. R. (1953). Notes on the theory of schizophrenia. In: *Second Thoughts* (pp. 23–35). London: Heinemann, 1967.

Bion, W. R. (1957). On arrogance. In: *Second Thoughts* (pp. 86–92). London: Heinemann, 1967.

Bion, W. R. (1959). 27 July 1959. In: *Cogitations*. London: Karnac, 1992.

Bion, W. R. (1962). *Learning from Experience.* London: Heinemann.

Bion, W. R. (1963). *Elements of Psychoanalysis.* London: Heinemann.

Bion, W. R. (1965) *Transformations.* London: Heinemann Medical.

Bion, W. R. (1967a) Notes on memory and desire. *The Psychoanalytic Forum,* 2: 3; also *Cogitations*, p. 392.

Bion, W. R. (1967b). Commentary. In: *Second Thoughts* (pp. 120–166). London: Heinemann, 1967.

Bion, W. R. (1970). *Attention and Interpretation.* London: Tavistock.

Bion, W. R. (1974). *Brazilian Lectures*. Rio de Janeiro: Imago.

Bion, W. R. (1975). *A Memoir of the Future.* Volume I: The Dream. Rio de Janeiro: Imago Editora.

Bion, W. R. (1976). How to make the best of a bad job. In: *Clinical Seminars and Four Papers* (pp. 247–257). Abingdon: Fleetwood Press, 1987.

Bion, W. R. (1977). *A Memoir of the Future,* Volume II: The past presented. Rio de Janeiro: Imago Editora.

Bion, W. R. (1979). *A Memoir of the Future* Volume III: The dawn of oblivion. Strathside: Clunie Press.

Freud, S. (1900). The interpretation of dreams. In: J. Strachey (Ed and Trans., with A. Strachey and Alan Tyson, in collaboration with A. Freud), *The Standard Edition of the Complete Psychological Works of Sigmund Freud,* SE 4–5 (pp. 7–622). London: Hogarth, 1958.

Freud, S. (1910). Leonardo da Vinci and a memory of his childhood. In: J. Strachey (Ed and Trans., with A. Strachey and Alan Tyson, in collaboration with A. Freud), *The Standard Edition of the Complete Psychological Works of Sigmund Freud,* SE 11 (pp. 59–108). London: Hogarth.

Freud, S. (1911). Two principles of mental funtioning. In: J. Strachey (Ed and Trans., with A. Strachey and Alan Tyson, in collaboration with A. Freud and A. Richards), *The Standard Edition of the Complete Psychological Works of Sigmund Freud,* SE 12 (pp. 213–226). London: Hogarth, 1958.

Freud, S. (1914). Remembering, repeating and working through. In: J. Strachey (Ed and Trans., with A. Strachey and Alan Tyson, in collaboration with A. Freud and A. Richards), *The Standard Edition of the Complete Psychological Works of Sigmund Freud,* SE 12 (pp. 145–156). London: Hogarth, 1958.

Freud, S. (1926). Inhibitions, symptoms, and anxiety. In: J. Strachey (Ed and Trans., with A. Strachey and Alan Tyson, in collaboration with A. Freud), *The Standard Edition of the Complete Psychological Works of Sigmund Freud,* SE 20 (pp. 77–178). London: Hogarth, 1958.

Freud, S. (1937). Constructions in analysis. In: J. Strachey (Ed and Trans., with A. Strachey and Alan Tyson, in collaboration with A. Freud), *The Standard Edition of the Complete Psychological Works of Sigmund Freud,* SE 23 (pp. 255–270). London: Hogarth, 1958.

Green, A. (1993). Two discussions of "the inner experiences of the analyst" and a response from Theodore Jacobs. *International Journal of Psychoanalysis, 74*: 1131–1136.

Sandler, P. C. (1997). The apprehension of psychic reality: extensions of Bion's theory of alpha function. *International Journal of Psychoanalysis 78*: 43.

Sandler, P. C. (2005). *The Language of Bion: A Dictionary of Concepts.* London: Karnac.

Sandler, P. C. (2011). *A Clinical Application of Bion's Concepts. Volume II: Analytic Function and the Function of the Analyst*. London: Karnac.

CHAPTER ELEVEN

Supervision D11

This supervision was conducted in Spanish and English in Brazil with a group of Argentine analysts. In the text that follows, A stands for Analyst; P1, P2, P3, P4, P5, and P6 stand for participants in the audience.

A: We want to tell to you some of our ideas that we're preparing for a paper which we're going to present in the next Pan-American Congress. It refers specifically to dreams: dreams and the actual practice of analysis. We should like to know your opinion and your ideas. To ask you some questions and also to know ... well, to know even the dreams of psychotic personalities, or neurotic personalities, even the difference between dreams and hallucinations and so on ...

Bion: Well, I will find it a very interesting discussion. I'm quite at your disposal whichever way you'd like to go, whatever you want to discuss. I'll say what I can about it, from my point of view.

A: We'll start with this fact ... Concerning sleep and dreams from the psycho-physiological point of view, there is R.E.M. (rapid eye movement) sleep and non-R.E.M. sleep, periods of sleep with dreams and periods of sleep without dreams.

Bion: Yes.

P1: Now, our idea was to introduce the understanding from the psychoanalytical point of view of new knowledge about the constancy of dreams during every night. The physiological facts are that for a normal eight hours of sleep, there is about two hours more or less of R.E.M. sleep. From that point of view, there may arise many new ideas. For instance, will this change our understanding of the dream work, and the creation of the dream images, the projection of the dream?

Bion: May I make observations as we go? The point that strikes me about this work is: that one is looking at it from outside and the findings of that investigation are from an external point of view or, as I put it, an external vertex: physiological, medical—whatever it may be—or psychoanalytic. So, I think that one needs to have a very clear idea in one's mind as to which the vertex is, from which this matter is discussed. I think that you make that perfectly clear there and then, the next point is: when you start investigating it psychoanalytically, because we don't know until we do that, what the facts that you're mentioning feel like to the infant or the adult, as the case may be, whichever way you're leading it, whether it's a child analysis or any other. Now, where I find a difficulty about this is that I see mostly adult patients, people who are well, twenty-five onwards and I'm quite used to statements that the patient is giving: that I am the breast or the mother, as the case may be and such and such … Now, I don't think I have much difficulty about that point when I make the interpretation. I have a great difficulty in explaining to you *why* I make it and this seems to me to be a big problem here, when you are communicating these findings to other people: the lateral communication, because you give a certain objectivity when you are dealing with this matter from the biological sense, in the way that you described. When it comes to the question of your psychoanalytic finding *that* I think is very difficult to pass on to other people. So the question of communication arises to give it to your colleagues.

P1: To make yourself understood or to convey the shades and meanings of a personal experience.

Bion: Well, let's take a crude example: a patient comes into the room and accuses you of being hostile, unfriendly, and all that. Now, an analyst might have no difficulty at all saying: this patient is very anxious. He could have no difficulty about that when confronted with the actual situation. He could actually also tell the patient that, and the patient could know what the analyst was talking about, because he was feeling it and he could disagree or he could agree. But, if you told somebody who had no analytic intuition, he may say: "Why do you say this?" The patient is angry, he was not anxious and you're at a deadlock. Now, one hopes that when it's a question of a psychoanalytic audience, then, they know what you are talking about. But, of course, you're talking about things which are much more sophisticated, and they may or may not follow you.

Do say if I'm not answering the question that you want to put.

A: No. I think it could be a starting point for some ideas ... There are different kinds of dreams, and then, to go back into the questions, to enter probably a few ideas about dreams and your last papers, because a certain kind of dream, the main function of which is to rid the psychic apparatus of accretion of affective contents, which are not tolerated by the dreamer's ego, given the intensive activity involved. We have called these dreams "*evacuated dreams*," because we believe that they are basically dreamt to discharge this context into inner or outer object containers.

Bion: This rather resembles a theory of Freud's, which he rejected. If you remember, in the *Interpretation of Dreams*, he talks about the evacuative function of dreams, as a theory, but then he rejected it.

A: Do you know why?

Bion: No! [lots of laughter at this point]

A: We asked ourselves the same question: why he rejected it.

Bion: Yes. I think that there are many of these theories, which Freud mentions and rejects, which we ought to treat like *free associations*, which patients reject. I don't think that one should regard the question as closed.

A: Yes.

P2: What are the differences between ejection and projection?

Bion: I think that I would say that *ejection* is less differentiated. It's just getting rid of it. I think *projection* has got a bit more direction to it, not quite. It's not the same thing as *projection into* an object, not quite like Melanie Klein means with *projective identification.* Put it to scale on this: it's undifferentiated. Here there's a sort of direction, there it's precise.

P3: So, do you think that dreams are projections, hallucinations? … When we dream are we projecting something or perhaps gathering up something from the inside and externalizing it as thought images?

Bion: I don't know, but, I think that it is very important to be in a state of mind where one can pick up as much as possible from the patient. Now, for example, a patient says to me: "I was in the bus and although I wasn't driving, I held out my arm to indicate that the driver was going to turn. My arm fell off and I saw it lying on the ground." Finished! No free associations, nothing more. Now, that dream, as I experienced being told, was, to me, a psychotic dream. Now, I still don't know how to describe the difference between that dream and another one, which a patient tells me—I don't know. I haven't got far enough. I've only got to a point where, being present when it is recited to me, it is a dream which is clearly differentiated in my mind, from the dream which a neurotic patient will ordinarily tell you. Now, there are bound to be lots of dreams between those two, which is much more difficult; but, even taking the dream which is markedly different, I do not know, still, how to describe that difference. I could describe it to the patient, I could say to the patient: "We have a dream but we can't make use of it, because it has no free associations, it has been mutilated, it is a useless dream, because it's got no free associations."

P4: This is why you said this is a psychotic dream?

Bion: No, no, it isn't. That is what I could tell the patient, because the patient was there and the patient knew what I was talking about.

P1: And why do you think it was a psychotic dream?

Bion: I can't tell you, I do not know. It hasn't evolved in my mind clearly enough.

P4: But, yet, in a way, you contradicted yourself in regard to what you said before, because, you managed to convey to us that it was an entirely psychotic dream; when you told us it.

Bion: Yes, but you have more experience. I'm talking to a sophisticated audience. Now, when you get these patients, I don't know who you are going to talk to. Some of them may understand you, but some of them won't.

A: Yes.

Bion: It is easier to put this over to somebody who's had that experience, like the patient, who knows what I'm talking about. Luckily the patient, being there, has a chance of knowing what I'm talking about, but when it comes to lateral communication, it depends whether people have had that experience or not. That's the trouble.

A: I remember in one of your papers you said that: when a psychotic patient speaks of having a dream, he thinks that his mental apparatus extends something from his mind, in a similar way that he can evacuate something from his bowels, and he's got a fantasy that his dream is an evacuation.

Bion: One gets into endless difficulties with this. When you say the unconscious mind, I find it difficult to know whether this is applicable to the psychotic patient or whether it's a correct intuition. I think it is a useful description for ourselves, because, one is falling back on the analogy of a neurotic patient. One's already in the state where one is having analogies of analogies, which is a terrible nuisance, and I think that one could probably put up with it, but I think that one has to bear this in mind if one's using one's analytic experience to provide an analogy for the psychotic patient—as it seems to be.

A: Yes.

Bion: I may mention that I don't know what a psychotic patient means, when they say they've had a dream. For example: this one that I've just recounted. The patient said that he had a dream: I don't know what he means.

P5: Can this happen to a neurotic patient too? That he, instead of speaking of a dream, he's speaking of a hallucination?

Bion: Yes, certainly. Certainly.

P5: Do you mean for us to make the difference?

Bion: You've got to make the difference in the analytic situation. Here we can only talk about it. There it is the *thing-in-it-self* and I think one hopes that one gets sufficiently sensitive to be able to feel that there's a difference. In the one sense, this sounds like the way that a neurotic patient talks: "I had a dream last night" and all about it, etc. But, in the other case, similarly, it is more disguised. But, I think I would pay great attention to the reaction which you feel to this question, as to whether hallucination is being masqueraded as a dream or what?

P5: But, in this case, the structure is the same in the dream and in the hallucination.

Bion: The structure is the same?

P5: The same!

P4: The structure of the dream, the phenomenon, the dream or the hallucination?

P5: It's the same phenomenon in the dream conditions and in the psychotic. If it is presented as a dream or it is presented as a hallucination, but the structure is the same.

Bion: They resemble each other and it's very difficult to discuss this point, because, in a dream, one could say: anything can happen. Therefore, any dream can resemble another. It becomes very difficult to say why you think they don't, why you say one dream is psychotic and the other one isn't. Now, when it comes to the question of structure, I don't know whether this has got anything to do with it or not, but a psychotic patient will say, from time to time, that they have an experience in which all the colors became very beautiful. They were in the country or something and there was this intense and pleasurable experience, where all the colors became very clear, very bright, very beautiful!! Now, something of this sort applies to the dream that I have just been recounting. It's very clear, even when the patient is telling you the dream; you will appreciate that it is very clear. He conveys to you something of the clarity of his own visual image. Now, with other patients when they tell you a dream, it somehow seems different … [At this point the microphone falls and some words were blocked out.]

Like in the patient I mentioned, I know the patient was traveling in a bus and so on, but it's something which one feels, it's got the sort of vague edge—that a dream has got. I can have a dream of that kind, I know that experience. But, this thing which is so sharp that the verbal transformation of a visual image which he's had, he's seen, comes over to you very clearly.

P4: But, I don't know if you've got, the question that Dr. X is asking right. Can we infer that basically, at the bottom, what has been projected as a dream, has the same structure as a hallucination? Is that the correct assumption? Is the basic stuff of the phenomenon the same?

A: Yes, especially considering the visual meaning.

Bion: Yes. Well, I think I did get the meaning and I was trying to get towards it, by this idea of the clarity and the brilliance of the color. I think it depends whether you manage: here's the psychotic, here's the neurotic, to go back to a point where they have common origin, if they've got one. Now, to take a somewhat obvious point, one would feel about the hallucination—anyway what you call the visual hallucination—that it's related definitely to the sense of sight. That tells one pretty well nothing, I'm afraid, but I think that there is a convergence there and I think it is furthermore related to omnipotence and if the infant can't get the breast. It can see the breast when it is away and it can take it into its eyes, if it can't take it into its mouth. Now, I think that it is legitimate to suppose that the ordinary person, if there is such a thing, knows the difference between the sort of wishful fulfillment and having the thing inside. Now, what's gone wrong? Is it the breast, or is it confusion with the eyes and the mouth? Where is the hallucination? Where does the mistake occur? It seems reasonable to say that the patient has taken it, the breast or the milk, anyway, through the eyes. We use that as an ordinary expression. In the ordinary way, a person says: "I'm talking metaphorically when I say I understand what you say: I *took in* what you have said" or "I *took in* the appearance of the girl I saw" or "I *took in* the breast." That's understood to be metaphorical. But when a psychotic patient says: "I *took in* the breast," he seems to think he did so.

P2: Somebody that has dreams thinks the same way.

P3: Has the conviction?

P2: Yes, I think so.

Bion: Yes, I suspect so.

P2: Somebody that dreams takes the object inside of himself. He sees a breast, he sees a girl, he takes the milk of the breast, the breast of the girl through his eyes inside of himself.

Bion: Yes and now …

P2: What do you think about this?

Bion: I think that you have to bear in mind that it might be *taking in* or *putting out*.

P2: Yes, that is the question! That is our question! Yes!

Bion: Now, I think you can only decide in the actual contact with the patient; that you hope to pick up some sensation which tells you which way this is going. I would like to be able to talk, some time, about the need for having some expression for *direction* which, I think, we very much lack in psychoanalytic talk; because, it makes a great deal of difference to an association, or an interpretation, as to which *direction* that is traveling in.

A: This is the topic of our problem, of our paper.

P1: One of the main topics.

A: I will follow with this question: in a hallucination and in the dream, the object is not outside, to be *taken in* (i.e., the breast is absent). It's necessary to have been there previously (i.e., memory of past good feed) in order to *put it out* (in the form of a dream image or hallucination).

Bion: That can, I think, be done. I think that if you want to know what your hand is, you can shove it in your mouth and find out, more or less, and then you can take it out and look at it, so that you can bring to bear two senses: the tactile sense and the visual sense—you get a binocular vision. One can put it like that: a bi-sensuous vision, which gives you a certain depth, perspective.

P2: Reality.

Bion: Reality, yes. I think that that is another question. I think …

P1: It's mono-focal …

Bion: Yes, I think so. The peculiarity of this is: there's actually a science which is mono-sensual—that's *astronomy*. The whole of it cannot be validated by any other sense, apparently. It is all by direct vision, or by photograph and so forth … the whole basis of it lies on mono-sensual appreciation. I don't know whether that's of any significance, but I think that it makes one think about the validity of the astronomical discoveries, which everybody accepts as being scientifically sound. I don't see any reason to doubt them either. But, on this question of the dream and the patient saying they've had a dream, I would like to be able to know what he means. For one thing: let's take the psychotic patient, that I'm talking about, he has learned that I call certain things *dreams*. So, to keep me quiet, he says he had a dream. His contact with me is good enough to tell him that I would probably think it was a dream. But, he may know quite differently; he may know that his arm was lying there on the grass and he could see it.

A: Perhaps you can say, for instance, that there's a constipation and when he speaks of having a dream, he's evacuating some material that he's been taking in before, in waking hours, or asleep and that the first function of the dream is to put out this material, that he has taken in before.

Bion: Well, again, I'm sorry but I have to say: I don't know, because, I think that that question in any instance could only be answered by a psychoanalyst in the session. Now, if you take the dream that I have mentioned, I believe that that is what the patient saw, when he was telling me. I don't think it was the previous night, or anything else. I would think it is *present*. Now, the question would be … well, I'll give a tentative answer, namely: the patient felt that I was wrong in my interpretation. If he tried to put me right, he would be castrated. Now, that is an analogy—it's an analogy from neurosis. It is different from what one would say would happen with a neurotic patient. To start off with: this is a statement that the patient saw this and was seeing it while he said it—in full waking life! Well, if that is true, why didn't he tell me that he wouldn't dare to put me right because he'd be afraid of being mutilated or attacked? But, he didn't say that; he presented me with a verbal transformation of a visual image.

P2: Would this be one of the most important facts: the transformation to visual images?

Bion: In this particular instance and in what the patient has called a dream, but which I think is a way of making it fit in with my sort of ideas: he dreamt it, he dreamt it last night. No, he saw it that moment at that time, when he was with me in broad daylight!! But, it is very difficult to show that there are two quite different sets of ideas about the fact, because he knows that I'm in the consulting room with him and, presumably, I have my ideas of what's going on and he has his ideas and that's what he saw—only in the same way as the neurotic patient has an experience, one doesn't know what—he has a dream and he verbalizes this thing and then says he has a dream. After all, the reported dream is really a *free association* of the experience that the patient has—what that was, only goodness knows! Neither he, nor any of us, will ever know! Because, when he formulates the dream he's already awake and when he repeats it, it is always some hours later. Now, what this patient has done is really attempted the transformation in the opposite direction. He has seen this occur in the session and is on the way to turning it into a dream last night, which makes it more the kind of thing that I would like to hear—that's my theory. So, one could say about that: if that is correct, it has got something to do with *direction*, it is going in the opposite direction. It is manufacturing a dream out of what? Hallucination? What are you going to call it? One doesn't know what happens when he goes to sleep and so forth ... but, really, one doesn't know what happens when he's awake, because one can't see this. I couldn't see him putting out his arm and it dropping off and so on ... but, he could. One could put it this way, perhaps: it's by way of being secondary elaboration, in the daylight before your eyes, whereas in the neurotic dream, one hopes to interpret the latent content, starting with the manifest one. But this one is the process of transforming a hallucination into a dream and getting rid of it—into the previous night, getting distance.

P5: From the clinical point of view, it's important to make the difference between a *real dream* or a *hallucination.*

Bion: I expect so. But the question is: when and how? That is why my interpretation simply was: "This dream in which you lose a part of your body—which was very important for telling me something—is itself a dream which has lost its free association. So, you can't tell me anything by this and I can't understand anything."

P1: In this case the loss of the free association is connected with the loss of the secondary process? Lack of integration of the ...

Bion: I wouldn't say the loss of it. I would say that it hadn't happened yet.

A: Not the integration?

Bion: No. If it was a neurotic, then, you could say; it's a loss, it's a loss of integration. But, this one is more ... I think that it hasn't happened yet. He is having a secondary process in front of him, but he hasn't *had it*. Indeed; if one gives an interpretation, in my experience, the probability is at first, at any rate, that the interpretation is used as a secondary process by you.

A: But you can speak of different kinds of dreams, as you can speak of different kinds of hallucinations and it depends on the content ... there are more aggressive kind of dreams, more primitive. Dreams in contrast with more elaborated dreams and the latter often occur after a lot of work has been done in the analysis.

Bion: You are probably referring to a relatively integrated patient, aren't you?

A: Yes, integrated.

Bion: Yes. Now I think that one could say that.

A: You can see the difference when he brings the dream and the contents: the manifest content and latent content.

Bion: I think because his degree of integration makes it possible to have dreams and when he reports a dream it's a pretty good description of what he experienced. It's the kind of thing that other people could understand.

P4: If we understand correctly more different categories of dreams A, B, C, D—a sort of ranking—and that Dr. Bion is not so much keen on the idea of a specific ranking or types of dreams.

A: No, no I'm not speaking about ranking dreams but of different kinds of … let's say, more regressive or more psychotic dreams and more developed, more integrated dreams—if we can put it like that. That means for instance … I think now, I'm wondering whether this kind of dream, that we call a dream, maybe they are not dreams. Maybe they are a kind of hallucination, a kind of phenomenon, that the patient dreams at that moment, like a colorless picture.

Bion: I still think that this has to be determined in the contact with the patient.

P1: In the contact!

Bion: At present, because our means of lateral communication are so bad, whereas the communication with the patient, are far better! So that, I think that you would be able probably to distinguish this point with much greater certainty in the consulting room. Whether you would persuade anybody else or not, I don't know, because, I think people hate it so much, they can always argue against you! But, I think that when you've had the experience in the room, it carries a conviction which is unmistakable and whether other people can grasp the point or not, does not help it. You can only repeat it and hope for the best.

P2: That conviction can be true. But can it be in error, also?

Bion: Unfortunately, yes! I think that one is dogged by that. I think that this point is not appreciated. That the psychoanalyst in order to be a psychoanalyst has really got to get to a stage where he can put up with ignorance, half truth, mysteries, and so forth ... This Language of Achievement that I was talking about which Keats describes, I think that it is one of the striking things about Freud's life, that he was haunted by the feeling that the whole thing was a failure and some kind of misreading of the facts that he's misperceiving everything. I don't remember where, but perhaps you remember the time where he speaks about his doubts getting to an intensity, where he feels inclined to throw the whole thing over. Well, he doesn't, he goes on. I think that the only thing that could substantiate him with that would be the internal consistency of his system. I don't think that he could get any reassurance from outside. Now, I think every psychoanalyst is in that position, because while you've got a big volume of experience, which is shared, you haven't got any experience, at all, with that patient, the one that you're actually dealing with. So that every actual analytic session is fundamentally a frightening position in which the facts are not available to you, reassurance is not there. Again, I'd say, you can get a little bit ... a sort of assistance from the patient, but you needn't get even that from the patient because maybe he's quite disturbed.

A: Well, that answers the first question that Dr. X tells us: that you can make the distinction between a more regressive dream and a more integrated dream, in the consulting room. I agree with that. It's in the emotional experience, in a direct emotional experience with the patient. Is it possible to say that the patient, at that moment, has a dream, or a kind of hallucination with regressive elements with part objects and, in another occasion, in another session, another patient, a more integrated patient, brings a dream with more ... it is nearer to the present position, that say, with more total objects, more integrated elements? Is it possible to make a distinction between these different kinds, or categories, of dreams?

Bion: Well, I think it is. I think it is in the consulting room and in the contact with the patient. I don't know how far it is possible to make the distinction in such a way. For example: you can convey that distinction to us, but can you make the distinction in such a way that you can convey it to an international Congress, even of psychoanalysis. I think that's a very different, a very difficult proposition! But, I think that you can make this differentiation, although it requires a very great deal of discipline. I think that the analyst not only has to go through this terrible lengthy procedure thing, the present time of being analyzed. But, after that, his troubles start and this is the kind of trouble, as I've said before, that makes this job worthwhile. It's a *tough job*; it can't be done by anybody. There are people who distinguish themselves at warfare and all sorts of fields, but they can't do analysis … because it's *too tough*. Once you enter into the canvas of mind, you enter into something, which is extremely alarming and this question depends on some sort of discipline, it depends on your having the good fortune to have the right patient and it really depends on your fortitude. Analysis only takes you some of the way, it clears up some of your obsessions and so on … But, after that, it brings in this whole question of whether the analyst can be tough enough to stand what is, fundamentally, about as big a strain as you've been subjected to.

A: I'm sorry I missed the last point.

Bion: It depends on whether the analyst can be tough enough to stand almost the biggest strain to which you can be subjected. Here, for example: everything is ordinary, life goes on, people do these various things and you go straight from your consulting room to the everyday world and there's an enormous gap. The domain of the mind, where you are dealing with matters of this kind, is a matter of reality; it's a psychoanalyst's reality. To bring that into relationship with the things that you have to do the moment you leave the room is quite difficult. You don't think it's certain to speak about qualities of regression in this case. To become … Well, I don't know. Well, I'll say what my difficulty is when I say to the patient: "You are feeling that I am the breast and the analysis is a kind of meal," etc. This is really using a primitive analogy, because the patient isn't at the breast, he's not having a meal, he is having what one calls an ordinary conversation. But, thanks to that analogy I can say it is as if you were doing this. Now, when you start on the subject that we're talking about, you have to use *the analogy of an analogy* and it is very difficult to know what this is. For example, *regression* has now become—for us here—something that is like talking about the breast. It's much more abstract. It is really a theory. It is a theoretical concept, which *we* have to use as if it were as concrete as the statement: "the breast." Now, the question there is: is this a good word to use? Or, will people think you are talking about something or other that Freud said in 1911? That's the trouble. Because, I don't think you are using *regression* in this way. You are using an old term to express a new concept. Now the question is: will that term, will that expression hold it?

[Melanie Klein] admitted to me in a conversation that regression was a bad term and so it is.[1] You can't do anything with it, you can't say: "I object to be identified as X." There's no grammatical future for it, it's a bad word and she always regretted it and of course, it's too late to alter it. If she had the luck, she'd have found perhaps a better term, I don't know. Because, with all its defects, it begins to have the meaning to some people, which it is intended to have. Now, this is your problem here: are you going to use this term? Now, are you sure that it hasn't got such a number of associations that it will not express what you want to express, but, will obscure it? It's very difficult to know what language will work and what language will do.

As psychoanalysts trying to use words, we are in a position of people like Galileo who had to invent and make a telescope before he could see anything. We have to make a language with which to do our job, whether it is talking to a patient, or whether it is communicating to each other and this is the trouble here. You've got this job, which you've set yourself about dreams and so on, but you have also to make the language to fit it.

P4: Sorry, but I think we might have been making the wrong questions to you, not in form, but in framing them, because I felt ill at ease with this dialogue somehow. Now it struck me, when I heard you answer that ... it seems to me that you found more difficulty actually in the experience of communicating with others and of conveying the precise meaning that is always the use that comes, than the actual experience with the patient. Because, as you said at the beginning, when the patient is there with an emotional experience with you, some kind of problems, are less difficult.

Bion: I would certainly agree. I would say that paradoxically it is easier to communicate this to the patient, than it is to put it into the language of communication for other analysts.

P1: Yes.

P4: My feeling is that you are being overly cautious with us, with a fear that we are not going to understand your meaning as it is meant.

Bion: Well, I'm sorry if you got that impression, because I don't feel like it. I feel, on the contrary, at greater ease in putting these things over to you, than I would to another audience, in the psychiatric field, in which I would be—and I am, in fact—in trouble, because I use a language which they all think they understand … Now, I haven't had that feeling. I get much more the feeling that I can use ordinary conversational phrases and so forth … and you know what I'm talking about. But, I dare say that I give you the impression I can't … I would like to deny what you're saying about it, but it is not. In fact, I expect to be understood here more, than I usually expect.

P4: Maybe we are taken by your first reactions, you said: "I don't know and then …" [a burst of laughter at this point]

Bion: Erh … yes! Because … well, frankly, I think that's the right answer. I don't like it much, I don't like feeling that. But I truly don't know.

P4: But I think that we all share that basic assumption that we don't know … that this is something that may have some parallel with what's actually taking place.

Bion: One's got to get involved, to make an attempt, sometimes, to say something, even at the risk of being premature and wrong.

A: Will you give us, then, some tentative explanation, even if it is not still certain, about your present idea of *regression*, about the new cause of regression?

Bion: I would say that when I feel the patient is regressive, if I were to discuss it as I'm discussing it here, I can't—not with the patient—I would say what is involved is: what is the patient saying and why is he using it? Now, supposing the answer to that is: he's using it for the purpose of *regression*. I'd want to know why. Now, I've come across the situation in which the patient is perfectly conscious about certain things about myself, which he's afraid of, which in fact, he regards as being his fault. Now, he avoids mentioning them, because he could only get a confirmation, or perhaps, one could say he avoids *not* mentioning them, because then it would be dealt with. So, what he does, sounds very purposive, but, of course, it isn't. If he regresses to a level in which he can say the same thing, but he has the privileges of a patient … Now that is only one use of regression and when you get this happening I think that the important thing to know is: what is the outside event? What is the stimulation here, which leads psychopathology and the unconscious to be preferable to the conscious? Now, it is this kind of thing, which I think, really, needs to be investigated with regard to regression. The moment you feel that the patient has launched on that kind of progress: Why?

P4: The dynamic of the regression!

Bion: Yes, yes! Whether there's anything in the situation, which could reveal why that is the case and why he is going back to a state of mind, which one would think would be particularly suitable for what he's got to do the moment he walks out of the consulting room.

P1: Well, this is the problem especially in connection with dreams.

Bion: Well, I think that if you get that kind of dream, it is certainly a problem which you've got.

P1: But in general, evidently, if the possibility is to solve the situation with all the intelligence possible, then the dream gives the possibility for the expression, in that patient, or for the disintegration.

Bion: Well, to my mind, it depends on what was dreamed, because, to go back to what I was saying, I think that the patient was trying to go through the *secondary process* with me out of something which was really *primary:* his way of seeing the session. In point of fact, that patient, after a time, began to have dreams, which had faces. It took a long time, it took ... oh, I don't know, over a year, anyway, to get to that state. But, what one was doing there, or what I was attempting to do was draw attention to what was going on in the consulting room and try to elucidate this process, which, then, seemed to have the effect of leading him to have dreams. Now, I take it that when you are talking about a patient who is sufficiently integrated to have what we ordinarily call a dream and which would be susceptible to interpretation and so forth ... Now, all that seems to me to be in a particular direction—you needn't worry about that—but, the problem is: have you got patients who are doing the same process, but are starting much earlier? Starting where the capacity for *secondary process* and so forth ... hasn't been developed and is part of the therapeutic process.

A: To integrate?

Bion: Well, whatever it is ... I, again, have a difficulty, because I think that one has got to observe this business and try to make up one's mind about how somebody reasons. Let me put it this way: the patient has some alarming experience and so forth ... it's not mentioned in the analytic session, but the patient has a dream and then you're able to interpret that dream, and it goes back to this alarming experience, which he already had. Now, the process that I'm drawing attention to, is the process in which, the patient has the alarming experience *in the room* and then, in the room goes through the whole process which the other patient has done between the time of the session and when he slept that night—he can do that. But, the patient that I'm talking about can't. He has the alarming experience in the session and he has to develop—thanks to analysis—a capacity for the *secondary process*, which *then* enables him to have a dream. Of course, one very big difficulty is: when you have—if you are fortunate enough to reconstitute his capacity for having dreams—he has such terrifying dreams that he finds them difficult to tolerate.

P5: Now, going back to the common answer about regression, don't you think it's important to investigate the phenomenon that produces the convulsions between the patient and the analyst? What precipitates it?

Bion: Yes, absolutely, absolutely.

P5: Is there something you could say about what happens to the analyst, in order that the patient could again make a regression, in the session?

Bion: I think it is difficult, because it is so individual with the analyst, it is hard to say how much responsibility the analyst faces. It's obvious that one could do analysis so badly, that the patient hadn't got any choice except to regress. But I'm rather skeptical about that. I really find it difficult to believe that one could talk to somebody in such a way, that they haven't got any choice except to regress. One assumes that one could do analysis badly, as well as one could do it well, but I'm very doubtful about the contribution being of that major order. I think it is true to say that there is a difficulty, because you give an interpretation, which is really drawing attention to states of mind which belong to regression—they belong to states of mind in which the patient would regress. But, they are given when the patient hasn't regressed. Now, why should a patient, one patient, profit by that, to be able to discard these methods of thinking and so forth … which are no longer any use and another patient uses the interpretation to get back to them and stay there? For example: if the patient has fears of the analyst, fears that he will be swallowed up, fears that the analyst's inside, fears of the analyst's vagina and so forth … then, I think that one would say: "You are frightened of psychoanalysis and there must be some reason why you are frightened of it—why you are afraid of going into a state of mind from which you cannot escape." It's too often covered by phrases like: *negative therapeutic reaction*. Then, it's too late!! In the actual session, when you get a constant repetition of this sort of material, I think it is time to be alarmed.

P5: When there is a regression in the analytic process, then everything can become confused?

Bion: Not what an analyst would call regression, because I think that one should preserve that term for a pathological process and I think that in my experience, when I've had the misfortune of having a patient who regresses, I've had a terrible time to get out of it again, or get him out of it. So, I do feel that this is a great defect, I think it is a great difficulty, because unless one deals with these things, the patient can never get cured. You can't reform it. So, you haven't got an easy way out of this, you've still got to get these interpretations, but the problem is: what use will the patient put those interpretations to? And I think that one would like to be able, at a fairly early state, to draw attention to the use, which the patient is making of the analysis. He isn't forced to use analysis in order to get better. He can use it to get what we are accustomed to call analysis. I can draw attention to the fact that the patient, he's feeding at the breast. Well, but then, the patient promptly behaves as if he were. This is a misuse of the interpretation. That's not the analyst's intention.

P4: I want to find out about the level of regression … I was thinking of something that might be, in a way, the opposite. Namely, I have in mind a very fascinating dream a patient had, a very rich dream, which I feel was dreamt in order to convey something of an order of complexity that, otherwise, could not have been said. So far, we have spoken about very primitive regressive psychotic backward movements. Take the example of a very sensitive person, who is trying to convey something that's very painful, but very complicated and that … Do you want me to tell you the dream? It's a very fascinating dream. It's a man who is inside one room where he links up with radioactive material. There are those arms that move objects that are radioactive, which you put an arm inside the arm to get inside there and through a spy glass—we call it "the ocular way"—like in boats but … the name is: "the eye of the bull," that is the name for it.

Bion: Yes.

P4: He sees through that from outside, like … a mask of death and he feels, as a free association, "born by the crowd." There is a part where the crowd is dreaming dreams of the devil, but he says: "If the devil had a dream, it would be the dream in which the breast is good" so that …

Bion: This was part of the dream?

P4: No, a free association. So, here you have a dream where there is the eye of the devil outside looking at him, but having dreams which … because he's the devil and has to be good, which are being seen through the eye of the bull, an ox, by being an ox, probably, are dreams of potency … [Many people speak together which blurs the sound.] So, you see the complication: there is a mechanical eye having good dreams outside, in the middle of the eye of the ox, having a dream and himself.

Well, it's such a complicated structure, but it's fascinating. Maybe he was trying to lure me into a merry-go-round, but maybe not. I wonder if such material cannot be expressed in any other way, but only with a dream. Maybe, as you said, I failed to convey my conviction.

P1: With whom?

P4: With the patient. When the patient told a dream, I felt it was very significant.

Bion: Yes. I'm not sure that I got the problem that you are posing.

P4: That the logical structure of the thing that he was trying to say was of such enormous complexity, that it was very difficult to put it in other words, in other ways, but could only be expressed in this very significant dream.

Bion: That, I think, is the important point. That your experience is the corroboration. Then, the dream itself has got the quality in which you can feel that it is communicative. I can put the problem more widely this way: when patients are free associating, telling their dreams and all that, are they doing that because it is the shortest and quickest and clearest way to put it, or because it is the most complicated, the most difficult, the most open to misinterpretation? What is the point? I think that you get it in literature, because there's no merit in obscure poetry, or obscure language. The only point that's important there is whether the poet or writer is expressing himself in the clearest possible language known to him, which may happen to be obscure, or whether it is just to hide something in front of the reader. I think that what you've just described sounds to me like the corroborative dream. Therefore, when he wishes to tell you something which can't easily be conveyed verbally, then I think that he resorts to a visual impression and a transformation of the visual impression into words, so that you get a verbal communication, admittedly but, it is a good transformation of a visual impression. The visual impression, in turn, is the clearest way in which he can communicate with you—since you can't be there and you can't have a dream. So, I think that your interpretation of this dream now becomes very important. You can be reasonably sure that you're not wasting your time on a befuddling sort of dream, the befuddling communication.

You're spending time on somebody who's trying to tell you something. So, I think that that itself gives you a classification, if you want it. I don't know how you classify it … like myself trying to use this grid and so forth. But, I think you've got to invent your own way. You've got to produce an arrangement of this kind, in which you classify this dream, classify others, have a look at them and then see if you can produce a grid, which would take in a number of these different things.

P6: Regarding the grid, where would you put this thing?

Bion: Well, C category and probably four, C4. Because, I think that this dream—as I gather it, from your account of it—has got a direction, it has got a tension. It has got direction towards some object. It's not just a notation. It's not just a record of an experience, it's more than that. It's forward looking and it belongs to this primitive kind. Now, what category do you want your interpretation to be in? This point I ask, because I don't believe that it is helpful to think of these things in terms of: "Oh, yes, those are free associations, that's a dream, this is the interpretation." I think that's nonsense. But, I think that there may be more in saying: this is the category of the dream and the category of the interpretation ought to be somewhere around here. So that the distance between the two is not too great; or to put it in other terms, enough to produce bi-focal vision, bi-intuitive vision, not say … mono-analytical.

P4: I told the patient something like: I felt that it was a very rich dream—I'll explain why—and that he might be afraid that whatever I might say could be turned wrong—following this idea that the crowd has good dreams. But stating first that I was taking his dreams and make sense of his material.

P4: I wondered after I said that, if I was perhaps acting something out because my comments seemed to reassure him.

Bion: I'm not adverse to that; on the contrary I think it ought to be done. I think that sometimes I would say to a patient: "You may think that this is a reassurance; it's not my intention, but I need to tell you what I'm going to say, because you must know it." Now, in my opinion, this is a compact and communicative dream. I think it is only right that the patient should be told that. If you've got the evidence supporting that,

I think that you should say so. But, you can repeat that it isn't your intention to reassure them, although they'll probably be reassured. The reassurance is a sort of accidental cure, it's not one's intention. But the fact remains that an interpretation of that kind is reassuring and I don't see any harm in drawing attention to that fact. It's not one's intention, but it so happens that it is so. What one is really trying to draw attention to is the peculiarity of this statement and the peculiarity of it is: that it communicates. Now, there is a reason for this too, I think, because in asking really, or telling him in one's action, one is acting on a theory that it is somehow worthwhile to bring reason to bear. Well, now, if that is right about frightening things, I don't think that this should be excluded by something, which isn't frightening. Your patient may well be frightened of having dreams at all. It is, therefore, as important for him to know that it's a frightening dream and has a frightening meaning and so forth ... as important as that to know that this dream is not frightening, except before he had it. It's taken him many years before he had that dream and told you. So, you can draw attention to that fact that it must have been a very frightening dream. It's taken him all these years before he's dared to have it. But, when he has had it, then I think it's important to show him that they've got these qualities—if you think so—and a dream with qualities of that kind has taken many years before the patient gets enough courage to have it.

A: Well, our time is up. Thank you very much!

Note

1. This attribution to Klein is not certain as this part of the tape was not clear. However, from the context of the discussion, the previous comments made by Bion and the participants, the fact that the Argentine analysts seem to have been writing a classical Kleinian oriented paper about dreams and Bion's having been in analysis with Klein, the editors are making a presumptive conjecture that the subject of this sentence was in fact Mrs. Klein.

Supervision D11 commentary

Renato Trachtenberg

In my comments, I hope to convey the stimulating character of this interesting supervision and describe some of the thoughts that spontaneously occurred to me "without any irritable reaching after fact and reason." I will then expand upon them with reference to other texts, seminars, and conferences by Bion. Finally I will make some observations, which hopefully may extend the discussion of the themes addressed in the supervision. Obviously, I make a choice when selecting only what appealed most to my attention, "a non-pathological splitting," as Bion would have it.

From the description of the dream that Bion recounts and the fact that he mentioned the same dream in two other supervisions that took place in Brazil in a particular year, I assume that this session occurred in 1973. The group seems most interested in discussing some points in the theory of dreams with Bion in preparation for the paper that they are hoping to write for an upcoming FEPAL Congress. To this extent, they seem more concerned with issues around knowledge *about* psychoanalysis, rather than with the experience that might be emerging within the group, because from the outset they ask questions in search of answers. These questions deal with dreams of psychotic and neurotic personalities and the difference between dreams and hallucinations. They seem to want to make sure that the theories they propose, based on ideas by Bion, are correct. Questions such as "Do you know why? You know why?!" are repeated, provoking laughter among the participants. They bring neurophysiological research about dreams, including statistics:

> The facts are: for a normal eight hours of sleep, two hours more or less. From that point of view, there is a lot of new ideas. For instance: every dream of the night … in such a way that almost fifty percent of the dream to as much as eighty percent …

Bion's response is to begin to talk about the concept of vertex, pointing to the presence of a psychophysiological–biological–medical vertex concerning dreams. He also calls it an *external* vertex. According to him, communication from this vertex is objective, in contrast with the psychoanalytical vertex, where it is extremely difficult to communicate findings to other people. This difference between vertices becomes one of the central themes of this interview/supervision. There is a caesura between them, making it difficult for the group to cross from one to the other, in spite of Bion's efforts to facilitate this crossing.

Bion gives as an example the dream of a patient, which seems to me an attempt to provide clinical material in view of the many theoretical questions of the group. That is, an attempt to lead the interview towards a supervision or at least a more psychoanalytic vertex. The dream goes as follows: "I was in the bus and although I wasn't driving, I held out my arm to indicate that the driver was going to turn. My arm fell off and I saw it lying on the ground." Bion says there were no associations and that, in the way he experienced it as it was told him, it was a psychotic dream. He says he isn't able to describe the difference between this particular dream and any other told by another patient:

> I don't know. I haven't got far enough. I've only got to a point where, being present when it is recited to me, it is a dream which is clearly differentiated in my mind, from the dream which a neurotic patient will ordinarily tell you … . but, even taking the dream which is markedly different, I do not know, still, how to describe that difference. I could describe it to the patient, I could say to the patient: "We have a dream but we can't make use of it, because it has no free associations, it has been mutilated, it is a useless dream, because it's got no free associations".

The group asks: "Why do you think it was a psychotic dream?" Bion replies that he can't tell, that he doesn't know: "It hasn't evolved in my mind clearly enough."

At this moment, someone points out a contradiction in Bion's speech, for prior to narrating the dream he had said it was entirely psychotic. Bion replies:

> Yes, but you have more experience. I'm talking to a sophisticated audience. Now, when you get these patients, I don't know who you are going to talk to; some of them may understand you, but some of them won't ... It is easier to put this over to somebody who's had that experience; therefore, like the patient, knows what I'm talking about; luckily the patient, being there, has a chance of knowing what I'm talking about and when it comes to lateral communication, it depends whether people have had that experience or not—that's the trouble.

Next, a question is asked: "Do you mean for us to make the difference?" Bion insists that the difference must be detected in the analytical situation:

> Here we can only talk about it; *there* it is the *thing-in-it-self* and I think one hopes that one gets sufficiently sensitive to be able to feel that there's a difference in the one sense, that this sounds like the way that a neurotic patient talks: "I had a dream last night" and all about it, etc ... It becomes very difficult to say why you think they don't, why you say one dream is psychotic and the other one isn't.

Confronted with the issue as to whether it is important under the clinical point of view to differentiate between real dream and hallucination, Bion comments it is, but the issue lies in when and how. That's why, he says, his interpretation had simply been:

> This dream in which you lose a part of your body—which was very important for telling me something—is itself a dream which has lost its free association. So, you can't tell me anything by this and I can't understand anything.

However, Bion stresses once more, this must be determined at the contact with the patient and in the present:

> I think that when you've had the experience in the room, it carries a conviction which is unmistakable and whether other people can grasp the point or not, one does not help it. You can only repeat it and hope for the best ... I don't know how far it is possible to make the distinction in such a way; for example: that you can convey it to us and how far you can make the distinction in such a way that you can convey it to an International Congress even of psychoanalysts ... we are in a position of people like Galileo who had to invent and make a telescope before he could see anything. We have to make a language with which to do our job, whether it is talking to a patient, or whether it is communicating to each other and this is the trouble here. You've got this job which you've set yourself about dreams and so on, but you have also to make the language to fit it. ... I would say that paradoxically it is easier to put this over to the patient, than it is to put it into language of communication.

As may be noted, Bion is talking about the difficulties in communicating when the vertex is psychoanalytical. The group, however, in seeking quickly to find a transformation into K, somehow once more places itself closer to what Bion referred to as the external vertex. Later, Bion will claim more emphatically the uselessness and even the language distortions of trying to employ words such as psychotic or neurotic, restraining the field of psychoanalysis as a thing-in-itself with the intention of achieving communication among colleagues. This point seems very relevant during this discussion.

In a previous supervision (Junqueira de Mattos, 1992) where Bion also mentions and uses the dream of the severed arm, he develops very similar reflections about the difficulty making interpretations in the absence of free associations:

> It has no dimension, none of the qualities that make it eligible for analytical interpretation ... Thus, when the patient has what he calls a dream, I think the analyst needs to be someone who doesn't care about this thing he calls a dream, but who can decide for himself

> whether it is really a dream or not ... We may think this is a psychic reality, or a psychic fact, but for the patient it is a fact and it is all, a simple fact ... It doesn't matter whether it has happened while he was supposedly asleep or supposedly awake—there are no free associations. So, under the analytical point of view, there's no use for this weird dream. (Junqueira de Mattos, 1992, pp. 450–451)

Going back to the language issue, Bion says he wouldn't call "it" a dream, delusion or hallucination:

> Very well! What could I call it then? I don't know. I don't know what I should call it, because I don't think there is a name. This is a difficulty we have as psychoanalysts, having to invent the language to be spoken as we progress. (Junqueira de Mattos, 1992, p. 451)

Here he again refers to Galileo We may therefore paraphrase Antonio Machado: "Speaker, there is no language, the language is made by speaking." Bion notes that language was invented as much to disorient and defeat enemies as to communicate with friends. It is very hard to use the same language, which is well-adapted to lie, to deceive, to elude, for the purpose of approaching the truth.

One might feel it somewhat strange to claim that the lack of free associations serves as a reason to not deepen the interpretation of a dream. Bion doesn't furnish details about the session's context, what came up before, etc. However, the dream itself (in Bion's own association/interpretation) seems to indicate something which is happening within the group: the "impressive" caesura (fallen arm) that responds to every attempt to change the interviews direction towards a supervision. As I understand Bion, the group itself doesn't make free associations (internal vertex). The group wants answers (external vertex).

In 1973, at the third Brazilian Lectures, Bion mentions the same dream and speaks of similar problems. Here, however, he introduces a subtle difference. The lack of free associations is not the core of the problem. He says that when a patient tells him he had a dream, he may think it isn't a dream as it does not entail free associations. That, he says, may be a wrong perception. The patient may be able to have a concrete dream, exactly as he may see that a concrete pair of socks is a series of holes that have been knit together. Why shouldn't a patient have the same experience regardless if asleep or awake? Bion says that he might think there is a difference, because they would be different experiences for him, Bion. Not for the patient—the events are the same in both states:

> Freud gets near to this when he says that a dream is wish fulfilment. That is to say, there is no "dream" (readily communicable formulation) which is not a "wish," in contrast with the original, unknowable, unknown "dream." In other words, there is no nightmare so terrifying that it is not better than the thing-in-itself ... The real thing is the dream which happens *exactly* as he said—he held out his hand and his arm fell off, and there it was lying on the ground. It is not a dream without free associations; it is the *real* thing. Similarly, a mystic may be able to say that he has direct relationship with God, without the intervention of any other agency. (Bion, 1973/1990, p. 24)

Returning to the issue of the limits of language, Bion will later state once more in *Caesura* that an analyst is not able to become familiar with the experience another analyst has with a certain patient, no matter how much experience the first analyst may have.

> No terms—"autistic child", "psychotic", "borderline", are of much use because the experience in an analysis is more subtle, detailed and difficult to divide up into these somewhat crude divisions available to us when we borrow from the practice of medicine, or existing philosophies, or analytic theories. (Bion, 1975/1989, pp. 54–55)

He comments that this is one of the difficulties about the type of communication possible in conferences, supervisions, or discussions among peers. A supposition, guess or suspicion may appear to offer a simple explanation for something extremely complex: "What I am putting forward as a mere suspicion or conjecture may be turned into a theory, or treated as if it were something which could be used for immediate translation into an interpretation."

In addition to this vast topic of human language and its limitations, which I consider a key point in the D11 supervision, I don't want to leave uncommented another very important point addressed there. Based on some issues related to the theme of projection/introjection (to bring inside or outside) in dreams such as the one described, Bion brings us the notion of "direction" as a very important idea in psychoanalysis:

> I would like to be able to talk, some time, about the need for having some expression for *direction* which, I think, we very much lack in psychoanalytic talk; because, it makes a great deal of difference to an association, or an interpretation, as to which *direction* that is traveling in ... Now, what this patient has done is really attempted the transformation in the opposite direction. He has seen this occur in the session and is on the way to turning it into a dream last night, which makes it more the kind of thing that I would like to hear.

I think that with the apparently simple idea of direction Bion is approaching what he will soon thereafter define as caesura. We may then state that caesura would be "the expression for *direction* which, I think, we very much lack in psychoanalytic talk." Indeed, the term "direction" or its sense would later appear frequently in the texts contained in *Caesura* and *Four Papers*:

> Using my hand I suggest something of this sort: look at it from one side, there is a psycho-somatic complaint; turn it round; now it is soma-psychotic. It is the same hand, but what you see depends on which way you look at it, from what position, from what vertex—any term you like ... (Bion, 1976b, p. 318)

Also:

> Picasso painted a picture on a piece of glass so that it could be seen on both sides. I suggest that the same thing can be said of the caesura: it depends which way you look at it, which way you are travelling. Psychosomatic disorders, or soma-psychotic—take your choice—the picture should be recognizably the same whether you look at it from the psychosomatic position, or from the soma-psychotic position. (Bion, 1976a, p. 306)

In *Caesura*:

> Can any method of communication be sufficiently "penetrating" to pass the caesura in the direction from post-natal conscious

> thought back to the pre-mental in which thoughts and ideas have their counterpart in "times" or "levels" of mind where they are not thoughts or ideas? That penetration has to be effective in either direction. It is easy to put it in pictorial terms by saying it is like penetrating into the woman's inside either from inside out, as at birth, or from outside in, as in sexual intercourse. (Bion, 1975, p. 45)

Therefore, we may note the continuity between what Bion was saying in 1973 about direction and what he would say about caesura starting from 1975. By then the notion of direction had been included in the concept of caesura.

Linked to the theme of caesura and in view of the limitations of language, Bion will propose—based on what he calls "language of achievement" (Bion, 1970)—a language for the psychoanalyst which approaches the language of poets, such as Shakespeare, and which is able to decalcify a little the impenetrable, or "impressive," caesuras produced by the calcareous matter created simultaneously with the production of a new idea. As we know, this language would be strong enough to cross both the caesura that separates emotions from speaking about them and the caesura of time, producing significant effects in times much later than its formulation. Introducing an aesthetic model, he suggested on several occasions that the analyst should go to his office as an artist goes to his studio, imaginatively conjecturing formulations which might be played as a musical instrument, painted as a painting, or narrated in a literary fashion. "Which kind of artist are you? ... In my experience, a large amount of analysts don't know really which kind of artists they are" (Bion, 1978a, p. 95). In this sense, Bion has had to go beyond Freud, who feared the poetic language in psychoanalysis. Although he did write poetically in many occasions, Freud oscillated between including psychoanalysis in his time's ideal of science and the aesthetic model (specifically literature) as reference and interlocution. In the method's origins, it is the patients' fantasy and imagination that provide him the instruments for the discovery and investigation of the unconscious in psychoanalysis. Freud's suggestions regarding analytical listening and the work performed by the analysand in the session are analogous to the mental state required for any creative process. Nevertheless, Freud reacted ambiguously to comments praising his writing, which in its turn matched so much the subject of his investigation. Examples of this are his letters to Schnitzler—his much feared and admired *doppelgänger*—as well as the impact suffered on account of the famous comment by Krafft-Ebbing upon the presentation of his first clinical stories: "That's nothing but scientific fairy tales." Bion would later say: "A hostile critic could easily say: 'That's all pure imagination!' I would say: 'Yes, but it's high time we accept Pure Imagination as entitled to a place in scientific work'" (Bion, 1978b, p. 224). In *Taming Wild Thoughts* (1997): "Similarly, these speculative imaginations, however ridiculous, however neurotic, however psychotic, may nevertheless be stages on the way to what we could ultimately regard as scientific, psycho-analytic formulations" (Bion, 1997, p. 41). Or: "… Unless the analyst allows himself the exercise of his speculative imagination he will not be able to produce the conditions in which the germ of a scientific idea can flourish" (Bion, 1997, p. 46).

In contrast to Freud, who sought to establish the scientific status of the new science, Bion, more distant from those early concerns, referred countless times to words that wear down with everyday usage and are no longer effective to convey an idea or emotion. The experience we would like to approach has no color, smell or flavor. That's why he emphasizes the need to search in the metaphors of the great poets for the instruments to try to revive fossilized terms, for theories transform our language into a repetitive jargon, unable to affect the one who hears it. Meanwhile, says Bion, the mental pain is as alive as it has always been; ailments don't wear down.

The issues of language and direction may in fact be considered two vertices for approaching the same problem. Without naming them, Bion is talking about the "impressive caesuras" and its expressions in analytical work. The limitations of language are related to some very ossified and restrictive caesuras, mentioned by Bion in this supervision/interview, between language grown stale by habit and a language that allows the creation of meanings not yet born or the awakening of those asleep, or between the one used in session with patients and the one to be transmitted to other colleagues etc. The latter was the very difficulty that the group had in order to cross the caesura between the interview (external vertex) and the supervision (internal vertex).

As mentioned by Chuster, the creative aspects of the mind, resulting from or representative of the psychoanalytical function of personality, are revealed in the radical nature of the concept of caesura:

> If we don't let ourselves be impressed by the elements of memory, of desire, of the need of comprehension and of sensorial impression, our mind recovers the plasticity of movement, travelling across the

> time split, establishing unsuspected links, creating conjectures, ultimately using the imagination. Everything may be the subject of metaphor. (Chuster, 2001, p. 106)

Thus, the caesura, recovered and transformed by Bion and based on Freud, ceases to be impressive, either at birth or death, and allows us to devise unforeseeable crossings across the shibboleths of the established. The biblical story (Judges 12) about the fratricidal feud between Ephraimites (who said "*sibboleth*") and Gileadites (who pronounced it correctly, "*shibboleth*"—ear, stalk or twig, in Hebrew), living on opposite banks of the Jordan River, inspired Freud to use the pass-word that led to the demise of the men of Ephraim in order to identify those who were and those who weren't psychoanalysts, the supporters of psychoanalysis and its enemies, as said Freud some times. The Oedipus complex as the core complex of neuroses, the unconscious, the child sexuality, and the theory of dream interpretation were for Freud the shibboleths of psychoanalysis. Therefore, the psychoanalyst has an identity established, defined by the "shibbolething" limits (theoretical, professional etc.). It's a "being/am." With the fetal-term *caesura*, which in an earlier paper I contrasted with the fatal-term *shibboleth* (ac-cursed word), the analyst in session is for Bion a "to be-being," a "becoming," transient, transforming the Jordan of mind crossable in any direction.

Today we would receive Krafft-Ebing's criticism of Freud as something generous and stimulating, because thanks to Bion we know that there's more continuity between the world of science and the world of fairy tales than the impressive caesura of *shibboleths* could lead us to believe.

Nonetheless, if psychoanalysis does not encourage the psychoanalytic group to develop the possibility of experimenting and playing with creative formulation that recover the not-yet-born, revive the devitalized, and transgress the decorated in all of us, we may say, paraphrasing Horace, that many heroic thoughts will remain buried and forgotten in the bottomless pit of time, with no psychoanalyst to sing them.

References

Bion, W. R. (1970). *Attention and Interpretation*. New Jersey, NJ: Jason Aronson.

Bion, W. R. (1973). *Brazilian Lectures*. London: Karnac, 1990.

Bion, W. R. (1975). Caesura. In: *Two Papers. The Grid and Caesura* (pp. 54–55). London: Karnac, 1989.

Bion, W. R. (1976a). On a quotation from Freud. In: *Clinical Seminars and Other Works* (p. 306). London: Karnac, 2000.

Bion, W. R. (1976b). Evidence. In: *Clinical Seminars and Other Works* (p. 318). London: Karnac, 2000.

Bion, W. R. (1978a). A seminar held in Paris. *Revista de Psicanálise (SPPA),* VIII: 91–102.

Bion, W. R. (1978b). Bion in Sao Paulo. In: *Four discussions with W. R. Bion and Bion in New York and São Paulo* (p. 224) London: The Roland Harris Educational Trust.

Bion, W. R. (1997). *Taming Wild Thoughts*. London: Karnac.

Chuster, A. (2001). Comments about Bion's lecture in Paris. *Revista de Psicanálise (SPPA),* VIII: 103–106.

Junqueira de Mattos, J. A. (1992). Interview with Bion. *Revista Brasileira de Psicanálise, 26:* 443–464.

CHAPTER TWELVE

Supervision A2

In the text that follows, A stands for Analyst; P1 and P2 stand for participants in the audience.

A: This patient I am bringing is a patient with whom I feel I have great difficulty; a very complicated case. My feeling, at almost every meeting, at every session is that I am making a mess. Very seldom do we manage to meet. Usually he doesn't come. We miss session and the losses … When he does come, he suffers terribly during the sessions and he manifests his suffering physically. He sneezes, he moans, he sighs, he cries, he gets very desperate. I always have the feeling that I have failed to understand what is happening.

Bion: What is he talking about, when he does that? When he behaves like that?

A: Very often he's not talking, he's just dreaming.

Bion: Just … yeah!

A: And he puts his hands on his head and says "Oh my God" in English. He says it in English: "Oh my God." He gets desperate and I can't reach him. I have here yesterday's session. There are other sessions, in which perhaps things went better than yesterday, but this is one that happened yesterday.

It is something that happens often—also when he walks by me he looks at me very nicely, smiles at me nicely with a happy expression, then he lies down. There was a long silence of some ten minutes. I tried to observe him during this silence.

Bion: But this is when he comes into the room?

A: Yes.

Bion: I see. So, when do you think that the session starts? Are you waiting for him in the room?

A: No, I go fetch him, in the waiting room.

Bion: I see and that is when the contact starts?

A: Yes.

Bion: Would you give any interpretations when you meet him? … And, how does the session end?

A: Well, I say the time is up. I get up …

Bion: And what happens?

A: He goes out and he usually—not usually, but very often—after a very bad session, he looks at me smiling and goes out, seeming happy.

Bion: And you go out with him or …?

A: No, he goes out by himself.

Bion: I see. So the session …

A: There was only once I went out with him, three days ago, by accident, the light went out—his session is the last session of the evening—so, I had to go with him, with a candle.

Bion: Some patients want to prolong the session, so, when they stand up to go they'll go on talking. I don't like, ever, giving an interpretation then, because then, they don't go at all. They prolong it, prolong it, prolong it, and so, it becomes a prolonged good bye. When I have said: "The session is over," I stop. I don't give interpretations after that, because that prolongs the idea and then, they go on free-associating. I think it's well to be clear, in your own mind, when you consider the session stops. For example: would you give any interpretations when you are bringing the patient from the waiting room to the couch? Or simply leaving it out, until he settles on the couch; until you're set, or rather, until you are settled in your chair. Because, he mightn't lie on the couch. So, it's a good thing to have, in your own mind, when you think the session has started and when you think it has finished; and not prolong it by interpretations, or free associations, whatever the thing may, be beyond the boundaries.

A: He once—I remember now—complained that he is the one, who has to start the talking in the session.

Bion: Well, that's his misfortune, he just has to put up with it, because he might complain that the session ends at the time when he's got a lot more to say and he hasn't had a chance of saying it. Whatever you do, there are disadvantages about it. For example: when he has settled himself on the couch—he lies down—and if I were to say to him: "Your expression has altered from what you were, when you were coming into the room." Then, you have yourself extended the session by referring to something that's outside the session. So, there again, you have to make up your mind about it, as to when you feel entitled to say it. Personally, I think that you could, because if you are going to fetch the patient, then it's quite legitimate to refer to what you've seen in there. You can say: "A moment ago you seemed to be quite happy or cheerful; so something has happened."

However, I was just considering this point about when does the session start and when does the session end. It is also a matter of importance when you are dealing with a possible suicidal patient. For example, if during the session the patient can throw himself out of the window, I think it is safe, or it is wise to see to it, that you are between him and the window. So the arrangement of your room is of such a kind, that you could be in the way. Otherwise, if some disaster of that kind occurred, the coroner or whoever it is might say: "But, Doctor, why didn't you stop this patient?" or "Didn't you do anything to stop him? You mean to say that you let a suicidal patient be so near a window, which he can throw himself out of?" and so on ... But it's quite different if you say: "Yes, I knew that, that's why I stand, or sit, in the way. So that, he has to pass me to get to the window, but then, he's very powerful, or much more stronger than I am and I couldn't stop him." Well, that's quite comprehensible, but, what is incomprehensible is negligence, if you failed to take the precautions that you might be expected to take about the patient. But on the other hand, you can say about such a person: "you can only be responsible for the time in which the patient is with you so, somebody has to be responsible to bring him and to take him away."

You can do nothing about that. Because if you're going to be responsible for the patient after they've left your room, or after they're out of your care, then your mind is taken up with what this patient might do, but this is somebody else's time; instead of attending to your next patient, the time that you ought to be spending with your next patient, has been occupied by the previous one. So, a greedy patient can see to it that he occupies your mind, when it is somebody else's time. So, I like, if possible, to make it quite clear that I'm only responsible for the fifty minutes, when he is within my sight and within my reach; I can not be responsible for him when I've got no power at all, when I can't even see him. But anyhow, I won't talk too much about that, because we're talking about this particular patient. I was thinking of it, in more general terms, of patients in general. So, it is important to be quite clear in your own mind, when you are prepared to be responsible for the patient.

A: Yes, but what you say is very correct, because very often, when he leaves, I'm very worried about letting him leave.

Bion: So, the other patients don't get a fair deal!

A: He's the last! [the analyst said this laughing]

Bion: Well, if he occupies your mind during the night and so forth … it is still taking up time. Analysts think that they *can* do that, but you *can't* do that. If you're going to have your mind occupied with your practice, during night and so forth … then, we have not got a leisure to think, such and such a person exhausts himself, they are not in a fit condition to be doing work. So you have—in a sense—to be capable of forgetting the patient and all your various preoccupations and cares about them, so as, to give your mind a chance of refreshing itself, recovering.

A: But, during the session, in his silence … gesturing in this way … [at this moment the analyst seems to have forgotten the word "sigh" in English, so she sighs, to show how the patient did it] in a very disrupted and very desperate way like that. Then he started talking, and said, that when he was coming up the stairs to my office, he felt relief, but in his house, before, he was sure he was going to quarrel with me, to fight more than quarrel. He was going to fight with me, but when he arrived he felt relieved. But now he says: "I don't know why I want to send you to hell."

Bion: Yes. Now shall we just pause there a moment. What's your impression of this? I'd like you to imagine that you yourself are seeing the patient for the first time. The patient has been referred to you, that's what you gather. Now, do you want to take him on or not? Yes or no? Are you going to have this patient, or aren't you? You've got no more to go on than that. In the first session, you don't know anything about him apart, perhaps you've been told: "Oh yes, he's very clever, a very nice man—just the patient for you! You'll do very well with him." Yes, that's what they say, but only you know and you've got four minutes, five minutes, ten minutes, in which you decide. Now, knowing this little bit, what are you deciding? You don't have to tell the patient but you have to tell yourself. Do you want him or not? Are you going to say: "Yes, we can start next week" or "No." Can anybody offer any suggestions? I don't ask you particularly because you've already contributed [here, Bion was talking directly to the analyst].

A: For two years and a half!

Bion: But the rest of us can ask ourselves a question like that.

P1: I'm in doubt to take him or not, just thinking.

Bion: Anybody else? I'm probably doubting as much as you are. Anyone else?

A: I think it is my doubt also, whether I should go on with him, or suggest that he change to another analyst.

Bion: Yes, in that way, every session is the first session—every session. The twentieth session, the fortieth, the sixtieth, the hundredth, two hundredth, it's always the first session. Should you go on? Should you not? Of course, by the two hundredth session, you have gained a lot of impressions, which sounds like an advantage, which is also a liability, because people change. So, the patient that you see on the two hundredth session, is still your first session, only you are now prejudiced by what you've seen in the previous a hundred and ninety nine. Now, by the hundred and ninety-ninth sessions you may be saying: "Ah! My God!"—that's you doing that—not him, but you! He may not; so this: "Ah! My God!" is a state of mind. Whose state of mind? Who's state of mind is it and when? Who is feeling like that? Is it him, or is it the analyst at seeing him again? Or, is it his mother or his father, or his aunt or somebody? Or, is it what you are going to feel like in the next session? Or, as I say, the two hundredth one. In other words, what are you looking at: a historian or a prophet? Is this a person who is writing with his body about the past history or times to come?

A: He said it in a certain moment: "I think you can't stand me any more."

Bion: Well, now that means that at this moment it is you. So, you can say: "I think that you are feeling that you are not taken in by the fact that, as far as I know, I behave in quite a polite or civilized manner, but if I was sincere or honest, then I'd be feeling and acting in a kind of way, that you are suggesting."

A: Because when the patient said: "I think that you're fed up"—I think he wants to come to me and say: "Doctor, this is no good any more, you go and look for another kind of therapy. Analysis is not for you."

Bion: Yes.

P2: You said that? Ah, he said that!

Bion: Has anybody got any idea, what they would say to that?

P1: I think that the patient is just trying to put inside the mind of the analyst, the feeling he just felt. He can't stand all the feelings that he is feeling in the relationship. He's trying to induce the analyst to feel just that and when he says: "I think the analyst should send me to another therapist, because I think she will not stand me," he's just trying to induce these feelings in the analyst.

Bion: Hum, yes. Now, what would you say to the patient?

P1: Now? I have to think!

Bion: This is why I'm asking the question, because here we can think about it; we can think anything you like. In the room with the patient, you can't. In the room with the patient, you have to say something at the moment. Here we can go all through this discussion; in the analysis itself you can't. There is nobody to discuss it with, except the patient and there's no time in which to discuss it—this sort of way. So, the advantage of thinking about it now is: if we all could say, what we would say, then, we could have several different ideas, as to what to say to the patient. And then, when you have a patient who behaves like this, you already have a very considerable vocabulary available. You've already played the psychoanalytic game, which is not any more a game, than the game that children play. It's serious and it's also amusing. But it's got a serious intention, because if you play fathers and mothers, then, by the time that you are a father or mother, you know a bit more about it, because you've played these games. You've quarreled with your brother, or sister or fought with him, over who is which and so on … So you're in a better position actually to be a real father or mother. But for our purposes here, now, it's better if you'd say anything you like, which you think you'd say to the patient, it doesn't matter very much, whether it is right or not. It'll be something that we can all hear and think of. Anybody want to volunteer any suggestion, of what you would say, or how you would put it to the patient in practice?

A: I was feeling that he wanted me to tell him to do something—about what he would do … . He wanted me to send him away—that was what I felt, he wanted me to send him away.

Bion: I'd like to make one or two suggestions about this. It may be that this is a reminiscence, that it is something which he felt, that his mother felt: too tired to deal with such a troublesome baby—always active, always requiring attention, always expecting to be loved and wanted. It may be that, he had a brother or sister, who also got tired of playing games with him. They might be able to say: "Oh, my God" but they could feel: "Where's my father or mother? I don't want to play this game any more." The same thing could be true about his girlfriend either that he didn't want to marry her, or that she didn't want to marry him, or go out with him and so on. Or it may be that his analyst, similarly, doesn't want to go on with the analysis, when he wants to have more analysis. Or he doesn't want to have analysis with this analyst, but with a better one—in case there is a better one. Or it may be: "No, this can't come to anything, because I don't want to marry this analyst. There's somebody else in mind." Anyhow, the analysis cannot end happily, you don't live happily ever after with your analyst. Now, that's just a few possible stories, which one shall I tell him? There are two people in the room; who is going to get tired of the other one first? And what is the game that's being played? That is the sort of question, which you have to answer on the spur of the moment; there's no time to go through it like this here, where you can take your choice as to what you say next. When the number of choices is pretty considerable like that, you can see that the chances of choosing the right one, are loaded against you, really. You don't know whether to give it in terms of past history, or present, or future. Shall we go on?

A: This person doesn't have a fixed relationship with anybody, with any girl. He had a fiancée years ago, when he broke the engagement …

Bion: He did?

A: He did. He does the same with his professional activities, he's always breaking off what he's doing. He's always changing jobs. He's always changing the career he chooses to do. He was an X, he left the profession to get scholarships in Europe. He spent three years in Europe, in different countries and he came back, came to work in laboratories as a researcher, then he had three jobs in six months; that is when he came to analysis. He made such a mess in the places that he was in: first he changed the jobs, because he wanted to earn more, but he made such a mess, that he was sent away. Now I don't even know what he is doing, because it's very vague and confused, but he also is attending the Faculty of (Y).[1]

Bion: Can we just stop a moment? Now, the situation gets a bit more complex. It's not that, but it's wider, because it isn't to be a question of choosing his doctor, or analyst, or husband, or wife, or father, or mother. It is also a question of choosing his profession—it's just the same. He's always being unfaithful to the profession that he's chosen, trying another one, the new one is no better than the old one, because sooner or later he's saying: "My God, this [X profession]!" or "My God, this [Y profession!]" or "My God, this analysis!" So, at the present moment, he's doing all those things—he's confused. He's saying: "Take all this rubbish and choose the best one out of it." When he goes … huhmm, then [A long sigh sound.] he's evacuating his breath. He's evacuating faeces, and when he talks, he's evacuating ideas. But the responsible person has to be the other one. It's the analyst, or his husband, or his wife who has to choose what of all these: loves, hates, sighs, groans and so on are that you want to get married to.

A: But these sort of things, when I say them to him, don't produce any … when I say that he's evacuating his ideas, that he doesn't think. Yesterday, when I asked him whether he ever considered, that he had a head to use, to think and not like a bowel, or intestine full of shit, because he had said: "Oh, I'm full of shit!" But it doesn't make any sense for him.

Bion: Hum … the point there is: he doesn't want to be to blame, so *you* must choose. Now, if you choose a man who's full of care and trouble and worry, then it's your fault. If he complains and is miserable and unhappy: it's your fault—it is the fault of his father, mother, sister, brother, wife, children, because they chose him. On the other hand, if you choose him, because he smiles and is pleasant, then it's your fault for choosing a person like that, because you made a mistake, anyway, he has to be smiling and nice and agreeable and polite and civil. So, it's your fault for making him carry this heavy burden of being agreeable and nice—whatever he's feeling like. He doesn't want to have to be working, cooperative, and friendly—whether he's got a headache or whether he's ill or tired; he doesn't want to do that. So, it's the fault of the person who chooses him, thinking he's got somebody who would be nice and agreeable. So he could say: "If you want to analyze him, or if you want to marry him, then you can't complain that he didn't say how terrible he is. You can't complain if you've got somebody who's bad tempered and tiresome. He warned you that that is what he was like."

In short, the problem here is: how to avoid being responsible for your own behavior and how to find somebody who will take the responsibility. Now, just consider, for a moment, the ramifications of that; it's even, one could say, the business of the job itself, to be interesting, it's not unreasonable. One would like to choose a job, one would like to choose work which is interesting, so, he carries in review all these that he can talk: he tries being a patient, he tries being a baby, he tries being a child, he tries being grown-up, he tries being a doctor, he tries being and so forth, but what he is looking for is a job that will be interesting. Now, contrast that though with this point: is it the job that has to be interesting, or does he have to be interested in the job? There's a big difference.

A: Yes, because at a certain moment of analysis, at the beginning, he was absolutely convinced that I was in love with him …

Bion: Oh, yes!

A: … And that he was there, he came there, because I wanted to be there, with him.

Bion: I know, but it's a particular sort of love. You are absolutely the person who would be interested in him, who would love him; not you are the person that he wants to love or be nice to. He doesn't want to have a wife that he has to look after or children that he would have to look after. He wants to choose a wife, or children, that would look after him—that's different. He wants to choose a job that'll look after him, that'll provide him with a living. But, that's different from choosing a job, in which you are interested, or a wife in whom you are interested, or children in whom you are interested. It's awkward if you want the kind of children who you can love—whatever they are like, whether they are deformed mentally or physically, or whether they're ill, or naughty, or good and so on or not. This is one reason, just to revert to our job here, where analysis and talking, speaking in analysis, that job we have to make the tools with which to do it and one of these tools is to do with *directions*, one could say: I wouldn't ask him, of course, but as far as one's own mind is concerned, when he says that he loves his wife, or children, what does he mean? Love that way or love this way? When he loves his food, has the food got to love his digestive system? Do him good and so forth? Or does he mind to have the sort of love and to love the food, in a way that it would love his insides and would eat him back again from inside? In other words: he wouldn't mind a meal but the meal mustn't give him indigestion, mustn't give him ulcers. In short, it mustn't eat him up.

A: Because: "I burn stomach." That I understood he says his stomach burns. When he comes to the session very often he starts feeling the stomach burn.

Bion: I expect you have the similar idea in Portuguese as in English, where you can say: I'm inflamed with love for this girl or boy. His love for the partner is like a flame, the flame of everlasting fidelity; not the sort of flame that burns him up, not the sort of food that gives him what medically we would call indigestion, burns his insides; not the sort of food which turns into a cancer and starts eating his insides off. I could say this to you more simply and more pictorially, if I wasn't talking articulate language and I could say to you: look at the Prometheus myth. When the patient talks like this, can you see the Prometheus myth buried in what he's saying to you? Something eats out his liver. Now is that anatomy or physiology or psychoanalysis or philosophy or lab work? A Chinese person would understand it, because a Chinese could say about his lady friend or his boyfriend: "You're my heart and liver"—the liver is the seat of the affections. That isn't medicine, not as we understand it, but that myth could explain what he is saying, when he talks about his insides being hurt or even: might have a gall bladder infection. He might even drink so much wine that he got jaundice, still talking the same language. So, I suggest that it's a kind of myth which *pictorializes*. So, when the patient is talking like this, you might be able to see that myth or be reminded of it—then, you could make up your mind to what part of the story he was telling you.

Well, as always, the story continues. We have to stop, but this story doesn't!

Note

1. The name of the actual field has been omitted for purposes of confidentiality.

Supervision A2 commentary

Dr. Carmen C. Mion

These supervisions, transcribed directly from unedited recorded tapes, give us the opportunity of entering into contact with a group experience where it is possible to visualize Bion as analyst, thinker, and supervisor: approaching the clinical material, interacting with the colleague presenting the session, and relating to the group. They have been very useful, even precious, in the illustration and realization of concepts presented both in *Transformations* (1965) and *Attention and Interpretation* (1970), as well as in his trilogy *Memoirs of the Future* (1991).

In my reading of the supervisions, I have privileged neither the clinical material, the supervisee questions, nor what happens in the group, but have chosen to focus instead upon how Bion approaches these three possible vertices in a clinical seminar. I have never read one of these transcriptions without a certain emotional impact, without being surprised, without having a feeling of "psychic expansion." And this supervision was certainly no exception.

This personal experience of reading, its repercussions in me and its effect on my evolution, my continued "becoming" and developing as an analyst, is what I will bring forward to you so that, as Bion suggests at a certain point we may play, as seriously as children do, this "psychoanalytic game." And in "playing this game" we can not only know a little more about psychoanalysis and expand our vocabulary in order to better speak about psychic phenomena, but also be amused as well.

Before the moment Bion introduced the idea of "analysts playing a psychoanalytic game" one colleague (P1) had just presented a commentary about the clinical situation described by the supervisee. Bion then addressed him provocatively:

> *Bion*: Hum, yes. Now, what would you say to the patient?
> *P1*: Now? Well, I need to think!
> *Bion*: This is why I am asking the question, because here we can think … anything we like. In the office with the patient you can't …

Bion emphasizes that there is no place for ready theories and no time to think in the consulting room. We are irremediably alone and naked, trying to help our patients find themselves through psychoanalytically trained intuition, relying on the only available equipment though rudimentary as it is: our own mind. But it was not this observation that surprised me in this paragraph. It is true, but it is not new for me. To a greater or lesser extent, I believe we all know, through our own experience, what Bion is referring to.

However, by introducing the model of a child's game for the psychoanalytic clinical seminars, Bion surprises me, bringing back that familiar sensation I have named *"psychic expansion"* for lack of a better name. In my view, he is not only pointing out the importance of these exercises for the analyst's clinical practice (as *preconceptions*), but also suggests it is not relevant for this purpose if, when discussing a colleague's clinical material, we are in the field of fiction, phantasy, knowledge or even hallucinosis, providing the group is aware it is *"playing a psychoanalytic game."* Certainly, for the game to be as amusing as Bion suggests, the predominance in the group of links of love, respect for truth and ethics becomes a necessary condition.

I find a correspondence between Bion's playful suggestion—and metaphor of play—in this supervision and a passage in the introduction to his book *Learning from Experience*. There he says: "… In psychoanalyst's methodology the criteria cannot be whether a particular usage is right or wrong, meaningful or verifiable, but whether it does or does not promote development" (Bion, 1962, p. ix). He will resume the theme in *Transformations* (1965/1983, p. 2) signalizing that some explanations though valid in their sphere, may not promote development in the domain of psychoanalytical investigation.

Here, I realize once more with Bion that the patient's associations may represent phenomena related to one another in an infinite universe, and that they may not correspond to any realization in the finite universe of analytic discourse. In other words, the realization will always transcend the theory. Therefore, the apprehension of a constant conjunction in the field of human experience, whether it be poetry, phantasy, dream, myth, theory, music or even an informal observation from a colleague, seems to me very useful providing it can be part of the analyst's equipment as in the column D4 of the Grid (preconception/attention) (Bion, 1975b), that is, that it can be significant but unsaturated enough to receive its meaning from the emotional experience of the analytical couple in the session.

I think that the theory of Transformations, including the turbulence aroused by the ideas contained therein, refers primarily to the *psychoanalyst's* practice. As Bion (1965, p. 73) points out, the idea that a constant conjunction has a cause or an element causes an effect is derived from forces acting on the observer and is not necessarily part of the observed conjunction. "Consequently, the content of the interpretations depends on how the experience from the session, "O", will be deduced from the clinical material according to the analyst's personality and his theoretical pre-conceptions, including his own analysis and his life experiences." I believe that non-discrimination between clinically observed phenomenon, a constant conjunction, and the theory utilized to organize the experience, to give it meaning, contributes significantly to our "psychoanalytic Tower of Babel" (Green, 2002).

Through his propositions stated at the end of his book *Transformations* (Chapters Eleven and Twelve), that the polarity conscious↔unconscious be replaced by finite↔infinite and the transformations in "O" (*"becoming"*), Bion introduces an infinite/id with neither form, nor time or space categories. He makes it possible for us to approach the unknowable, the void, and that which is nameless in our clinical practice. That is, to approach not only the manifestations of the knowable (Freudian) unconscious, but the formerly unthinkable in psychoanalysis, approaching the very nature of the unformulated unconscious.

Right at the beginning of the supervision Bion asks a question to the supervisee: "Bion: ... So, when do you think the session begins?"

Accordingly, we may ask ourselves: When did our meeting begin? Today at 11:30 a.m.? Two weeks ago when we received the text? By the time the supervision first began to be translated? Thirty-one years ago when the supervision took place? When does any human experience begin? (Bion, 1975a).

Inevitably, these questions lead us to think of Bion's suggestion of a transparent mirror as the model for caesura (Bion, 1978, p. 108) and the diagonal in Sapienza's theoretical diagram (Sapienza, 2009), which derives from Grotstein's formulations (2007). Each of these models, metaphors, and images allow us to conjecture the impacts of "O" as infinite, ultimate reality, unknowable or God in the oscillations (conscious/finite ↔unconscious/infinite) ↔ (PS↔D).[1]

In the last two chapters of *Transformations* Bion quotes the beautiful lines of Milton twice, first (p. 151) to represent "O" and to differentiate transformations O→K from *becoming*, then (p. 162) to assert that the verbal expressions intended to represent the ultimate reality are contradictory within themselves.

> The rising world of waters dark and deep
> Won from the void and formless infinite.
> John Milton: *Paradise Lost*, Book III. (Quoted in Bion, 1965, p. 162)

These infinite spaces are too vast and frightening to encompass. For Bion, tolerating doubt and the feeling of the infinite, negative capability, the potential for reverie and oscillations PS↔D are the necessary conditions for optimal functioning of the analyst's mind within the session. It is what makes waking dream thoughts possible. Then, abandoning memory, desires, and comprehension, in a certain way blinding himself in order to see in the dark (Grotstein, 2007) with patience and psychoanalytical faith, the analyst can wait for the emergence of a "selected fact" which gives coherence to the "O" of analytical experience, opening further to the possibility that a "catastrophic change" might become a "creative change." Even more, the possibility that creative changes in K (Knowledge) might move in the direction of becoming in the infinite unknown and vice-versa, in continuous oscillation (K↔O).

In this context, we observe that sometimes, movements in the direction PS→D may lead to obstruction to knowing, "tranquillizer understandings" (K→–K), as a Grid's F3 formulation (Concept/ Notation) used in column 2 (Ψ), that will interrupt the continuous cycle (PS↔D) in the analyst's mind. The freedom and intactness of the latter is a necessary condition for the oscillation (K↔O) to occur. Movements in the direction PS←D, are fundamental for a progressive dimension of *not-understanding* (i.e., dissolving known relationships between psychic elements) and thereby opening transformational access to the unknown infinite (K→O). In this situation the interpretation (O→K) may be maintained by analyst and/or analysand as a "barrier" against the psychological turbulence expected to occur with the emergence of "O", from K→O. According to Bion (1965, Chapter Twelve) only when the analyst feels aware of this kind of resistance in himself, that is, when he can see the column 2 elements in his own thoughts, should the interpretation be made.

Bion has repeatedly pointed out that the analyst's main concern must be with the material for which he has direct evidence, namely the emotional experience of the analytical couple, the emotional experience of the analytic sessions themselves. Thus, Bion opened up and added the task of articulating the intersubjective in the analytic relationship to Freud's descriptions of the intra-psychic. Consequently, in the consulting room, the presence of the analyst's subjectivity begins to have the same importance as that of the patient and the session is considered as a succession of movements resulting from the interaction of the two minds from the beginning of the meeting. It follows that the session's elements shall include the emotional atmosphere, the analyst's emotional state, his dream thoughts and the emotional experience of the couple. I believe it is in this direction that Bion conducts this supervision.

Just before his question ("… So, when do you think the session begins?"), the supervisee colleague had brought up the emotional atmosphere of the meetings with the patient:

> Difficulties, incompatibilities, "we lose each other."
> Doubts …
> Pain, desperation: moans, sighs, crying.
> Lack of understanding.
> "Oh my God", hands on the head, "I cannot find him."
> "Just dreaming …"

Bion then continuing his unusual dialogue with the supervisee asks a series of questions seemingly related to the setting:

> Where the meeting and the separation takes place?
> When the contact starts?
> In the waiting room? When he comes into the room?
> When the patient lies down?

The supervisee answers Bion's questions and quickly resumes observations on the emotional state of the patient. For example, the contrast she has noticed between the patient's happy facial expression when he passes by the analyst in the beginning or end of the session and the suffering, the moans and sighs when he lies down. Yet Bion insists:

> ... some patients want to prolong the session ... it's a good thing to have, in your own mind, when you think the session has started and when you think it has finished. And not prolong it ... whatever thing may be beyond boundaries.

It seems to me Bion is calling attention to the analyst's condition in his daily practice, relating setting to limits and responsibilities. Each analyst is responsible for the determination of his working conditions, and this is only possible if he does not disregard who he really is. Bion does not set rules or standards: he proposes, above all, that the analyst attend to and be aware of himself; get in touch with his feelings and limits, to know who he himself is once he has the intention to know his patient.

The supervisee, on the other hand, continues to focus on her patient, apparently trying to understand a situation of great anguish and suffering. Bion then gently directs the focus of the analyst's attention to herself. Though he refers to the patient's question and the supervisee's observations, even making a suggestion about what might be said to the patient, he still goes back to his initial issue: *when does a session begin and end?*

This is a very interesting moment in the supervision, because, without apparent relation to this session or the patient in question, he brings up a "possible suicidal patient" and the window of the consulting room. (Perhaps this relates to the window opened or closed at the beginning of the meeting that has now been incorporated into Bion's dream-work-alpha?). It seems he is calling the group's attention to the analyst's responsibility in relation to the patient in the setting, mentioning questions of common sense, incomprehensible negligence, the need to be attentive, but only to re-emphasize the issue of the *analyst's limits* in his practice, the choices he has to make and his responsibilities to himself, to his mind, his working equipment. He brings back the greedy patient, who is able somehow to occupy the analyst mind and finalizes: "So, it is important to be quite clear in your own mind, when you are prepared to be responsible for the patient". That is, when a session begins and ends.

The supervisee now says she continues to be really worried about letting the patient leave the office but, I believe, she is still not apprehending what seems to me Bion is trying to convey, or rather, not accompanying him in the *direction* he is pointing: to herself. She seems concerned, naturally, with her patient's suffering and desperation.

Until a certain point when the supervisee relates an observation made by her patient (p. 7): "I don't know why I want to send you to hell"[2]. At this moment Bion proposes a pause to the supervisee and, in the sequence, practically leads her in the direction of her feelings awakened by the patient, but in the *here and now of the supervision, in the present time*:

> *Bion*: What is your impression of this? ... imagine you are seeing him for the first time ... you don't know anything about him ... Are you going to have this patient or aren't you? ... You don't have to tell the patient, but you have to tell yourself.

By gently mentioning his own doubt to the supervisee, Bion helps induce a state of mind or an environment in which the colleague can feel comfortable with her own doubts. From this moment on, it seems that both, followed by the group, are moving in the same direction. Bion then, utilizing the *language of achievement* (Bion, 1965), introduces into the room, the minds and hearts of the group, the binomial, finite↔infinite:

> *Bion*: Whose (is this) state of mind? Who's state of mind is it and when? ... In other words, what are you looking at: a historian or a prophet? Is this a person who is writing with his body about the past history or times to come?

> *Bion*: ... Anyhow, the analysis cannot end happily, you don't live happily ever after with your analyst. Now, that's just a few

possible stories, which one shall I tell him? There are two people in the room; who is going to get tired of the other one first?"…

Bion: … you can see the chances of choosing the right one are loaded against you, really. You don't know whether to give it in terms of past history, or present, or future.

Bion: … it's your fault. … it's your fault. … it's your fault. So, it's the fault of the person who chooses him … how to avoid being responsible for your own behavior and how to find somebody who will take the responsibility.

Bion: … Now, contrast that thought with this point: is it the job that has to be interesting, or does he have to be interested in the job? … When he loves his food, has the food got to love his digestive system?

Bion: … look at the Prometheus myth. … can you see the Prometheus Myth buried in what he's saying to you? Something which eats out his liver. Now that is anatomy or physiology or psychoanalysis or philosophy or lab work?

The direction of the psychoanalytic investigation overlaps Pascal's infinite spaces, and proceeds until it reaches the deep recesses of Hades. The session's emotional atmosphere, the analyst's impressions of the session, the emotional state of the analyst-analysand couple, the analyst's own dreaming thoughts are the compass we have at our disposal. In this supervision, Bion put us in touch with the anguish of living with uncertainty, tolerating mystery and doubts; with the perception that we may be blind, misled by our own perceptions, choices, and decisions which will bring inevitable repercussions in the future, but also knowing that this limited perception is the only equipment we have (Mion, 2006).

Notes

1. Subsequently I have evolved the theme in the paper "Conjectures about caesuras, memories, and dreams", presented at the Bion Conference in Los Angeles CA, 2014.

2. It is impossible not to recall Bion's observation: "The likelihood of meeting old friends there makes the prospect of Hell less frightening than the prospect of Heaven for which life on earth has given no adequate preparation" (Bion, 1975a, p. 49).

References

Bion, W. R. (1962). *Learning from Experience*. London: Heinemann.

Bion, W. R. (1965). *Transformations*. New York, NY: Jason Aronson, 1983.

Bion, W. R. (1970). *Attention and Interpretation*. London: Karnac.

Bion, W. R. (1975a). Caesura. In: *Two Papers—The Grid and Caesura* (pp. 35–56). London: Karnac, 1989.

Bion, W. R. (1975b). The grid. In: *Two Papers—The Grid and Caesura* (pp. 1–33). London: Karnac, 1989.

Bion, W. R. (1978). *Bion in New York and Sao Paulo*. London: The Roland Harris Educational Trust, 1980.

Bion, W. R. (1991). *A Memoir of the Future*. London: Karnac.

Green, A. (2002). *Key Ideas for a Contemporary Psychoanalysis: Misrecognition and Recognition of the Unconscious*. New York, NY: Routledge, 2005.

Grotstein, J. S. (2007). *A Beam of Intense Darkness: Wilfred Bion's Legacy to Psychoanalysis*. London: Karnac.

Mion, C. C. (2006). The stranger. *International Journal Psychoanalysis, 87*: 125–143.

Sapienza, A. (2009). II Jornada de Psicanálise: Bion. Da clínica às teorias possíveis [II Psychoanalysis Conference: Bion. From clinical practice to the possible theories]. 2–3 April 2009, São Paulo, SBPSP.

CHAPTER THIRTEEN

Supervision D8

In the text that follows, A stands for Analyst; P1 and P2 stands for participants in the audience.

A: Last week I made a mistake at the end of Thursday's hour. I told her "until Tuesday," instead of "until tomorrow." The next day was a Friday and I was coming here, so I had changed her appointment and I was seeing her in the morning, very early in the morning. I forgot and I said "until Tuesday."

Bion: Yes, yes.

A: Monday, was a holiday!

Bion: That was the time that you mentioned?

A: Yes. Then, she didn't come Friday. Tuesday she came. When I opened the door, she looked at me laughing, in a superior way. Then, she said that she understood that I set her free: "You don't need to be here tomorrow."

Bion: You don't need …?

A: "To be here tomorrow," what she understood about what I had said.

Bion: Umhm.

A: She felt as if I had said: "You are free, you don't need … ." Then she told me a lot of complaints about her husband. She gave him a … a …?

P1: Loudspeaker.

A: Loudspeaker.

A: He wanted it very much, for his birthday. His birthday was actually later, but she gave it to him early, because she saw it and then she gave it to him. She said it was something that he didn't have. She was thinking he will be glad to have it. It was a very good loudspeaker. Then she complained a lot about her husband. I said to her that she was talking about him, in order to show me what she was feeling here. Then she said, very worried: "Bah! I want you to help me with my husband and you say things like that?"

Bion: Ummhmm.

A: And she said, "It's not true, this story has nothing to do with us. I can't accept this," and the rest of the session was more like that.

Bion: Yes, do you give any reply, when the patient says … well, what she's just been saying to you? Because, it seems to me, that it's worth while asking a patient: "Why do you suppose I should waste your time and mine here, by telling you something, unless I thought it was right. I'm not saying my interpretation is right, but why do you think that I would say it unless I thought it was correct?" I think that now and then, it's a good thing to remind the patient that, after all, one is attempting to be an analyst! Otherwise, one accepts ideas as if one was just being perverse or stupid. I think that it's a further point that, in fact, what she says fits in, quite well, with your being a bad husband. But, I'd leave that aside, at the moment, to take up this point: "What do you think would be the good if I were to tell you, to give you interpretations, which I did not think were correct? They may be wrong, or they may be right, but, what makes you think that I would tell you them, unless I thought they were correct?"

A: Yes.

Bion: Because, this sort of thing seems to me to happen over and over again in analysis. Gradually, it edges into position as if one were really quite prepared to give incorrect interpretations!

A: Sometimes, also, people used to say, many patients: "I don't feel like that. If I had felt it, then, I could have accepted what you said, but I didn't feel …"

Bion: Yes!

A: It's something like that.

Bion: Yes! Well, again, I think the answer to that is simply that: "Well, it seems to me that that is how you feel. I've told you, so that you can compare it with what you really do feel and we have to accept it, that in this instance, you don't agree that my interpretation is correct," and leave it as a matter not for argument at all, but simply … well, possibly, the future will show in one way or another, whether it is right or not. Because, it's hopeless to be put in a position where you are forced to defend an interpretation—that's endless, there's no end to it, at all. The analysis is just brought to a standstill. You could say: "Well, it seems to me that is how you feel, but it doesn't seem to you to be so. We'll just have to leave it at that." After all, the only reason one has ever given these interpretations is: "You feel such and such," because it gives the patient a chance to understand what you are talking about and either to agree—"Yes, you're right"—or not; this will happen quite often. It is very helpful, because a psychotic patient—if a psychotic patient replies at all what you say—will sometimes say "correct" or "right" those were the cases, interpretations like that, which one wouldn't know, unless they said so. Sometimes, the psychotic patient, or borderline psychotic patient, seems to be more cooperative than a neurotic.

A: This was Tuesday; she came more or less … and the interesting thing is that when she arrives she nearly every time began the sentences with "but" as if that "but" was the continuation. Even this Monday she begins: "but."

Bion: Just going on from last session.

A: Yes. She said "but" and Tuesday also, Wednesday also "but" and she began Tuesday again: "I don't know why I came, I am coming here and I don't believe in you. But, you are the only person, the only one I have." Then, I said …

Bion: The only … what has she? She doesn't believe in you, the only X?

A: What I said to her was this: "Yes, now in this moment I am the only one you have. Now we are together, but I am not the only analyst; but now, yes! Now, we can see why you are here."

Bion: But, what I meant was: what is this only one that she's got? Is it a husband, wife, daughter, what is it?

A: I don't remember exactly the way she said it, but she said that I was the only analyst she has: "This what I have," something like that, "It's the only I have. And it is for that that I came here."

Bion: One of the things that I've been trying to reply to that is: "I don't think that this can be true, because for most of your life, you haven't even known that I existed. So, I can't really be the only one that you have, unless you're feeling that I am some particular person; but I can't be the only analyst, because you only heard of me recently." Is there any reason to suppose she knew you before? You never had any reason to think that she did know you before she came to a professional relationship?

A: She heard me speak once before in a professional setting that described some of my background, but we never had met socially.

Bion: Yes, yes! But none of that explains the reason why she has come to you for analysis.

P2: Yes, that's right, but she knew something.

Bion: That's what one needs to establish there: this can't really be a true story—not as it stands. There's no reason why she should come, or go on coming, if she doesn't like it, because she's always been able to do without the analyst. So, there must be some reason why she's come again today.

A: Yes, I talked more about this, showing her that in this special moment it was true, but we were alone together and the hour we could work was in that moment! I took this point, because I, we talked about why she was coming: "Many weeks now you are repeating this."

Bion: Yes … yes, yes!

A: Then, I made this point: I didn't say why you are coming …

Bion: Now, it's quite useful to have in mind that she needn't be there; but, she is there and all this talk about objecting to your interpretations being wrong, all that, may be perfectly true. This may be how she feels, but they don't explain why she's in the room.

A: What she needs!

Bion: No.

A: Then, this Wednesday, she said: "You are not understanding me. What I am saying is that I want help." She said that; she's changed, she said: "I want help. I decided that there is no reason to continue like that." Then, she said something about "intention," and it's meaning was ambiguous, because that word can be written in Portuguese with have a "ç" or an "s."[1]

Bion: Yes, yes!

A: Then she said: "Intention" can be written with a "ç" and an "s" and I am showing you the difference between these two expressions and one is "intention"—that is real intention—and the other is linked with intensity, intense quantity." She is always speaking like this. The way she speaks is so difficult, even to write. This week was very difficult, I wanted to write after the session, but she kept going round and round. It was more difficult than in the other weeks …

Bion: Yes.

A: Then, what I felt at that moment, what I took was exactly the intention with "s"—the force. I said to her that she was trying to show me that what counts was the intention with "ç". But what I was feeling about this was that I was remembering that she said to me about how she felt capable of killing and she wanted to kill. She said: "I learned with Dr. X (a previous analyst) that I have to use my feelings and I learned that I can be able to kill, that I can break a person." Then, I took this and I showed her that I thought that what she wanted to do was something like that: to break, to kill.

Bion: This very often happens. I think it will happen more as people need to come to you, after having had other analytic experience. But, I think the only thing that you can bear in mind about that is … well, the sort of way I would try to deal with it would be: "Yes, but when you were with Dr. X, that's not the same thing as when you are with me. I am not Dr. X and you are not the same person with me as with Dr. X, or one would need to know why you treat me as if I were an entirely different person." Now, the point about this is: what we are supposed to interpret is the *relationship*. Now, the relationship between you (A) and me, is not the same as a relationship between me and you (P1), or between you and me (P2). If it is, one would wonder what's gone wrong. What is the matter? That one person is just the same as anybody else. The thing that one is talking about is what Freud calls a transference—it's a peculiarity of a relationship between two human beings. It isn't, really, about the two human beings; the transference is a relationship between A and B, it's not about A and B, or about either A or B. So, the question, which would arise with her is: why is the relationship the same? Or, why does she expect it to be the same? You ask this, too, when you are analyzing a student, because students think this and one would say again: "When you see patient X, you are not me and patient X isn't you. Therefore, what I say to you about your relationship with me is not applicable to the relationship which exists between you and patient X." If it was the same, one would say: "There's something very queer about this." Of course, that might open up further. How is it that she still speaks as if she were having a relationship with Dr. X?

A: She is speaking a lot about this, but really, that day I showed her something when she said: "I don't know why I am speaking about this"—about what happened because, I said: "Until Tuesday."—Why speak about this? This is not important. Then I said to her something linked with relationships. I said: "Look, it's very important because you are speaking about feelings, about what you really felt about this."

Bion: Yes.

A: "It is our relationship." I said something about it: "Is our relation that we are speaking about, that I think is important."

Bion: Yes. The only thing about that is: when one makes these mistakes, it's always a nuisance. But one tends to regard them as very important, because we know about the importance of being accurate and so forth ... patients don't know that.

A: Yes, but she is bringing this in—all the time!

Bion: Well, then, you can say to her: "You've brought in this, you've brought in that, you've brought in this other thing and you've brought in ... all these seem to me to be very similar. Now, I wonder what has happened?"

A: You shouldn't say important?

Bion: I think that's alright. I think you've got to use any language that you've got at your disposal. In fact, one of the great things about practicing analysis is that it's a great advantage to get a sort of basic language of one's own. It's a horribly difficult business. Envy! Well, everybody knows what envy is and so forth ... but, one doesn't mean what everybody means—not sometimes. Sometimes you can say: "The feeling of envy that you have here is what I want to draw your attention to." The patient will say: "Envy? What about it? Yes, yes. I'm envious; it often happens." I think the only thing you can say is: "You are really making a distance between what I said to you about your envy and you; you are telling me that your envy is like every other person's envy; that isn't what I've said."

P2: Dr. Bion, this is really important: we have a basic language with each patient. I mean, it's not enough that you know what you are saying, it's necessary that you can exchange with it.

Bion: You've got to have a flexible basic language.

P2: Exactly!

Bion: But, you can not really change over and over again, because one's seeing patients all the time and the more you have to depart from the kind of language you use, the more time and so on ... is occupied in dealing with that point. So, the main thing is: for you, the analyst, to satisfy yourself. Now, after a time, you may feel that there's some word, which is a very useful word and you'd like to bring it into your vocabulary. Well, there's no harm in doing that, none whatever! Then, you can see how it goes. Fundamentally, it takes time before one knows one's own basic language. It's like any other art, really: the painter has to get used to his particular palette, the sort of brushes he uses, the kind of knives he uses; this suits him, but it wouldn't suit another person. A very good thing, taking up that sort of example: a painter can do very well with about five colors. He can make an enormous range of mixtures and it's a good thing to limit oneself to that, to those few, not forever, but till you can feel that you'd like to begin another one. Then, you've got six and so on ... Then, you can use quite extensive colors, that's because you know how to use them.

So, I think that, with the verbal vocabulary, I would tend to keep it down to what is in your experience manageable, without too much argumentation and so forth ... For example: on this business of envy, typically, all these fundamental words like: love, hate, and so on ... everybody thinks they know what you're talking about, but it's quite important to say to them: "I don't think that you know what I'm talking about." Why is this woman going on talking as if the relationship between her and Dr. X was still in existence? Why doesn't she admit that she, for good or ill, she is now with another analyst? You've got a perfect right to be yourself! The patient doesn't have to come if they don't like you, or your character, or your personality, they don't have to come! But to maintain—as she's doing—that she's got to come and, at the same time, it's a bad analyst … well, that is, really, trying to say two obvious things at the same time, without any acknowledgement.

P2: Dr. Bion, we know what she said about Dr. X, how wonderful he was, etc., etc., but she doesn't think, so much, that he was so and so … because, it's so difficult for her to admit something so human as dying—I don't know if I was clear enough.

Bion: No, I think that I would be inclined to say: "I don't really feel that Dr. X is the actual person, so much as a very useful weapon which shows, how bad I am."

A: Yes, I said that. Yes, yes! I used this one day. She was using Dr. X like a weapon against me.

Bion: Yes, yes!

A: And this day she really changed a lot, really.

Bion: Yes, yes. Well, I'm sure it comes back in different forms, different ways of attacking the analyst.

P2: It was very important to her.

A: Yes, very important.

P2: Last time it was important to her, because she reacted to it.

A: This day, it was almost the same, because when I showed to her that she could kill somebody, could break somebody, that I was near what she wanted to do with me, then she changed her mind and said: "Dr. X, in response to anything I used to bring, he used to say something straight forward. And you, you don't say it in a straight line." I say: "I didn't understand what you said." She said: "It is a straight line, if you want to know if I am in this side, or that side. If it is a circle, you want to know also in what side I am." Then, suddenly she said: "Look, I would like that we could be like a crystal." Crystal, do you know?

Bion: Yes.

P2: A glass, a very nice glass!

A: Like a crystal! I didn't understand ... I asked what she meant by this: "like a crystal." Then, she said: "A crystal you can see all the faces and you can see inside." Then, she pointed to a teapot on my desk and she said: "Like this, because it is reflecting both."

Bion: Yes.

A: Then, she said: "I have the impression of the infinite." Really, I didn't know how to work with this. I only said to her that she was speaking to me in a completely different way.

Bion: I think that's good enough; because if you can draw her attention to that, then she herself may produce something, which shows the difference. I think it's a great nuisance feeling that there's a *correct* interpretation. All one can hope, is that the "*correct interpretation*" will get a bit clearer if the patient will keep on coming. So far, this patient has been coming.[2] What impression did you get about what she thought, you were doing instead of seeing her? Why you were missing the session?

A: She knows that I am coming here.

P1: All the patients know.

Bion: Yes.

P1: I don't know how they know.

A: They speak with each other, they know!

P1: It's something terrible!

A: She knows and I think she's very envious of this.

Bion: There can also be a great deal of hostility, if the analyst appears to attach some importance to another person, because I think it's important to realize that the patients do want to believe—in spite of all the hostility and so forth—that *their* analyst is somebody who matters. So, appearing to behave as if there were somebody more important is quite a blow to the patient.

A: I have another patient who said directly this. He said: "I came to you because you look so well, so good, you came from X city and so on … and I want you. But I was thinking that if you are going to see Dr. Bion, then it's because you don't know so much, you need to learn, then, perhaps, you are not so good!" He said that directly.

Bion: It's a very direct interpretation, isn't it?

A: Yes!

Bion: You might be coming to see me, but there's another reason why you should be coming to see me, for any but private reasons of your own. Why should the patient assume that you're coming to see somebody who knows more than you; after all, one can meet anybody.

A: Why can't people change ideas and talk? Why do you have to be alone? I interpreted also this other side.

Bion: Yes, yes.

A: Why be isolated? In this case I would know everything!

Bion: You could say about it: "You are free to feel what a bad analyst I am, you are free to feel what a good analyst I am, if you feel friendly disposed, but that doesn't really tell you about how much I know, or how much anybody else knows." It's like the supposition that this world that we live in can easily be known, or undisturbed, but, in fact, it's extremely unlikely. It's awful! Look at it, just consider the astronomers themselves, with these vast apparatuses: radio telescopes, optical telescopes and so on … I would be the last to say that they've discovered the universe yet. Even taking our own galaxy, they can't even see the centre of it. Yet, there seems to be very good evidence to suppose, like the Nebula and Andromeda, take the Crab and Nebula, again it is just not visible, or at least, it is visible, but you'd have to have a very powerful telescope to see it. Well, the effect of all that sort of thing is simply not understood. Now, the patient is talking again, as if we think that the human mind is just a sort of tiny little thing like that.

A: Why can't we learn!!

Bion: But, as a matter of fact, why we investigate it, is because we feel that there's a lot to learn, not because we think we know all about it.

A: She said also how she felt about our relationship, how she was surprised because she was not like that, with her friends, they understand together very well, she's not so aggressive. She is a teacher. Well, with other teachers, with the pupils, I said to her, and with friends, they are social relationships, colleagues. But ours was a private relationship like … with her husband. I said the husband, because she had brought in her husband, and with me. This was something private, intimate, you know, very close, different. Then she … she waited a moment and … I thought she was thinking something but it was … she said something like "really," but it was the end of the session. After that, she came in in a completely different way. Yesterday she brought the theme of the crystal again, in a different way. She said again about Dr. X, that she was feeling that Dr. X gave her the structure of the crystal, because the crystal had lines.

Bion: Yes!

A: He gave her the structure and she was feeling that I was giving her the *feelings* about the crystal. Then, I said something that she was, perhaps now, she was making an integration of two things: structure and feelings. Then, she began to speak about her father and her mother, how she felt many times that her mother used to be upset in their relation. Very different from her father, different from her brothers, that when they are together, they could communicate, they could speak. But the mother was always, when they were together, making it difficult to have a conversation. She said that she would like to be able to speak, or to try to speak with her mother to make a dialogue, to have a dialogue with her mother.

Bion: Did she say what she wanted to say to her mother, if it were possible?

A: She didn't say anything special. She really gave an example of the difficulties of the mother to follow a conversation. For instance, if she's speaking about something she wants to change in her house, then the mother instead of staying in this dialogue, wants to act, to help, trying to get a person that comes and does something. She wants to act, to help, but not …

Bion: Yes, yes.

A: Not a dialogue.

Bion: Do you know anything about the mother, except what you've heard in the analysis?

A: I don't know nothing about her. But, I remember that she said a lot that the mother is very afraid of everything. I remember that the mother was very afraid that her son could kill her. Then, I said that it had a relation to me. Because the day before we spoke about the intensity of her hate, that she was able to kill, to break someone. Then, I linked those things and said how she was feeling that I am so afraid of the relation between her and me, how she thinks that I am afraid of the feelings stirred up between us. The day that I said: "Until Tuesday," she was speaking about the statue—do you remember?—of the two women.

Bion: Yes.

A: When she was very excited, speaking about the two women, she spoke about her mother, how it was difficult to have any contact with the mother. That she was so afraid of many things related to the son and so on … in the moment I said: "Until Tuesday." I linked them: to be afraid and the feelings about me.

Bion: Yes, I think that I would let her expand more of this material, give her time to give you quite a lot of information because, I think, again, one errs very often by being too anxious to give an interpretation rather than to wait until one's got some evidence to go on. The pressure which is brought to bear by the patient, it's everyone's own wish to push along with the analysis. I think it makes one, sometimes, rather prone to be working on inadequate information and you have to have some respect for your own feeling that you don't understand, that you are going to wait for more information. I think that on this, one could say about it: "Well, she is afraid of her destructiveness, she is afraid that she is destroyed out of her envy and hatred of the penis, both: of herself and of her mother—that's why these women have no penis." Well, there may be some moment, at which such an interpretation is the one that feels right; but I think that very often it's premature and precocious. So, I would say to her about this: "You must be feeling anxious to have a good relationship with me and for me to have one with you, but something is going on which makes you think it's impossible, what is it?" Well, I don't know what she'd say about that, but it could very well be something like this sort of feeling, where a kind of overwhelming importance is placed on the male genital and then that gives rise to destructive impulses and so and so forth ... But, fundamentally, there is really the transference of the tremendous importance, which is felt to exist with regard to the breast, which is, then, transferred on to the penis as being some sort of appropriate organ which is the counterpart of it. But, these theories are extraordinarily unsatisfactory to me compared with what crops up in the course of analysis. So, I think that I would be content with a bit more coaxing here and coaxing there ... getting a word or two out asking her: "Can you expand that? Can you state this more?" That sort of thing, just to ... as to a fact or question.

A: She speaks about her father and her brothers much more than about her mother.

Bion: Yes.

A: Her mother is always fighting. When she thinks about her mother is always complaining: poor mother, feeble; and sometimes hating—but hating because she's not strong.

Bion: That's right. I think that there can be a feeling of resentment about this overwhelming importance of the male. Her brothers, her father, Dr. X. Why aren't there any female analysts? Something of that kind comes in, somewhere. There must be a kind of reaction to a situation in which, apparently, the world is populated by one sex and one sex only! Biologically, that's just nonsense. Any physical, physiological, anatomical point of view is pure, is pure rubbish.

Now, this is sure to reflect itself in the character or personality of any intuitive woman, who must, after a time—although she will praise the father and the brother and so on—really, get very hostile about it and hostile to you, if you seem to fall in with it. Of course, mind you, if you don't, you're sure to get accused of being jealous or envious or something of that sort ... but, that doesn't matter! There's always an objection to any interpretation. I think that this woman is a woman with a woman inside of her trying to break free, that she'd like to say, what she has to say, as a woman, not as a man, or a counterpart of a man, or something of that sort. This very sort of cultural dominance stands very much in the way of the establishment of a good relationship between man and woman. It's one of these sound barriers that people can't breakthrough! You have to have a sort of upheaval to act through this sort of cultural conspiracy.

Of course, there are certain characteristics for which a male is obviously necessary, or seems to be the case; for example: fighting is a characteristic, the mere waging war. One would expect the male there to get idealized, put on a pinnacle and so forth ... but that, of course, also involves idealizing war, as if it were, really, a kind of activity, which the human race can afford! But I think I should go for that point, but give yourself time because, there again, you don't want to get maneuvered into a position where you have to think and interpret and so on, like a man would do so. What you have to discover is how *you* would do an analysis. That's why I say: find out what your vocabulary is and so on ...

The same thing applies to the man; after all, we derive from both sexes, so there's always a big component of female and male in each. That it isn't, all together, a simple matter; but what is essential is: that you should know how you do the thing. One *real* defect of analytic training—which I think is very good—is the idea of everybody undergoing analysis and so on ... is that: it hides from the trainee that the really important person, whose way of doing analysis that he's got to learn, is *him* or *her*—not somebody else. Takes a long time before you recover from the predominance of your analyst, until you do that you never get any real satisfaction out of the pleasure of doing your own analytic work. It's when it begins to be *you* analyzing somebody, then it's important.

So, I should leave yourself room to get the information that you want.

Notes

1. In Portuguese we have "intenção" which means "intention" and "intensão," which means "intense." We may also say "em tensão" which means to be in a state of "tension" "tense."
2. This concept by Dr. Bion about interpretation that provokes or evokes feelings or ideas that are always becoming ... always becoming something else ... always evolving towards something else ... like the ultimate truth that we never touch ... has a profound significance in the practice and theory of psychoanalysis.

Supervision D8 commentary

Ney Marinho

If any ordinary clinical discussion usually raises a great number of questions, it is easy to imagine how many will occur when one of the participants is W. R. Bion! So, I will take this opportunity to list a few highlights of my responses, thoughts and feelings, with short comments about them.

1. Link theory (K, L, H, –K, –L, –H) as a tool for understanding the analytical experience

Beginning with the analyst's first remarks, attention is called to the preoccupation about misunderstanding. How to deal with the patient's reaction in regard to the analyst's mistake in saying "till Tuesday" instead of "till tomorrow." This worry will take form in the *interpretation* given by the patient that the analyst actually meant: "You don't have to come tomorrow."

In relation to the link theory, I think this situation (patient's *interpretation*) is a typical manifestation of –K link. Namely, a categorical statement which doesn't allow dialogue, although at the same time is a provocation for a growing misunderstanding. Further on there appears another sign of the prevailing –K link. It is when the patient says: "That's it! I want you to help me with my husband and you say things like that," replying to the analyst's interpretation about their relationship in the session.

Bion's comment "Why do you suppose ..." calls our attention to another link: –L, that is present. I think that under the influence of the death instinct, the love link can become distorted, as is shown in the patient's attitude. Bion's next comment on this page reaffirms this understanding. In other words: –K would be a function and –L one of its factors.

I would like to emphasize my understanding that all the links are permanently active all of the time. However we only observe the results, like in physics when we deal with many forces acting simultaneously.

2. Negative therapeutic reaction

There is a comment where Bion describes the impasse that this kind of clinical situation leads the analyst to. Bion: "... it's hopeless to be put in a position where you are forced to defend an interpretation—that's endless, there's no end to it, at all." Similar situations appear again in the text, patient: "... I don't know why I came, I am coming here and I don't believe in you. But you are the only person, the only one I have."

This reminds us of the *reversible perspective* described in Chapters Twelve and Thirteen of *Elements of Psychoanalysis*. We are dismissing the different descriptions—the noisy disagreement, which appears in the clinical seminar, and the silent one described in the *Elements*—to call attention to a common point: the impasse, the analysis at a standstill. We know we are talking about something that will be very familiar to any practicing analyst; a clinical situation so familiar and so difficult to cope with. I think that when Bion discusses the character of the *reversible perspective* he offers us elements to formulate ways of escaping from this labyrinth, where we and our patients are ensnared.

"Reversible perspective is evidence of pain; the patient reverses perspective to make a dynamic situation static" (Bion, 1977, p. 60). Further on, in the same thirteenth chapter of the *Elements*, Bion says:

> In reversible perspective acceptance by the analyst of the possibility of an impairment of a capacity for pain can help avoidance of errors that might lead to disaster. If the problem is not dealt with the patient's capacity to maintain the static situation may give way

> to an experience of pain so intense that a psychotic breakdown is the result. (Ibid, p. 62)

If we concede to pain the relevance which it deserves in these situations we will have the hope of achieving a *language* which allows the patient to get in touch with his own mental pain in a hopeful way. For the patient, this will be a new—and hopefully more productive—way of experiencing mental pain.

3. Language

The theme of *language* is a constant in this clinical seminar. I would like to remind ourselves how often Bion raised the question to the participants: "what could we say to this patient?" In this seminar Bion offers a great many considerations about the personal choice that each analyst should consider in regard to his particular vocabulary.

I would like to question the traditional conception of *language* as an intermediary between thought and reality. This way of seeing the role of *language* leads to paradoxes and misunderstandings and this is a common point to philosophers, psychoanalysts and … patients, keeping in mind what Bion said in a certain moment: in cases of disturbance of thinking, old philosophical problems become, for patients and their analysts, decisive questions of life or death. I am thinking of the search for meaning and its vicissitudes, among them its destruction. My contention is to consider *language as an activity*. So, it may be an activity for understanding, or mis-understanding, for expressing pain or pleasure independent of the meaning of the terms of discourse.

Following this proposal, it would not make sense to evaluate an interpretation as *right* or *wrong*. We could see an interpretation as promoting the dialogue, investigation and mental development or not. In this way, we could cite the use that the patient makes of her recollections about Dr. X: many times as a *weapon* against her current analyst and, it is possible, in other times as a hope of having a good experience again. Her statements achieve meaning only in specific context.

It is important to remember that Bion, discussing reversible perspective and impasse, suggests the use of *the grid* to think about that clinical situation. The grid is a remarkable epistemological tool, which exemplifies—see the horizontal axis—the function of use of the language (any language: pre-verbal, verbal, non-verbal). It is for this reason that I believe that the grid is a more revolutionary contribution to the epistemology of psychoanalysis than it is usually considered.

4. Turbulence

The clinical material does not follow a determined order and sometimes information is not clear. However, we do not see this as a necessary handicap, but as a datum. In continuity with the last topic about language I would like to remind us that a lot of things in life *cannot be said, but may only be shown.*

I have the impression that Bion suggests that the analyst should better tolerate and offer more support for this state of turbulence in order to allow the patient to bring more data. This attitude would better help the analyst avoid giving a theoretical interpretation, even if the latter is correct. Theory, even correct theory, cannot substitute for whatever "... crops up in the course of analysis."

I think this attitude can be applied to many other situations. I am referring to the possibilities of transformations in O, experienced by the analyst. At the very end of the seminar, Bion says: It

> ... takes a long time before you recover from the predominance of your analyst, until you do that you never get any real satisfaction out of the pleasure of doing your own analytic work. It's when it begins to be *you* analyzing somebody, then it's important ... So, I should leave yourself room to get the information that you want.

5. The search: a recollection

In 1978, returning by bus overnight to Rio from São Paulo, where we had been participating in clinical seminars and lectures with Bion for one week, we had a conversation. Fernanda Marinho, Robert and Vivian Perecmanis, and I became aware that we had just been with the most important Brazilian analysts, presenting our clinical material, sometimes in a not so good English, asking questions and giving opinions without fear, with a spirit of enthusiasm produced by the lectures, that stimulated a great deal of thinking. We laughed, remembering our boldness! During the thirty-six years that followed, we have tried to maintain in ours hearts this experience of respect, in regard to human suffering, allowing no room for criticism or hierarchy, for judgment of *right* or *wrong. What mattered most, was the continual search for truth. To this end, we have tried to keep our minds and hearts open to receive thoughts without a thinker.* Hopefully, readers of this clinical seminar will share in these ideals.

I will end with Bion's last sentence: "So, I should leave yourself room to get the information you want."

Reference

Bion, W. R. (1977). Elements of psychoanalysis (1963). In: *Seven Servants* (pp. 60–62). New York, NY: Jason Aronson.

CHAPTER FOURTEEN

A journey's notes

Leopold Nosek

I

Wilfred Bion first landed in our midst in 1967, invited by Frank Philips, one of the founders of the Sao Paulo Society, who had earlier trained in London and undergone analysis with both Klein and Bion. Our colleagues are unanimous in describing the profound impression this British psychoanalyst had upon our analytic milieu and the deep impact of his thought on the Brazilian Psychoanalytic Society of São Paulo. Almost immediately, his work came to predominate over the classical Kleinianism that had preceded it, offering a breath of innovation and stimulating ever deeper studies into the psyche and the analytic process. This situation lasted to the end of the 1980s, when its supremacy began to be questioned and was followed by an opening to other schools of thought and to a renewed interest in Freud's work. Bion, however, never ceased to be studied—and I believe it is no exaggeration to assert that to date his writings are one of the identifying marks of the São Paulo Society. The work of a great author instigates new intellectual adventures for those who investigate it—and this book bears witness to one of the products of this shared trajectory.

The psychoanalytic encounter, created by Freud and brought to ever expanding, previously unexplored dimensions by Bion, configures a situation never before lived: two subjectivities put themselves in contact, having as commitment the reporting of free associations on the one side, and the listening through free-floating attention, on the other. It feeds on narratives. Heir to humanity's cultural heritage, it creates a new narrative with which it returns to culture. Thenceforth, nothing escapes it; it is an omnipresent interlocutor, whose aim can be variously conceived of as being at rest under one's own skin, finding the comfort of inhabiting one's own unique psychic territory and somehow taking hold of one's own fate.

Although deeply ethical in its conception and performance, the analytic encounter has no moral objective, no intent at transformation, no presupposition on the part of the listener—and mysteries begin to spring up, be they from ancestral memories, the depths of the corporeal body or the mysteries of the world. Figurations arise, due also to the participants' courage and daring. A drama is enacted and re-enacted in an inevitable present and unique creation. Dreams appear at each encounter, as the analysand, upon lying down upon the couch wanders the endless adventure of creating the human. Most often, this journey requires, as its prelude, an impasse in the life of the one who seeks the psychoanalytic course—a course for which no other route would serve as substitute.

Training analysis inevitably takes analytic practitioners through the odyssey of an adventure of this sort. And the latter encompasses as well seminars and supervisions which, not linked with the institution, set out to create the passage of concepts into their incarnate forms—it is these navigation tools that enable our delving ever and once again, into unlikely waters. I believe it is this we come across as we experience and observe this peculiar trajectory, which the Brazilian students of Bion have presented us with here.

Bion's supervisions remind us over and over again that the analytic encounter is not about resolving dead material of some forgotten past, but rather, retrieving it, bringing it once again to life and memory and setting it in motion. To translate it into the inevitable individual language and, as the group participants likely would put it, produce an *emotional experience* with its possibility of figuration. This situation, despite its singularity and unrepeatability, allows through the accumulation of experiences, the building of an individual and group heritage. As readers will have seen, what is underway is not simply a homage or reverential approach, but a search for emerging and uniquely individual truth. Spoken material becomes written material and as such awaits once again that it be spoken, and regain life; that the word become incarnate …

II

In 1977 enthused by his experience with Bion with whom he had learned much, José Américo Junqueira de Mattos at the time already an experienced psychoanalyst and father to five children, went to Los Angeles to be personally analyzed by Bion.[1] His was a journey that has always been familiar to analysts, be it in the direction of Vienna, in the years of Freud, or later to centers such as Paris and London, and so many more. In our country, where the distances are inconceivable to Europeans, long trips within and outside Brazil in order to complete psychoanalytic training are still not infrequent. Various generations went the way of such routes and, in a sense, the pages of the present book pay homage to these adventurers. With great personal sacrifice, many Brazilians did their training analysis in so to speak condensed form; that is, four sessions in two days, during which they also attended clinical and theoretic seminars at the Psychoanalytic Society of São Paulo. To complete their training, across the years, they left their city, their family, their own professional practice. Their personal lives would also be "condensed."

For Junqueira, it was a radical adventure: He ends up having to sell his house for this to happen, transfers himself and his family to an unknown country where his activity will consist in undergoing a daily psychoanalytic experience. This experience extended over almost three years and was resumed during the subsequent visits of Bion to Brazil. It was Junqueira who was responsible for recording, preserving, and translating the majority of these Brazilian supervisions that document Bion's teaching and thinking in the last periods of his life and provide the focus of this volume. These are classic fragments of psychoanalysis, part of our analytic heritage and the universal history of ideas, fundamental excerpts of the development of psychoanalysis in São Paulo. It is with great pride and pleasure that we may now share them with the psychoanalytic world in general.[2]

III

Since it is impossible to comment on the whole set of these supervisions and reflections, I will keep to a few personal considerations on the course and ramifications of Bion's thought.

Upon his break with London and the constrictions he felt being seen as part of the Kleinian "establishment," Bion returns more closely to Freud, and this movement will have its reflections in our own milieu. In the Kleinian orthodoxy of his time, the concept of the unconscious phantasy was omnipresent. Which means we always assumed that we are confronted with a *constructed unconscious*. As I see it, this view is continuous with the first Freudian topographic theory as defined in *The Interpretation of Dreams* (Freud, 1900–1901). Without doubt the British school produced fundamental advances in the Oedipus complex sphere, in research on sexuality and its aggressive component—although perhaps it was a misconception to have equated aggression too completely with the death drive. One way or another, the Kleinian interpretive search took place, at least among us Brazilians, as though underlying the manifest there would always be an organized and structured unconscious to be discovered. This vested the analytic project with the aura of a hidden truth to be unveiled, and with the consequent tropism for positivist ideologies. True to his Kleinian origins, Bion's work presents moments in which he reflects this positivist outlook, while others increasingly allow a mystic interpretation. Nevertheless, what most stands out in this present compilation, reflective of the thinking of Bion's late period, is the concept of the unconscious coupled with the idea of the unknown and the infinite.

The concept of the infinite underlies the idea of a psyche always to be developed, the figuration of which we will never reach. And this takes us to the Freud of the second structural theory, wherein the definition of the Id alludes to an unconscious to be construed, a psyche that plunges into the inevitable abysses of the corporeal and the reality surrounding this individuality, the enigmatic music of the world and the inescapable questions arising from it. Could it be that the world imprints itself on the psyche, offering it a window that invites it to come in, or can it be that, as a mirror, the psyche stamps upon our sense of the world its internal laws of functioning? These are questions that humanity has been asking itself ever since the Pre-Socratics.

But whether as a window or mirror, there is the glass—and it is with this that our literary and scientific disciplines concern themselves. In the 1970s, this aspect of the Freudian theory somehow attracts the attention of various schools across the world. In France, for instance, reflecting on borderline disorders, "limit cases," André Green (1977, 1990) observes the scant building of the psyche and thus the unconscious that is yet to be built. Further, he proposes a correction to the course of the death drive, unbinding it from aggression and associating it with the psychic non-construction or even deconstruction that occurs in a frightening silence of the psychic void (Negative hallucination and de-cathexis).

Mindful of not for a moment in analysis neglecting the importance of aggressive factors, Bion's developments rest upon a keen listening to the infinite silences of psychic creation that are yet to happen and the enigmas that inevitably will perpetuate themselves. On this point, Bion seems to make a radical rupture with his milieu of origin and a departure from the so-called post-Kleinians. I like the idea that knowing is not a filling in of gaps, but rather an ascending in a way such that the unknown itself broadens as psychic apprehensions grow.

From this emerges another mode of approaching dreams. If before they were no more than the "*via regia* to the unconscious," as Freud said in the first topography, now with the unconscious to be construed, they cease being the first step in analytic working through and constitute the grandiloquent ending of a long journey, acting more as a stimulus to the production of new workings through. According to Bion, dreams with their two facets, one manifest and the other latent, simultaneously create the territory of the conscious and what Freud (1923) calls, in *The Ego and the Id*, the unconscious of the Ego. As such, the language of the patient not always reflects free association, but also functions more as a virtual action, which discloses a virtual happening between the participants. Here is announced what might have become the third structural theory, in which it would be fit to assert, *Where action was, there shall the unconscious be*. It is in this realm that the psychoanalytic adventure will occur in a virtual space and in time exempt from linearity.

Thus in the first texts of Melanie Klein, it is possible to apprehend the continuity of multiple psychosexual happenings taking place simultaneously. There is a break in the linear time of ascendant development and also with that of the eternal return. From such insight ensued a writing of lengthy paragraphs, a succession of phrases punctuated by an excess of commas, which variously gave rise to negative critiques of the writing style of the author. I do not share in this opinion: it is my view that the language used corresponds to the simultaneity, synchronism, and diachronism of psychic happenings.

In Bion the complexity of time is underscored: all layers are updated in an impossible present time, covering at once the time of the happening that is yet to take place, the time of the memory *aggiornata* in its current pulsional spreading, and also the time proposed by the ongoing situation. It is no longer fitting to think of anachronic primitive moments, but rather of the foundations and bedrocks of the being which emerge and present themselves as *a priori* data—lenses through which the current moment acquires some figuration. In the final analysis, the *a priori* Kantian lens will be provided by the pulsional world of drives that is always there.

The ubiquity of this pulsional world will inevitably lead our reflection not only to the patient's pole of the analytic dyad, but also the subjective world of the analyst and the happening arising from the confrontation of two psyches. To my mind, the analyst's binocular vision turns to the patient's internal world and as well to the product which the interaction between both parties reveals. A new reading of the Freudian concept of transference presents itself: no longer the revelation of denied memories, but rather *the overflowing of the internal situation of the participants in this singular encounter*, or adventure, which the psychoanalytic practice proposes. The storm strikes both participants, but from the analyst is expected a better preparation to act as Virgil in this crossing/passage.

Finally underlying the concept of the unkown or the infinite, such as it presents itself in the psychoanalytic space according to Bion, is an ethical proposal. By its very essence the infinite extrapolates the concept; the infinite is something that is beyond definition—otherwise, it would not be of the infinite that we are speaking. There is no word for God, any attempt at naming already constitutes a heresy. In this way the Other, the unconscious—whether the analyst's or the analysand's—if infinite, cannot fit into any definition, naming or figuration. There is an excess of experience that inevitably brings to the analytic scene the traumatic, but there is also always the grandeur of the unreachable, the epiphany of the wondrous, which will also express itself in the ambience of the excessive that the encounter with the infinite proposes.

Having traversed other routes of thought, the philosopher Emmanuel Levinas says that the inaugural gesture of all knowing is submission to the otherness of the infinite, and this constitutes an ethical and not an ontological gesture. Within this it is not unfitting to think that in our field of practice, psychoanalysis, free association configures the invitation for the Other to be, in all its radical altereity. Inevitably, one must succumb by means of free-floating attention, to the traumatic and to the wonder which the excess of the presence of the Other brings us.

So here once again we plunge into transitions from the domain of the spoken word to that of the written word, and from thence once again to the spoken word. Or better yet could we put it along with André Green: to the *territory of the word incarnate*. This locale of the memory, and not of habit, is the territory of Homer and those moments when Mnemosyne held her place in the pantheon of Greek gods, when writing had not yet promoted the dethroning of memory. From this period, bedrock of our humanity, it has left us the need always to return to the classics, have them revive in a new moment, accompanied by another reality and other associations. So, too, with Bion and with Freud.

May the written words once again regain their incandescence. This is our adventure.

Notes

1. For an elegant recollection of this experience, see Junqueira de Mattos, J. A. (2015). Impressions of my analysis with Dr. Bion. In: H. B. Levine & G. Civitarese (Eds.), *The W. R. Bion Tradition* (pp. 5–22). London: Karnac.
2. Junqueira's daughter, Gisele Brito, herself a member of the Sao Paolo society and a training analyst in the Minas Gervais Center of Belo Horizonte, has coordinated a monthly discussion group with analysts such as Cecil Rezze, Celso Antônio Vieira de Camargo, Antônio Carlos Eva, Julio Frochtengarten, João Carlos Braga, Evelise de Souza Marra—and so many others that the limits of this space do not allow me to name—who have dedicated themselves to the unending work of editing and discussing the supervisions, keeping them alive and present as a continued source of learning and study in the Brazilian context and milieu.

References

Freud, S. (1900–1901). The interpretation of dreams. In: S. Freud, *The Standard Edition of the Complete Psychological Works of Sigmund Freud* (J. Strachey, trans.), Vol. 4–5, First part (1900); Second part (1900–1901). London: Hogarth and the Institute of Psychoanalysis [1953–1974].

Freud, S. (1923). The ego and the id. In: S. Freud, *The Standard Edition of the Complete Psychological Works of Sigmund Freud* (J. Strachey, trans.), Vol. 19 (pp. 1–66). London: Hogarth and the Institute of Psychoanalysis [1953–1974].

Green, A. (1977). The borderline concept. In: A. Green. *On Private Madness* (pp. 60–83). London: Karnac, 1997.

Green, A. (1990). *Conferências brasileiras: Metapsicologia dos limites* [*Brazilian Lectures: Metapsychology of limits*]. Rio de Janeiro: Imago.

Junqueira de Mattos, J. A. (2016). Impressions of my analysis with Dr. Bion. In: H. B. Levine & G. Civitarese (Eds.), *The W. R. Bion Tradition* (pp. 5–22). London: Karnac, 2016.

INDEX